CHAPEL STREET

CHAPEL STREET

'The Bravest Little Street in England'

SHEILA BRADY

The
History
Press

Front cover: Courtesy of North West Film Archive at Manchester Metropolitan University.
Back cover: Courtesy of Geoffrey Crump.

First published 2017

The History Press
The Mill, Brimscombe Port
Stroud, Gloucestershire, GL5 2QG
www.thehistorypress.co.uk

British Library Cataloguing in Publication Data.
A catalogue record for this book is available from the British Library.

ISBN 978 0 7509 7042 6

Typesetting and origination by The History Press
Printed and bound by CPI Group (UK) Ltd, Croydon, CR0 4YY

To Dad

Our dad gave us the family's verbal history of the First World War. It was a duty he took seriously. As children, he wanted us to have an understanding and to make it meaningful he took us to the towns, battlefields, cemeteries and memorials of Belgium and France.

We visited the memorials of the Menin Gate, for the last post sounded by the Belgian Fire Brigade; the imposing monument of Thiepval; Tyne Cot Cemetery, where we signed the visitors' book and read the gravestones, and were informed of the work of the Commonwealth Graves Commission; and to Passchendaele, where he explained about Hill 60 and the Canadians' sacrifice; we saw Ypres, Mons, Loos, Lens, Lille, Arras, Nancy, Verdun, Reims, and we followed the River Marne to Paris.

It was his legacy.

About the Author

SHEILA BRADY is a former local town councillor who has a degree in Education Studies. She formed a friendship with the author Dick King-Smith after finding out that her great-uncle was awarded the Military Medal for carrying King-Smith's father through no man's land in the First World War.

Contents

Acknowledgements

I am indebted to the publishers The History Press and especially Nicola Guy, without whose interest in the manuscript and belief in the project, this book and its contribution to the worthy cause of the charity Walking With The Wounded would not have happened.

I am grateful for the kindness of Dr Nick Barratt who, when he heard about the book, instantly offered his help and support.

It is with gratitude and esteem that I thank the Chester Military Museum's Andy Manktelow; Geoff Crump, who made me very welcome and offered all his resources, knowledge and expertise and with whom I spent privileged time; and Bill Preece, who showed me how to use the IRCS site and who found Martin DeCourcy, who was a prisoner of war, and James Ratchford's heroic exploits; and Caroline as custodian of Peter Hennerley's trove.

I wish to acknowledge Mr Paul Nixon's site *Ask the Expert*, which I came across by chance and found an account of Private Vincent Maguire, and on further researching of records I realised that the name on the Chapel Street Roll of Honour was incorrectly recorded as McGuire. This led to a search for the DCM citation to ascertain the act of gallantry he was rewarded for. I also wish to make reference to Chris Baker's *Long, Long Trail* site with its detailed information of the Royal Field Artillery Brigades and batteries. From here, I found the account of the German sinking of the British transport ship *Kingstonian*, which Vincent Maguire experienced and which enabled a search for the relevant dates and finding the written accounts of the event in the war diaries.

I would like to thank Jon Harrison from Cavendish Press for his offer of help. I especially would like to acknowledge the time and expertise of Will McTaggart, of the North West Film Archives, who was very helpful in facilitating the stills for the book cover and with accessing the Chapel Street Victory Parade film. A special mention is accorded to Wigan Local Studies, whose auspices are a model of local authority professionalism. I am obliged to Andy Burnham MP, the Lord Mayor of Greater Manchester, who offered assistance when he heard about the book and with the Walking With The Wounded fundraising efforts for servicemen.

Special gratitude is due to Tim Mole of the Salonika Society, who went out of his way to furnish me with the official Courts of Enquiry findings. Thank you to all the people who have helped in many different ways, they share in the success of the book.

Thank you to my friend Zainab Bhatti, who kept me going through the long, hard days and nights and whose encouragement and constancy is equal to none.

Special recognition and gratitude is due to my son Christian, for the original idea for the book and for its compilation, and whose support at every stage has been hugely invaluable,

If I have missed anyone from the acknowledgements or have made an error in research, please accept my apologies.

Preface

One day, many years ago, my father showed me a local newspaper article about the Norton family of Chapel Street, Altrincham. As he passed it to me he acknowledged it with the words, 'Uncle Jimmy lived on Chapel Street.' I read the article, which was about a family with several sons who had fought in the First World War. Up until then I had not heard of the street, and did not know until some years after this of its part in the Great War.

However, I was intrigued to try and piece together Uncle Jimmy's military story. My father wrote down all the detail he could recall. We knew that Uncle Jimmy was awarded the Military Medal for saving an officer's life, so I wrote to the Chester Military Museum's Honorary Researcher and gave over the information we had. The researcher was Geoff, whom I met many years later whilst doing the research for this book. He sent me an account of a raid in Salonika along with detail, and a prisoner of war list.

It transpired that the officer whose life was saved was Ronald King-Smith. Acting on speculation, I wrote to Dick King-Smith, the highly popular children's author responsible for *The Sheep-Pig*, the film version of which had just been released by Walt Disney as *Babe*. He confirmed that Ronald King-Smith was his father. After the war Ronald married, and Dick, an only child, was born. The year was now 1998, and for many years Dick and I enjoyed a warm correspondence, and he would send copies of his new books for my son Christian. One year, he sent a homemade Christmas card with a hand-drawn postage stamp on yellow paper, which I was overwhelmed to receive. It was a family tree of himself and his wife Myrle (who had just passed away), and his children, grandchildren and great-grandchildren, all drawn as matchstick characters. He was very proud of his family, and it was amazing to think that it was due to Uncle Jimmy's heroic action that they were all born.

Some ten years later, I read that a blue plaque had been erected to the men of Chapel Street. Further enquires put me in touch with Mr Hennerley, who had been responsible for the commemorative plaque. We spent many hours chatting and laughing on the phone and he shared his reminiscences, including the fact that he knew of Uncle Jimmy. Peter Hennerley came from a military family background and close family members, including his grandfather, had lived on the street. He felt that the surface of the soldiers' wartime experiences had only been scratched. He had also discovered the fact that the council had an obligation to keep the Roll of Honour in a state of good repair, in memory of the soldiers who had volunteered; an obligation which, up until that time, had not been honoured. Sadly, he passed away, and a booklet with his collection of memorabilia, recollections and history of Chapel Street was published in his memory, with the proceeds going to the local regimental benevolent fund.

In 2015, I came across a play of the First World War produced by the North West Drama Services Limited, in which Chapel Street was referenced. I contacted the director and was consequently invited to see the production, which involved north-west primary schools enacting roles and events telling the story of the war. I was informed that the children of Middlewich Primary ('The Middlewich Pals') were very interested in Chapel Street and wanted to ask me questions, and so a visit to the school was arranged. The children were very enthusiastic and knowledgeable; some of them brought in their family research and heirlooms, one pupil brought in a wonderful embossed cigarette box, a Christmas gift from Princess Mary to soldiers of the BEF. The visit went so well that my son suggested that I should consider writing a book.

I held on to this idea for a few months, then at Christmas 2015 I ran into Ed Parker, CEO of Walking With The Wounded, who was doing a sponsored walk to collect donations for veterans' housing in Manchester. The charity was involved in a project that had purchased two Victorian streets and was renovating them to house ex-service personnel and their families. The project work had received a helping hand from the BBC One *DIY SOS* team, who filmed Princes William and Harry lending their services to the construction work. I thought, 'this is a coincidence!'

I hope that the book will resonate with all those who read it. The story is a familiar one of its time. A hundred years ago, the men, women and children of Chapel Street did not get the help and assistance they needed after the war.

The legacy of Chapel Street is to ensure that returning servicemen and women and their families are looked after, and that their sacrifices are recognised and valued by society.

Introduction

When I started to research the men from Chapel Street, I found that it was a peregrination of discovery. Initially, I began by enumerating the names on the Roll of Honour, however, anomalies arose as the number of names recorded and the official total are not exact but correspond. It would seem probable that the date of the commissioning of the Roll of Honour is the reason for this. A further consideration in studying the names was the use of phonetic substitutes, the translation of names into English and the variance of accent; also, the creator of the record spelling the name the way they thought it should be spelled and transcription error; all of which was a complication in the census-taking.

One of the first areas of research undertaken was an examination of the 1911 Census. This is the official register taken every ten years, which lists all the names, marital statuses, ages, occupations and birthplaces of people who spent the night in each household, either residing or visiting on the nights of recording. I also had access to the Census documents for 1901 and the decades going back to the mid-1800s. However, one of the problems was the fact that anybody who lived on Chapel Street between 1911 and 1914 was not officially listed. As the housing was predominantly lodging house accommodation, this meant that boarders moved frequently. After the war, many men did not return to live in Chapel Street for various reasons, and it is probable that some returned to Ireland. To compound the issue, there is the difficulty of cross-referencing names; under the 100-year rule of confidentiality, the 1921 Census (three years after the war) will not be released until 2022.

The Roll of Honour, whilst recording the regiments and armies the men volunteered for, does not give battalion or service number information. Another major difficulty is the fact that only 40 per cent of soldiers' service records or attestation papers survived the German bombing of the War Office repository during the Second World War. The attestation papers were either destroyed or suffered damage by fire and water, and became known as the 'Burnt Documents'. This resulted in trying to find soldiers by other means, such as online searches, which entails searching: Silver War Badge records, pension records, medal index cards, prisoner of war lists (many prisoners were not listed), Commonwealth war graves, Soldiers that Died in the Great War (SDGW), medal citations and anything else that might help.

War diaries are another search area. However, as the diaries are effectively the recording of events in the field of action, it is worth knowing that 'Other Ranks' are generally not mentioned by name, though officers may be. Not all the regimental or unit war diaries are digitised, for example those pertaining to Mesopotamia and Macedonia (Salonika), which can limit research. These diaries can be viewed, however, at the National Archive (Kew), which necessitates travelling to London. It may be that a personal visit to the relevant Regimental Military Museum would yield information from the battalion diaries; this would require an appointment. It is worth enquiring if the museum(s) are open or have changed address beforehand. For instance, at the time of writing, the National Army Museum has just opened after refurbishment, but an in-depth study of the Royal Horse and Field Artillery including the Royal Garrison Artillery could not be carried out as the museum at Woolwich has closed and is in the process of transferring to Salisbury; as is the Royal Marines Museum and the Royal Engineers Museum. This circumstance also affected the research of other regiments pertaining to Chapel Street. Whilst some museums keep material online, others do not, using this tranistional phase as an opportunity to develop the sites. Unfortunately, regimental museums do not keep lists of the soldiers who served with them, though some are endeavouring to do this along with the histories of individual service, relying on volunteers to carry out research.

Another factor to consider is that soldiers can change their battalion or regiment, as many of the soldiers did, either through manpower shortage or returning to battle after injury. Brigades and divisions also changed for differing reasons. If soldiers served in the Labour Corps they could be attached to different regiments, and this can present difficulties with the complexities of service number identification, especially if searching for a common surname such as 'Smith'. It is also worth noting that second names can be used instead of first names, which is a common custom in Ireland, i.e. 'Patrick, James' for 'James, Patrick'.

It can be useful to use a Soundtex converter when searching for difficult to find surnames. Soundtex is a system universally used to search through a phonetic index for names that sound alike but are spelled differently, such as Stewart and Stuart, and for names spelled with different vowels, or double letters. Soundtex tools are freely available online, and genealogy websites such as *Ancestry* and *Find My Past* now have free access at most libraries.

Another avenue to explore is the Local Studies centre in libraries, along with newspaper searches. It can be very useful to have a membership of societies and/ or associations, and to engage with forum sites.

The book contains a large amount of easily accessible educational material and resource links useful for teachers, educators and students in their study of the Great War. It is hoped that study of the narrative accounts will lead to the development of frameworks for further research and debate, and so to the deepening of our knowledge and understanding of the experience of the First World War.

There is more archival material available for research to the enthusiast than there has been previously, and I am personally very excited to find out the part the men of Chapel Street played in Russia; and the two-day march across the Sinai Desert undertaken by the 127th Brigade during the Battle of Romani, in defence of the Suez Canal from the Turks, which resulted in victory; and a telegram of praise from King George V.

It is amazing what can be revealed, as I hope the reader will appreciate from this account of the 'Bravest Little Street in England'.

Chapel Street: 'The Bravest Little Street in England'

At the outbreak of the First World War, Chapel Street stood as a long row of sixty Georgian and Victorian terraced houses in Altrincham, Cheshire. From here, 161 men heeded Kitchener's rallying cry and volunteered to fight for 'King and Country'. King George V, recognising their patriotism in a telegram, was moved to call it: 'The Bravest Little Street in England'.

In 1914, Chapel Street was home to some 400 men, women and children, mostly of Irish nationality and English heritage. The historical roots of this conurbation are largely unknown; however, there was a definite Irish presence in Altrincham in the latter eighteenth century. Probably this was due to the political and religious situation in Ireland at that time, and the conditions and penalties placed on the Roman Catholic population by the Penal Laws. These extreme laws prevented Irish Roman Catholics from intermarrying with Protestants; purchasing or leasing land; voting or holding political office; living within 5 miles of a corporate town; entering a profession; or obtaining an education. Ireland was part of Great Britain at this time and was benefitting from an expansion in its economy. However, in view of the imposed sanctions, disenfranchised Catholics may have considered it more expedient to leave the country and become economic migrants in a more tolerant society. This could have coincided with the employment and construction opportunities afforded by the building of the Bridgewater Canal in 1760, and its extension to Altrincham in 1765. In 1774, a new Act of Parliament removed the restrictions imposed on the textile trade. And by 1782, a new mill had been built and was locally auctioned with the claim, 'Plenty of hands to be procured in Altrincham for carrying on the cotton manufactory and on very reasonable terms' (Foster: 2013). Evidence indicates there were four mills in Altrincham by 1800. The 1801 census records the population as 1,692, and 340 houses.

Catastrophe struck in 1845 with the failure of the potato crop in Ireland, which was a recurring event from 1739, happening some eighteen times and leading to the potato to be recognised as an unreliable crop. This was a widespread blight coupled with poor weather conditions, leaving the Connaught area of Ireland the worst affected. The potato was a staple part of the Irish diet and was also grown for export to England. It set off a chain of events that led to disease, starvation and death amongst the population. During this time people lost their income and the means to pay rent, which led to evictions and homelessness. Families were left destitute, relying on workhouses and poor relief. The Poor Law had been extended to Ireland in 1838. From 1845–52, the population dropped by some 2 million. As more than a million people died from hunger, it came to be known as 'The Irish Potato Famine', or Gorta Mor (The Great Hunger). Many Irish leaders and orators saw capital being made from the disaster by landowners using it as a means to increase their lands, and the authorities using it to subjugate a rebellious population. They argued that food exports should be curtailed to feed the home population. At this time, Britain operated a protectionist economic system known as mercantilism. Though Ireland was part of the Union, it was at the same time considered to be a foreign country, therefore subject to tariffs. Under the Corn Laws, exports of grain were kept artificially high, and 'corn' was deemed to be any grain that could be milled, especially wheat. In practice, this meant that bread, another staple food, was beyond the reach of most. The Anti-Corn Law League sought a repeal of these laws, but this was not a popular political policy and was not immediately enacted. Exports to England increased during the famine and grain was plentiful. Consequently, 'Dissenters' believed it was a deliberate policy of genocide imposed on the population by the English. It was the cause of mass emigration to England, the USA and Canada by those who could escape its consequences.

A sea-swell of Irish arrived in England, and by 1851, Altrincham had a recognised Irish community with over 200 living in Chapel Street. Although this ingress of Irish immigrants was British, they spoke a different language (Irish Gaelic), and were regarded as foreigners; they were also seen to be politically dangerous. Altrincham during this period of time must have seemed a good prospect. The railway linking it to Manchester was under construction in 1846, opening in 1849. Work was available and Manchester was at the heart of the now thriving cotton industry. Opportunities for employment and a new life away from the countryside came with this first wave of industrialisation. The Chapel Street immigration was mostly from the counties of Mayo, Galway, Sligo and Tipperary (Connaught). These western counties were devastated by the failed potato crop, and lack of investment in constructive infrastructure and productivity. Passage from Ireland would have been from the ports of Dublin or Belfast and most would have been foot passengers, i.e. not reserving berths for the three-hour crossing to Liverpool. They would have had little luggage and relied on purchasing supplies on arrival. It was a diaspora, and entire families were leaving their roots behind.

The Irish brought with them their culture, and by all accounts Chapel Street was a very lively and industrious society. Chapel Street gained its slightly 'S' shape due to the apportioning of former agricultural strips of land which were sold off as building land (Bayliss: 2006/7). Terraced housing was ideal for housing large numbers of people (1820–40). A cartographic survey shows a combination of mixed housing ranging from groups of terraced houses, three-storeyed terraces, some back-to-back houses and semi-detached housing with stables, and included in this were sixteen cellar dwellings. The street was built on a slope, and photographs of the time indicate there were no gardens, trees or verges; the unpaved street was very narrow, approximately 11ft in width. Some of the houses had steps outside. The street was lit by a couple of gas lamps affixed to the walls of buildings. There was a general provisions store, a bakehouse and piggeries behind the housing, with a sizable market garden or allotments. A variety of trades and labour were employed by the residents, including lodging house keepers, coachmen, gardeners, labourers, railway workers, stonemasons and nail-makers. A contemporary account states that every house in Chapel Street had a handloom. Schooling provision for 'scholars', as the children were known, and place of worship was on a nearby street, formed by converting two cottages. St Margaret's Church opened a tea and coffee house at number 19, which proved very popular, leading to another property being purchased. Here, residents could read newspapers and books, and there was a smoking room. In 1880, number 42 was bought as a refuge. Here, religious, moral and industrial teaching was given to 'all children who are unprotected, or in circumstances of degradation'. At the top of Chapel Street stood a Wesleyan Chapel where John Wesley preached in 1761. It was sold in 1881, with some 512 square yards of land and erected buildings, and was described as one of the most valuable and improving areas in Altrincham. It was now known as the Congregational Church. There were two public houses: The Grapes (still standing under a different name) opposite the church, and The Rose and Shamrock situated in the middle of the street, which was the centre of activity. Here, everybody came for their socialising, drinking, music and entertainment; not least of which were the regular fights that broke out. Such was the reputation of the strong and resolute men that lived and drank there, that the local priest was sent for when things got out of hand.

In the 1800s, life was precarious and in Altrincham the mortality rate was high, outbreaks of typhus fever and cholera were an annual occurrence. The town had its own local Fever Hospital paid for by charitable means. Dysentery and other associated ailments were difficult to contain or eradicate. In 1852, Sir Robert Rawlinson was commissioned with presenting a report to the General Board of Health. This would be a preliminary inquiry 'Into the Sewerage, Drainage and Supply of Water, And the Sanitary Condition of the Inhabitants of the Town'. As part of the inquiry, a cartographic plan of all land and property in Altrincham and the surrounding areas would be drawn, to enable a local board to judge the propriety of applying the Public Health Act to the town and township of Altrincham. The report was exceedingly scathing in its findings, and it noted: the want of proper sewage, pavement and cleansing; the neglected state of the town and the dirty, unpaved, undrained and ill-ventilated squares and alleys; the faulty arrangement of cottages, yards and midden sand privies. Chapel Street itself was serviced by communal privies, midden, a few hand pumps and sink stones; there was also a long alley for drying washing running at the back of a block of houses. In submitting evidence to the inquiry, local working men from Chapel Street complained about the want of water and Mr Balshaw, a local builder, stated that he could not let ten new houses he had recently built on the street because they had no drainage. Another contention was the issue of keeping pigs close to housing stock. Rawlinson states to remove them forcibly 'would be resisted to the uttermost and would result in the Irish admitting the pigs as inmates'. Alarmed by this possibility, he states that other diseases such as malaria would be rampant in the town if this happened. Rawlinson was also unhappy with the overcrowding in the lodging houses, with the inquiry revealing four to ten beds in one room as commonplace. Rawlinson's proposals were accepted, not least of which was the establishment of a proper form of local government, proper sewers and drains would be constructed, a sufficient supply of pure water, and the paving and regulating of all streets, courts, alleys, lanes and passages liable to be used by the public. The number of houses on Chapel Street depleted from about this time from eighty-one houses to sixty, presumably as part of the sweeping proposals.

By the 1850s, Liverpool had developed as a port of strategic importance. From here, imports of cotton from India, the Middle East and the southern states of America made their way by the canal system to the mills of Lancashire. Manchester became known as 'Cottonopolis', and cloth spun from the cotton was exported to the Empire. It was said that Britain clothed a quarter of the world's population. But this was about to change. In 1860, Lincoln was elected President of the United States of America. However, because of his stance on the slave trade, seven southern states seceded to form a new nation: the Confederate States of America. By 1861, America was embroiled in what came to be known as the American Civil War: the Union (north) against the Confederacy (south). In April 1861, President Lincoln ordered a military blockade of the southern ports in order to prevent the export of cotton. He sought to starve the Confederacy of its income, which was financing its war effort. He justified his actions on the international stage on the grounds of humanitarianism, and called for the abolition of the black slave trade, which was used extensively in the south to pick cotton. If the Confederacy was to succeed, it needed support and recognition from Britain and France. The Confederate Congress believed that the way to remove the Union Blockade was through 'King Cotton Diplomacy', a cotton embargo. By limiting supply, it sought to upset the economies of its trading partners and put pressure on them to join in the fight against the Union. Diplomatic envoys were sent to London for meetings with Earl Russell, then Foreign Secretary, who was a strong advocate of laissez-faire, an economic system which is devoid of government interference such as embargos or sanctions, the opposite of mercantilism. Indeed, a decade earlier, as prime minister, he would not intervene during the Potato Famine regarding the exportation of food to England, preferring to let free trade take its own course.

The plight of the black American slaves of the Deep South struck a chord of solidarity with the millworkers of Lancashire, many of whom were Irish. They also had experience of being tied to autocratic landowners as economic slaves earning a potato wage; that is, earning just enough to cover sustenance and possibly rent for themselves and families. This was known as the cottier system (a peasant form of serfdom, which disappeared from Ireland altogether). They wholeheartedly supported the blockade of raw cotton by President Lincoln and refused to spin cotton. Another reason was probably the recognition of democracy and a government elected by its people. Ireland's own parliament was dissolved in 1800, and its governance came from Westminster, and though it had representation by MPs, its people did not have a free vote. Manchester had been at the forefront of demanding electoral reform with the Chartist Movement and the Reform League. These active organisations had great support from the millworkers, who demanded representation (the majority of working men did not become enfranchised until 1867). In 1863, President Lincoln wrote a letter to the working men of Manchester, in which he reiterated his terms of office stating that his government was one of integrity, founded on human rights. He argued that it should not be substituted for one which should rest exclusively on the basis of human slavery. He emphasised the values and sentiments of justice, humanity and freedom and acknowledged the sufferings the struggle had caused, stating that: 'Theirs was an act of sublime Christian heroism, which has not been surpassed in any age or any country.' This was indeed a time of struggle. 'King Cotton Diplomacy' had not worked; Britain did not give formal recognition to the Confederacy and maintained a position of neutrality, despite many manufacturers in Liverpool and Manchester demanding that it should be recognised. The consequence of this was a depression. Stockpiles of raw cotton lay in full warehouses. The price of cotton fell rapidly, and a loss of markets and idle looms all over Lancashire caused a situation which became known as the 'Cotton Famine', lasting from 1861–65.

When the Poor Laws were drafted, the Poor Law Commission did not take into account the situation in the north or the socio-economic effects of recession. The consequence of this was that the slump in cotton production meant thousands of people had no work or income; families had no breadwinner or means of paying the rent and buying food. The law that was intended for vagrants, beggars and ne'er-do-wells was now applied en masse to a population that had no control over the economic situation. This situation was mirroring the humanity crisis in Ireland. Richard Cobden MP (Anti-Corn Law League) stated that the cessation of employment represented the loss of £7 million per annum in wages. He saw this as a crisis which warranted national attention, and for which local poor relief could not meet demand. In England, the welfare provision for the poor was in two forms: the Outdoor Relief, which was administered by local charities, offering money, food, clothing or goods; or the state's provision for the absolutely destitute: the workhouse. Poor Law Unions were formed from small parishes coming together to build workhouses. Under the Poor Law system, they were paid for by levying a 'poor rate' on property-owning middle classes. Conditions of entry to the workhouse were dire; they were not to be seen as a soft option. In return for bed and board, the inhabitants did long hours of menial work. It was a humiliating system of degradation which included the segregation of whole families. Many poor people died in them from hard labour, illness and simply losing the will to live. The result was that people avoided them at all cost, which was an intended prerequisite of their provision. A codicil to the Poor Law was 'The British Laws of Removal'. This was a sectarian piece of legislation which was intended to reduce the burden on local rate payers. Irish people were required to have a residency period of five years before they could claim poor relief. The stipulation was that those who did not meet this requirement no longer quali-fied for residency in the country, and under magistrate's order they were forcibly returned to the original port of entry, and from there back to Ireland. The letter of the law regarding forced repatriation was loosely interpreted and Irish nation-als of even longer residency found themselves stranded on the dockyards of Ireland. Essentially, the Irish poor were deported, and this would have applied to Chapel Street. Records for 1860–62, show regular expulsions from Altrincham to Ireland until 1875. Ireland was also in the grip of depression, with 1879 being a marked year for failed potato harvest, and another famine known as *'Gorta Beag'* (mini famine). Although not as severe or long-lasting, and with relief in place, it nevertheless was a testing time for government and people causing unrest and consternation. A determined populace was not prepared to tolerate an English absentee landlord system, increased rents and evictions, and the income of these rents transferred to England. The Land League of Mayo was formed by tenants and it rapidly became organised as a protest party as membership increased, its title changing to the Irish National Land League.

Emigration also increased in that year, and many Irish came to Chapel Street. From 1871–81 the population of Altrincham in general rose by nearly 3,000. There were many reasons why populations moved around, such as war, displacement and employment.

Onomastic research reveals many surnames of the residents to be a mix of: Italian (Venice – Margiotta); Anglo-Saxon (Bagnall, Clarke, Oxley, Reeve, Wyatt); Old English (Barrett, Stocks, Starrs); English (Croft, Kirkham, Morley, Peers, Ratchford, Smith, Taylor, Turton); Old French/Welsh (Hughes, Caine); Anglo-Norman (Burke, King); Norman French/Germanic (Hulmes); English/German (Arnold); German/Irish (Lennard); Irish Gaelic (Kenny, Brennan, Murray, Naughton, Quinn); Anglo-Scottish (Johnson, Wood); Welsh (Jones, Owen, Prosser); Irish (Behen, Collins, Curley, Durkin, Dwyer, Egan, Gormley, Groark, Hanley, Kelly, Mahone, Riley, Rowan, Ryan, Scanlon, Sheehan, Shaughnessy); and Old Norse (Scarfe, McNicholas).

Habitational names such as the surname Hollingworth, taken from an area in Lancashire (Old English for 'hole and enclosure'), reveal how far populations move around, as do surnames specific to certain areas such as Corfield, indig-enous to Shropshire; as well as pre-medieval location names such as Featherstone, and local derivations such as Brownhill, believed to have come from nearby Sale in Cheshire in the late thirteenth century.

Many of the surnames reveal a royal lineage or aristocratic hereditary, such as Tyrell, a baronial name from Castleknock; Wickely, from the family seat at Brampton; Birmingham, who accompanied Strongbow to Ireland; Chesters, mentioned on the pipe roll between 1119 and 1216; Davis, a patronymic surname for the last independent ruler of Wales, Dafydd ap Gruffydd; DeCourcy, from the Carolingian Kings of France; O'Connor, considered the most important of all Irish surnames, an aristocratic Catholic family who were the historic Kings of Connaught; Hannon, from the Clan Hannon, associated with the Counties of Limerick, Galway and Roscommon and who, it is said, gave the names to Eire and Ireland.

Endogamy, the practice of marrying within a specific ethnic group, class or social group and keeping distinct as a community, was a custom of Chapel Street. Families intermarrying included: De Courcy, Oxley, Hennerley, Booth, Inion, Donnelly, Hanley, Hollingsworth, Shaughnessy, Brennan and Tyrell.

Capital investment came to Liverpool and Manchester in 1887, with the construction of the Manchester Ship Canal which would link Manchester to Liverpool, and via the Irish Sea would open a trade gateway for imports and exports with the rest of the world. It would bypass the railways and their charges, and merchants would benefit by avoiding dock and town duties at Liverpool. It was also a response to 'the Long Depression' (previously known as the Great Depression) of 1873–79, and was caused by the second wave of industrialisation. There were 12,000 workers employed on the 36 miles of excavation, rising to 17,000 at its peak. It is likely that the single men coming from Ireland and living in lodging houses in Chapel Street would have formed part of the workforce. Likely they would have been enlisted or recruited by 'gangers' on behalf of the company. These migrant men were known as 'navvies' (often used as a derogatory term) or navigational engineers. Historically they worked on railway construction, and then on canals. The work of the 'navvy' involved more than a man with a pick and shovel; essentially, this was an overarching term which involved the subtrades of drilling, mining, hammering, timbering and handling explosives. It was difficult and dangerous work and many lost their lives. Victorian enterprise was extended further in 1897: three years after the canal opened, its consociate, Trafford Park, began development to become the world's first planned industrial site.

This was also the age of Empire and world events would draw the United Kingdom of Great Britain and Ireland into war against the Transvaal Republic and the Orange Free State, known as 'The Boer War' (1899–1902). Records show that more men enlisted from Chapel Street than any other street in England, and they distinguished themselves with honours. The reasons for this can be speculated on: it is possible that the population explosion in Altrincham, with an increase from 4,488, in 1851, to 16,000 in 1900, and the short supply of jobs and income, were contributing factors. Since 1800, recruitment into the militia by the Irish was a known occurrence in times of economic decline. The Census for 1891 records single men from Knutsford taking abode in lodging houses on Chapel Street (the local workhouse was situated in Knutsford). Patriotic fever was running high in the country, with parades and marching bands in Altrincham including a visiting American brass band. The year 1887 had seen a popular royal visit to Altrincham by TRH Prince and Princess of Wales to mark the occasion of the Jubilee of Queen Victoria. It should be noted that in 1900, Queen Victoria had a very successful trip to Ireland, and it was thought that the long-awaited permanent royal residence would go ahead. It was also a time of sentiment and many Irish felt that her presence would bring about a new golden dawn of prosperity, enabling a return to the mother country.

Altrincham celebrations for the Coronation of King George V, 1911. (John Hudson)

In 1913, Altrincham held a by-election which saw the Unionist candidate George C. Hamilton easily win the contested seat with an increased majority. Hamilton was a local employer who would not pay union rates. Another controversial issue was Home Rule for Ireland. Many people living on Chapel Street at this time were born in England but had Irish heritage, and the Irish Nationalist leaders John Redmond and T.P. O'Connor were urging Irish voters to vote for the Liberal candidate. The Liberal Party had formed a minority government with the support of the Irish Nationalists, and they were attempting to introduce Home Rule for Ireland. At the time of the election there were concerns regarding the issue of plural voting (electors who appear on the electoral register twice), which both parties recognised and this may have influenced the outcome. Hamilton held the seat until 1923, when there was a swing to the Liberals.

George C. Hamilton was appointed Director of Enrolment National Service in 1917 (National Service is compulsory service: or Conscription).

In 1914, Britain declared war on Germany in response to the guarantee given to Belgium to protect its neutrality in the face of invasion. Germany issued an ultimatum to Belgium to allow free access for its troops to pass through the country to go to war against France. Belgium rejected this ultimatum. On 3 August, Germany declared war on France, and on 4 August, Britain was at war with Germany. This was a national call to arms. The reasons for volunteering can be speculated on. Public records show the population of Altrincham had now increased to approximately 18,000, and work and wages were still a primary concern. By 1914, evidence shows nearly half of Chapel Street was given over to lodging houses. In 1916, when the war was at its height, lodging houses at numbers 3 and 5 Chapel Street were sold as 'viable investments', attracting a letting income each of £26 per annum (in 1901, Welsh tenants made up a third of lets), and half of the male occupation worked as labourers of various sorts. However, war in Europe was different and invasion was a real threat. This time it was about peace and security, principle and values. Germany was seen to be ambitiously expanding its empire. Genuine patriotism and a feeling of protectionism were valid reasons to go to war. In addition to this was the urging and blessing of the Catholic Church in Britain and in Ireland, notably the Bishop of Galway and the Archbishop of Tuam (part provinces of Galway, Mayo and Roscommon), for men to enlist to fight against Germany. This was in retaliation to the devastation of Leuven, Belgium, where the oldest Catholic University in the world and its manuscripts were destroyed by the Germans. Leuven had enjoyed a close association with Ireland for centuries, and was the seat of the first Irish language institute. It was an attack on Irish heritage, religion, culture, identity and history. The Bishop of Kildare stated it was the duty of all faithful Christians to come to the aid of what was now essentially a Holy War. Playing on this attack of Ireland, and the empathy of nationalism towards a small country invaded by Protestants, the British War Office recruitment posters urged Irishmen to answer the call and come to Catholic Belgium's aid.

In August 1914, there was a political crisis in Ireland which threatened Civil War. The passing of the Government of Ireland Act 1914, which became known as the 'Home Rule Act', divided the country. Nationalists were in favour of independence and were largely Catholic. They wanted the restoration of an Irish parliament with distinct powers. The Unionists wanted to stay in union with Britain and drew on Protestant support. The implementation of Home Rule was postponed under the Suspension Act 1914, for twelve months, due to the outbreak of war. The war was generally acknowledged to be of short duration and the act had reached the statue books by September 1914. John Redmond MP, leader of the Irish Parliamentary Party (IPP), used political coercion to project the idea that militarily supporting Britain in its hour of need, in the form of enlistment, would strengthen the case for devolvement. This was widely supported by most nationalists in Ireland and could have been an influential factor in the enlistment of Chapel Street.

Eighty-one men volunteered for 'King and Country' on the first day of the war. Lord Kitchener's highly provocative poster doubtlessly was persuasive in stirring the emotions of the other eighty men. Some of the men of Chapel Street had previously fought in the Boer War and were decorated soldiers; to them, Kitchener was a heroic and valiant figure who had led them to victory at Mafeking. And he was an Irishman: a fellow countryman who could be trusted. With the ethereal finger pointing and the mesmeric stare giving a sense of urgency, the poster 'Britons: Lord Kitchener Wants You. Join Your Country's Army!' would have been a calling impossible to ignore. The poster sought to create a feeling of individual worth and a sense of collective nationalism, as well as a response to an emergency cry for help. The gravitas of the end line, 'God Save the King', to many would have seemed like the response of a bidding prayer: a prayer to God. Chapel Street answered the call-up and its husbands, fathers, sons, brothers, uncles, cousins and fiancés volunteered for 'The War to End All Wars'.

BUCKINGHAM PALACE

My message to the Troops of the Expeditionary Force. Aug. 12th, 1916.

You are leaving home to fight for the safety
and honour of my Empire.
Belgium, whose country we are pledged to
defend, has been attacked and France is about to be
invaded by the same powerful foe.
I have implicit confidence in you my soldiers.
Duty is your watchword, and I know your duty will be
nobly done.
I shall follow your every movement with deepest
interest and mark with eager satisfaction your daily
progress, indeed your welfare will never be absent from
my thoughts.
I pray God to bless you and guard you and bring
You back victorious.

Ireland and Politics

In 1914, the peaceful achievement of Home Rule for Ireland was thrown into doubt due to the failure of the Government to deal with the build-up of arms in Northern Ireland (it was estimated that the UVF [Ulster Volunteer Force] had smuggled in from Germany 24,600 rifles and 3 million rounds of ammunition; with the Nationalists also smuggling in from Germany some 900 rifles and 25,000 rounds of ammunition) and the public refusal of a cavalry brigade in the Curragh to enforce the Home Rule Act. Civil war in Ireland was looking increasingly inevitable, but was prevented when the First World War broke out.

Great War

When Great Britain declared war on Germany on 4 August 1914, the total army strength was 247,000 with 145,000 ex-regular reservists. Of these, 20,000 were Irishmen already serving in the regular British Army with another 30,000 in first line reserve.

The British Army did not have National Service or any form of conscription and relied on volunteer soldiers. When war was declared, Lord Kitchener, who became Secretary for War on 5 August 1914, informed the Cabinet that it would be a three-year war requiring at least a million men. The attestation papers that volunteers for the war were required to sign stated that it was a *short* attestation. However, these facts are contrary to the popularly held belief that the war would be 'over by Christmas'.

Thirty new divisions were incorporated into what became known as the 'New Armies' or 'Kitchener's Army'. The volunteers were assigned to new battalions of existing regiments of infantry with the word 'Service' added to the battalion number. When volunteer numbers began to dwindle conscription was introduced, but this was not applied to Ireland.

On 20 September 1914, the leader of the Nationalist Party, John Redmond, was widely expected to be the first prime minister of the new Irish parliament. He called on the 'Irish Volunteers' to enlist in the British Army. This created a schism within the organisation, which resulted in those following Redmond (approximately 168,000) changing their name to the National Volunteers. The remaining 12,000 retained the title of the Irish Volunteers (erroneously referred to as Sinn Fein Volunteers), and committed themselves to the objective of gaining full independence for Ireland, by force if necessary.

John Redmond, the leader of nationalist Ireland, was a consummate politician of persuasion: a man ahead of the game. He understood the need for popular support and financial donation, and the need for powerful political allies to the cause. He astutely combined this in declamatory speeches that drew on nationalism, patriotism, Catholic ideology, sentimentality and love for the 'old country', global identity and a unity of 'Irishness' and what that meant. On 17 March 1914, St Patrick's Day (a celebrated day of national holiday for Irishmen and their descendants), American President Woodrow Wilson sported a sprig of shamrock in his jacket buttonhole. Redmond's gifts of pots of shamrock were on display in the White House and around Capitol Hill. Reports of the time stated that big dinners, balls and gatherings were held, with some 3,500 attending Mass at St Patrick's Cathedral in New York.

Some five months later, however, the First World War had broken out. It was, as the Americans say, 'a game changer'. Redmond still believed in the ideology of an Ireland that would gain its freedoms and identity, from within the provisions of the Home Rule Act, which he saw as the first steps towards independence. He felt it important that Irish nationalists should support the king at this time, and gave his backing to the war effort. He believed that loyalty to the crown would be rewarded by the enactment of Home Rule. He mounted a campaign of publicity and oratory persuasion, travelling extensively to that end, giving speeches and attracting large crowds.

St Patrick's Day on 17 March 1915 saw Redmond deliver one of the greatest acclaimed speeches of the First World War at the Free Trade Hall, Manchester, England:

Mr Chairman: If there is one thing more than another which I most value about this meeting it is its character. I have often, in the octave of St Patrick, had to speak in Manchester, but I have on these occasions addressed myself only to the Irish people of Manchester, I am proud to know that the present meeting is one not of Irishmen alone; but of Englishmen as well-[cheers]-firmly united in a common purpose. [Cheers.] I am proud to think it is a meeting of the representatives of every political party which existed in this country before the war, and the mere assembling of such a meeting in this great English centre is a proof of the profound and ineradicable change which has come over the Irish question.

When this war is over, we will all of us, of all previous parties, go back to the consideration of political questions in a new political world. [Cheers.] Ireland has been admitted to the democracy of England, upon equal terms, to her proper place in an Empire in the building of which she had as much to do as England herself [cheers] and she has taken that place with perfect and absolute good faith and loyalty. In ordinary circumstances this St Patrick's Day of

1915 would have been for us a day of triumph, of universal congratulation and jubilation. But alas! For Ireland, the mother of sorrows, we are met today in a moment of suffering and deep tragedy. The moment for our jubilation is postponed. The shadow of war – ay, the shadow of death – hangs heavily over our people and our country, and our first and most immediate duty at this moment is not to give expression to triumph over our political successes, not to take part in jubilation or congratulation, but to do, every man and woman of us, what we can to see that Ireland bears her right and honourable part in the duty that is cast upon us.

[Cheers.]

From the day of the declaration of war to this moment I have not made one single controversial political speech, and I have spoken in every province in Ireland to the greatest and most united and most enthusiastic meetings that I ever faced in the whole of my political experience. My one theme has been to impress upon Ireland the duty of taking a part today worthy of her history and traditions. The one political hope I have ventured to express, and I express it again here with all the fervour of my soul, is that when the war is over the common dangers which all Irishmen of all creeds and all parties have faced together, the commingling of their blood upon the battlefield and their death side by side like brothers in a foreign land, may have the effect of utterly and completely and forever obliterating the bitterness and divisions and hatreds of the past, so that the new Constitution we have won may be inaugurated in a country pacified by sacrifices and amongst a people united by the memory of common suffering.

[Cheers.]

This is the first speech I have had the opportunity of making in Great Britain since the outbreak of the war, and I will confine myself to considering what the Irish race has done since the declaration of war. I am proud to make the boast that every section of Ireland has bravely and nobly done its duty. [Cheers.] I wish to draw no invidious distinction between one section of my countrymen and another. You will remember the circumstances of Ireland are peculiar. For more than half a century the flower of her manhood has been fleeing from her shores to distant lands. No part of Ireland has suffered more than another. The emigration from Ulster has been, if anything, greater than the emigration from the other provinces. In the last sixty years over 4 millions of people have emigrated from Ireland. Since the year 1900 over a half a million have emigrated, and two-thirds of the people who have gone have been young men of military age. I will not dwell on the sad political causes which ended in this emigration, but every man today must deplore the fact that for these reasons Ireland is not able to make a contribution in men towards this war such as she would have been able to make, if political and social and economic conditions had allowed her population even to remain stationary. Happily, for all of us, the drain of emigration has now been arrested. Last year, 1914, was the first year since the great famine when the population of Ireland actually increased. [Cheers.] The emigration for last year was 50 per cent, less than it was the year before. [Cheers.]

It must also be remembered that Ireland is purely an agricultural country, and at present there is a great dearth of agricultural labour in many parts. There are few great centres of population after Dublin and Belfast, and yet in spite of these facts Ireland's contribution to the army has been of a truly remarkable kind. [Cheers.] The Irish Government have given me some figures which they have laboriously collected from every parish in Ireland with reference to enlistments. These figures show that up to February 15 there were Irishmen from Ireland with the Colours to the number of 99,704. [Cheers.] Recruiting is going on at the present moment at the rate of about 4,000 a month. From December 15 to January 15 there were 3,858 recruits; from January 15 to February 15 there were 4,601 recruits. It has been stated that at the Grafton Street recruiting office in Dublin they are now getting over five times as many recruits as they got in August and September, and that the men are still coming in from all parts of the city and county of Dublin. There are so-called Unionists, so-called Nationalists, and – it is interesting to note – so-called Sin Feiners. [Laughter.] All young men now seem to be imbued with a new idea of their duties and responsibilities. There were with the Colours on February 15, 20,210 men who had actually enrolled and disciplined and drilled members of the Irish National Volunteers [cheers] and there were 22,970 Ulster Volunteers with the Colours.

The volunteers presented one of the most extraordinary spectacles ever seen in the history of our country. There are today in Ireland two large bodies of volunteers. One is called the Ulster Volunteers. They are partially armed and partially drilled, but they are all filled with the true military sentiment and spirit. Fifty thousand of them have joined the army, and of the rest many are not of military age, are not physically fit, or are prevented from joining the army by just the same reasons as prevented thousands of men in this country. But these men are quite capable of home defence. On August 3 in the House of Commons I told the Government that, for the first time in the history of the relations between England and Ireland, Ireland could be left safely to the defence of her own sons, and I appeal to the Government to allow the Irish to undertake that duty. At the same time, I made an appeal to the Ulster Volunteers to join hands with the National Volunteers in this work. I wish to make no complaint, but I think it right to say that I have received no response to either appeal. The Prime Minister on August 10 said the Government were seriously considering how the volunteers could be utilised, but that Lord Kitchener's first duty was to raise his New Army. Subject to that, Mr Asquith said, and concurrent with it, he will do everything in his power to arrange for the full equipment and organisation of the Irish volunteers. Up to this time nothing has been done. Early in the war the Irish volunteers made an offer whereby 20,000 men could have been made available for home defence, so that not a single regular soldier need to be detained from the front for that purpose. The offer has not been accepted. I have some reason to think that in military circles in Ireland there is a strong feeling that from a purely military point of view, enlistment for home defence should be permitted; 20,000 men of Kitchener's Army, who are supposed to be drilling and training for the front, are being wasted, by being engaged in defending various points on the coast, railways, bridges and waterworks. The whole of these men could be set free, if Irishmen were allowed to take their places.

I have told you that Ireland has sent from Irish soil over 100,000 men to the Colours. What about the Irish race in Great Britain and throughout the world? Some figures were recently published which showed that 115,000 recruits of Irish birth or descent had gone from Great Britain since the beginning of the war, and after making careful enquiries I am convinced that these figures err on the side of modesty. I have been told by responsible men in Canada, Australia and New Zealand, that an enormous proportion of the contingents sent by those countries to the army was made up of Irishmen. It is no exaggeration to say that at this moment the Irish race can number with the Colours at least a quarter of a million sons.

There are some places in England, where Irish recruits have been branded together in Irish brigades, and all that they do that is honourable and chivalrous will rebound to the credit of Ireland. But I regret that the great bulk of the Irish recruits have been scattered among the English regiments, and to those Irishmen who are going to enlist I would like to make an appeal. There are in Ireland three divisions. One has been called the Ulster Division, and I am told it is very nearly full. Another, the 10th Division, is intended to be a purely Irish division, but some thousands of English recruits have been drafted into it. The third, the 16th Division, we have come to call the Irish Brigade, not because we know the difference between a division and a brigade, but for reasons of history and affection. The term recalled the history of the old Irish Brigade, which for nearly a hundred years cast the light of its glory over all the battlefields of Europe. This Irish Brigade is not quite complete. It still requires about 2,000 men, and I hope that every Irishman in England who enlists will chose one of the regiments in the 16th Division. I have heard of some complaints of difficulties put in the way of Irish recruits who desire to enter Irish regiments. I have been told that recruiting officers have brought pressure to bear upon recruits to prevent them from going into Irish regiments and I should like to get hold of an authentic case. When these rumours first came to me, I went to the War Office, and I was assured that a recruiting officer who did anything of the kind was guilty of a gross abuse of duty. Any man who went into a recruiting office to enlist was entitled to choose for himself which regiment he would enter, and whether that regiment was stationed in Fermoy or Tipperary the Government would send him free of charge.

I do not want to make any comparisons, I believe every country is doing its duty in the best way it can. I make no claim for Ireland except that Ireland is doing its duty. Our record is one of which we can be proud. If we turn for a moment to the record of performances at the front, I think we Irish men can hold up our heads. [Cheers.] Sir John French is an Irishman [cheers] he springs from good old Irish stock. Admiral Beatty is an Irishman [cheers] from the County of Wexford. Admiral Carden, who is bombarding the Dardanelles, is an Irishman from Tipperary. [Loud cheers.] The Lieutenant commander of the destroyer that sunk the U–12 the other day is a Creagh from County Clare. And if we leave the high in rank and go down to the rank and file [cheers] I think the name Michael O'Leary [cheers] will be forever associated with the history of this war. If you look at the performances at the front from another point of view, and look at the casualty lists and see how whole regiments of Irish troops have almost been wiped out, I do not think any man will have been found in this country to deny that Ireland is doing her duty. [Cheers.] But, after all, we make no boast of it. It is nothing to be wondered at. It is all in keeping with the history and traditions of our race. [Cheers.] If Ireland had held back in this war she would have belied her whole history. How the calculations of the Kaiser have been falsified! He expected to meet a divided Empire. [Laughter.] It is easy to laugh. Ten years ago he might have done so. He expected revolt and disaffection in South Africa. He expected revolt and disaffection in Ireland, and in Egypt, and in India. But he forgot the march of events and the march of ideas in this country. He forgot the march of education and enlightenment in this country. He forgot that the rule of the people has been substituted for the rule of the ascendancy classes. And he forgot that the rule of the English democracy has united this Empire upon a firm and sure foundation of liberty. Principles of freedom have turned South Africa into a loyal, because self-governing, country. The principle of freedom has made Canada and Australia and New Zealand loyal, because they are self-governing. The same thing has happened in Ireland. [Cheers.]

We Irishmen feel that today, at least, we have entered on terms of equality into the Empire, and we say we will defend that Empire with loyalty and devotion. [Cheers.] For the first time in the history of the British Empire, we can feel in our very souls that in fighting for the Empire we are fighting for Ireland. [Cheers.] My own belief is that every Irish soldier who gives his life on the battlefields of Flanders dies for Ireland, for her liberty and her prosperity, as truly did any of the heroes and martyrs of our race in the past. [Cheers.] It was a blessed day when the democracy of Britain trusted Ireland. That trust has done what force could never do. That trust has done what centuries of coercion failed to accomplish. It has bound two nations together in a unity of common interests and common rights and common liberties, and it has given to us a watchword for the future, the old classic motto, Imperium et libertas-Empire and liberty. [Cheers.]

This was a keynote speech: its audience of some 10,000 people were both Irish and English; it was intended to be non-political, as Redmond points out, but was politically inclusive. It drew on the history and influence of Ireland's past and present contributions and its identity; it developed the idea of Ireland as a recognised nation within the British Empire – an Ireland with a 'voice' and democracy, through the realisation of power. Redmond's rhetoric carried the theme that support for the war was ultimately support for Ireland. It promoted national unity and solidarity in a time of world crisis, a calling to arms alongside the spiritual obligation of all Irishmen to support the war effort. In the speech,

Redmond calls on women to do 'their part', though it is interesting to note that this call of equality did not extend to women's suffrage after Home Rule, something Redmond was very opposed to. In a *Manchester Guardian* report some years earlier, he was quoted as saying that: 'It is necessary for the Irish Party in the interests of Home Rule, to save the Liberal ministry from the disruptive effects of women's suffrage.' However, his rallying cry was taken up by one Chapel Street lodging-house keeper, Mrs Bridget de Courcy, who enjoined her lodgers to volunteer to do 'their duty'. It is worth noting the problems Redmond associates with the volunteers' choice of Irish regiments and the drafting of recruits by the British Army: in establishing an 'Irish Brigade' (16th Irish Division), the British Government were suspicious Redmond might harbour plans for an Irish army at some future date. The sentiments expressed in the speech did strike a chord and recruitment figures show an increase in the numbers of men joining up in the following months.

Irish soldiers in the British Expeditionary Force had already seen action in Flanders. Some 80,000 men enlisted in Ireland in the first twelve months of the war, with 40,000 from Ulster alone. These Irishmen enlisted in the Irish regiments of the 10th and 16th (Irish) Divisions of the New British Army and the 36th (Ulster) Division, as well as English, Scottish and Welsh regiments. There were also English, Scottish and Welsh men assigned to Irish regiments because of their Catholic faith. This may have been the case for those of Chapel Street who, in all likelihood, did not make the journey to Ireland to enlist. Questions were asked in Parliament, however, with regard to volunteers in England who wanted to volunteer for Irish regiments but were informed that this was not possible. This allegation was denied, but Hansard (Official Record of Parliament) records that Redmond disputed this.

The recruitment figures for Ireland itself, for the period of August 1914–February 1915, show an enlistment of 50,107. In the period to August the figures dropped to 25,235, within six months the figure is 19,801, and for the period February 1916–August 1916, through to February 1917, they show 9,323 and 8,178, respectively. Factors affecting these figures include: the rush to enlist at the onset of war, for whatever reason; the Easter Rising of 1916 and subsequent turmoil and events; and the high casualty rates, particularly from the Battle of the Somme. The numbers continued to fall further, averaging at around 5,000 each half-year period up to the period August 1918–November 1918, when they show an increase to 9,843 within that three-month period. As the war progressed, Irish losses were replaced by UK conscripts. For example, the percentage of non-Irish soldiers in the 1st Royal Irish Rifles in 1916 was 23 per cent, but by 1917 the figure was 52 per cent.

Although many numbers of men who left Chapel Street to go to the Great War did return, some who had been lodgers did not for various reasons. An unspecified number of men did not return to England and it is probable that a proportion of these chose to go to Ireland. As demobilisation did not take place immediately after the war, the ex-soldiers, on retuning to Ireland, would have found a changed political climate.

In 1918, Ireland voted as one nation in the Irish General Election, held as part of the United Kingdom General Election. The election resulted in an outright win for Sinn Fein ('Ourselves alone'), who polled 476,087 (46.9 per cent), with the Unionists polling 257,314 (25.3 per cent), and the nationalist Irish Parliamentary Party (IPP) polling 220,837 (21.7 per cent) of the vote, respectfully. There were many factors which influenced this landslide victory: not least the increased number of people allowed to vote. Under the 'Representation of the People Act 1918', women over the age of 30 years (who met specific property regulations), were enfranchised for the first time: also, men over 21 years (military servicemen over 19 years). This increased the Irish electorate from 700,000 to approximately 2 million. Other significant factors were the sense of betrayal felt over the 'Irish Convention of April 1918', which sought to tie Home Rule with Conscription in a dual policy; the anti-conscription campaign and general strike; the probable partition of Ireland, and the execution of many of the leaders of the Easter Rising.

It is more than likely that it was the Women's Vote that carried the day. The census figures for 1911 show an increase in the population of women (specifically in the age group between 32-49 years), which had in general more than doubled since the Gorta Mor (The Great Hunger). For too long they had no representation, the leaders of the main parties – Asquith, Carson and Redmond – were against women's suffrage; their champion Francis Sheehy-Skeffington, a pacifist, was shot dead by the British during the Easter Rising. Now, for the first time in history, they had a 'voice' that could be heard; they now had the opportunity of representation and power to affect change. It was the males of their families who had gone to war, and either died or came back wounded. They were the ones now facing a future of no breadwinners, poverty and low expectation. They were the ones carrying the worries of eviction, workhouse, and the possibility of future famine. They were the ones who had been marginalised by politics, patriarchy, religion and the class system.

The election resulted in seventy-three parliamentary seats won by Sinn Fein, which entitled the ruling party to be represented in the House of Commons at Westminster. However, the elected members instead formed a breakaway parliament in Dublin – the first Dail Eireann (Assembly of Ireland) – and declared its independence from Britain.

The Irish Free State Constitution Act of 1922 was an Act of Parliament of the United Kingdom passed to enact the constitution of the Irish Free State, which formally ratified the 1921 Anglo–Irish Treaty of 1921. Under the conditions of the Anglo–Irish Treaty, Crown forces (army and police) would withdraw from most of Ireland. Accordingly, the following regiments of the British Army were disbanded on 31 July 1922: Royal Dublin Fusiliers; Connaught Rangers; Royal Irish Regiment; Leinster Regiment; Royal Munster Regiment.

On 12 June 1922, the five regimental colours were laid up in a ceremony at St George's Hall, Windsor Castle, in the presence of HM King George V.

With emotion in his voice, the king received the colours, saying:

> Your colours are the records of various deeds in war, and of the glorious tradi-
> tions thereby created. You are called upon to part with them today for reasons
> beyond your control and resistance. By you and your predecessors these colours
> have been reverenced and guarded as a sacred trust – which trusts you now
> confide in me. As your King, I am proud to accept this trust. But I fully realise
> with what grief you relinquish these dearly prized emblems; and I pledge my
> word that within these ancient and historic walls your colours will be treasured,
> honoured, and protected as hallowed memorials of the glorious deeds of brave
> and loyal regiments.

Statistical dispute surrounds the agreement of figures for the total number of Irish
soldiers who served in the British Army and Navy in the First World War; it is
thought to be in the region of 210,000, with 140,000 men enlisting in Ireland.
The names of the soldiers who died during the war show a figure of 49,400
recorded on the National War Memorial (these figures would not include the
men of Chapel Street that were Irishmen or of Irish descent).

It is important for the Republic of Ireland and its future generations to recognise the sacrifices made by its sons and families in the Great War. It should
rightly honour those who died and those who suffered ill health for many years
afterwards. The United Kingdom of Great Britain and Northern Ireland should
also recognise the supreme effort and sacrifices of all Irishmen (and families),
those of Irish descent, and emigrants of various political and religious beliefs, who
voluntarily answered the call-up; without whose service the war would not have
been won, and world peace brought to pass.

PART ONE

Lord Kitchener's Letter to the Troops

[This paper is to be considered by each soldier as confidential, and to be kept in his Active Service Pay Book.]

You are ordered abroad as a soldier of the King, to help our French comrades against the invasion of a common enemy. You have to perform a task which will need your courage, your energy, your patience, remember that the honour of the British Army depends upon your individual conduct. It will be your duty not only to set an example of discipline and perfect steadiness under fire but also to maintain the most friendly relations with those whom you are helping in this struggle. The operations in which you are engaged will, for the most part, take place in a friendly country, and you can do your country no better service than in showing yourself, in France and Belgium, in the true character of a British soldier.

Be invariably courteous, considerate, and kind. Never do anything likely to injure or destroy property, and always look upon looting as a disgraceful act. You are sure to meet with a welcome and to be trusted, and your conduct must justify that welcome and that trust. Your duty cannot be done unless your health is sound. So keep constantly on your guard against any excesses. In this new experience you may find temptations both in wine and women. You must entirely resist both temptations, and while treating all women with perfect courtesy, you should avoid any intimacy.

Do your duty bravely.

Fear God.

Honour the King.

KITCHENER

Field-Marshal.

Kitchener's New Army

I was convinced that, not only had we got to feed the existing Expeditionary Force, and maintain an adequate garrison here and in India, but further, we had to produce a new army sufficiently large to count in a European war. In fact, although I did not see it in detail, I must ask Gentlemen of the House of Commons to recognise that I had, rough-hewn in my mind, the idea of creating such a force as would enable us continuously to reinforce our troops in the field by fresh divisions, and thus to assist our Allies at the time when they were beginning to feel the strain of the war with its attendant casualties. By this time we planned to work on the upgrade while our Allies' forces decreased, so that at the conclusive period of the war we should have the maximum trained fighting army this country could produce.

Such an idea was contrary to the theories of all European soldiers, it had always been argued, could be expanded within limits, but could not be created in time of war. I felt, myself, that, though there might be some justice in this view, I relied on the energy of this country to supply deficiencies of previous experience and preparation ...

Kitchener's New Army was made up of the following Army Groups and Divisions. (These were not formed as actual groups of armies, but as divisions of similar size to an army.)

K1 ARMY GROUP
9th (Scottish) Division
10th (Irish) Division
11th (Northern) Division
12th (Easter) Division
13th (Western) Division
14th (Light) Infantry

K2 ARMY GROUP
15th (Scottish) Division
16th (Irish) Division
17th (Norther) Division
18th (Eastern) Division

19th (Western) Division
20th (Light) Division

K3 ARMY GROUP
21st Division
22nd Division
23rd Division
24th Division
25th Division
26th Division

K4 ARMY GROUP
Kitchener's Fourth New Army was formed from November 1914 with:

30th Division
31st Division
32nd Division
33rd Division
34th Division
35th Division

The divisions were not fully formed when the decision was made to use them to provide replacements for the first three New Armies. The division were broken up on 10 April 1915; the infantry brigades and battalions became reserve formations and the other divisional troops were transferred to the divisions of the Fifth and Sixth New Armies.

K5 ARMY GROUP
Re-designated K4 following breakup of original K4

30th Division – originally designated as 37th Division
31st Division – originally designated as 38th Division
32nd Division – originally designated as 39th Division
33rd Division – originally designated as 40th Division
34th Division – originally designated as 41st Division
35th Division – originally designated as 42nd Division

K6 ARMY GROUP
Re-designated K5 following re-designation of original K5.

36th (Ulster) Division – raised as the Ulster Division, numbered on 28 August 1914.
37th Division – originally designated as 44th Division
38th (Welsh) Division – originally designated as 43rd Division
39th Division
40th Division
41st Division

The Cheshire Regiment

MOTTO: 'Ever Glorious'

The Cheshire Regiment raised thirty-eight battalions for the First World War, fighting in Gallipoli, Sinai, Salonika, Mesopotamia, Palestine and the Western Front.

From the outbreak of war in August 1914 until conscription in 1916, almost half of the men from Chapel Street volunteered their services to the Cheshire Regiment. A sixth of this number would never return home to their families.

Cheshire Regiment Casualties
Killed, died of wounds, disease, and missing:
378 officers
8,420 WO, NCO and private soldiers

FIRST BATTALION (15th BRIGADE, 5th DIVISION):
Sgt James Arnold, service number 6463; Joseph Arnold, service number 1049; John Booth, service number 10168; Thomas Booth, service number 9715; Thomas Corfield, service number 10493; John Davies, service number 6300; Martin de Courcy, service number 10421; Michael Groark(e), service number 9278; Hugh Hennerley, service number 10426; Peter Hughes, service number 6974; Frank Collins, service number 10816.

Retreat from Mons

The first battle of the First World War for the British Expeditionary Force (BEF) was fought in late August 1914. Known as the Battle of Mons, it formed part of a subsidiary of engagements referred to historically as the Battle of the Frontiers. The BEF was the regular army and their numbers were added to by enlisted men with previous warfare experience. These ex-soldiers became known as 'Old Contemptibles', with numerous men from Chapel Street making up their numbers.

The BEF attempted to hold the line of the Mons Conde Canal against the advance of the German First Army. The British Army was forced to retreat due to the superiority of the German Army and the sudden retreat of the French Fifth Army, which exposed the British right flank.

The retreat from Mons lasted two weeks with numerous battles, including Le Cateau, taking the BEF to the outskirts of Paris, before it counter-attacked with the French at the Battle of the Marne.

The Retreat

At 11.45 a.m., 'GOC 5th Division personally told CO (Commanding Officer), that the Division was ordered to retire with the Norfolk Regt, Cheshire Regt, 119th Btty R.F.A. and Squad 19th Hussars.' The Cheshire Regimental Diary concurs they were to take up a position facing north-west along the Elouges–Audregnies road and act as a flank guard to the Mancheters and the troops entrenched round Wasmes in this retirement.

The troops were moved into position, with B Coy Cheshire Regiment holding the village of Audregnies. The diary notes that masses of the enemy were seen moving out of Quievrain; and their artillery and machine guns opened a very hot fire on the infantry and cavalry and R.H.A., who were operating against the German cavalry in the valley 1¼ miles to the south-east of Quievrain.

The official history records that consequently: 'Colonel Ballard sent to the Cheshire three separate messages to fall back, not one of which reached them.' The Major of L Battery receiving no orders and seeing no sign of the Norfolk, and having fired away all his ammunition, was meditating on withdrawal when the Brigade-Major of the 2nd Cavalry Brigade arrived and directed him to bring his battery out of action. 'The guns were thereupon run down close under the screen of the railway hedge; the limbers were brought up one by one at a gallop from Audregnies; and the battery limbered up and got away without further mishap.' The 4th Dragoon Guards retired from a house by the lane and, together with L Battery and the main body of the 2nd Cavalry, moved southward upon Ruesnes. The Cavalry Division had already fallen back towards St Waast and Wargnies, with the 4th Cavalry further to the west between Saultain and Jenlain.

Abandoned by the rest of the Allied army, this left the 1st Battalion and a small party of the Norfolk Regiment alone. The Commanding Officer Lieut. Colonel Boger was unaware of the general retreat, with the official history denoting that he was at a loss to know what was expected of him. With the Germans now pressing forward rapidly on both flanks, and while making dispositions to meet the movement, he was 'disabled by three wounds'. Shortly before this, part of the reserve company at Audregnies had been ordered by a staff officer to fall back, and after vainly trying to rejoin the fighting line (which was forbidden), made its way to Athis.

As the Germans came closer, the main body fell back to the Audregnies road, where they were fired upon by two machine guns placed in a dip in the ground, a couple of hundred yards away. They were immediately silenced by the machine guns of the Cheshire with a little party of men charging forward with the bayonet to dislodge the enemy from the vantage point. The Germans fled at the sight of them and during this short break the opportunity was taken to draw a small part of the battalion across country to Audregnies Wood, which they reached under heavy fire, making their way to Athis.

But the Germans, on seeing how few in number their assailants were, returned to attack, and 'there was nothing left for the remainder of the Cheshire, mere handful though they were, but to fight to the last'. They still had ammunition and could keep up rapid fire, but they were by now separated into at least three groups, continuing to defend themselves. But by 7 p.m., surrounded and overwhelmed on all sides, they were forced to lay down their arms and surrender. Only forty of the main body on the Audregnies road remained unwounded. During the retreat, the small parties also ran into trouble at Dour and Athis.

The indefatigable gunners of the 5th Division artillery came into action along the line Blaugies–Athis–Montignies, and further south at Houdain, which enabled the survivors of the flank guard to reach their bivouac at St Waast at 9 p.m., utterly worn by hunger, fatigue and hard fighting.

The cost was heavy. The 119th Battery lost 30 officers and men and the Norfolk over 250 officers and men. The Cheshire suffered the most devastating casualties of all. Out of nearly 1,000 men, only 2 officers and 200 men remained to answer roll call in the evening.

The flank guard had held off from the main body of the 5th Division, the pursuit of a whole German corps, preventing the retreat from becoming a rout. Their action delayed the German advance by four hours. It has been claimed that the actions taken by the 1st Battalion Cheshire Regiment saved the BEF from extinction.

The Western Front: Second Battle of Ypres, 22 April–25 May 1915

Men from Chapel Street:
Cheshire Regiment: 2nd Battalion
Joseph Booth Jnr, service number 8851, died 8/5/15; Charles Croft, service number 24973, died 8/5/15; Arthur Garner, service number 10419; Robert Hughes, service number 12291.

King's Own Royal (Lancaster) Regiment: 1st Battalion
James Ford, service number 6523, died 8/5/15; Ralph Ryan, service number 3508, died 14/5/15; John Norton, service number 9479.

Prince of Wales's (South Lancashire) Regiment: 4th Battalion
Lance Corporal Arthur Oxley, service number 200309.

Gordon Highlanders: 1st Battalion
Joseph Margiotta, service number 24140.

Somerset Light Infantry: 1st Battalion
Michael Hines, service number 44416.

Manchester Regiment: 2nd Battalion
Richard Ryan, service number 2643.

The commencement of the second battle of Ypres was marked by the initiation of gas warfare.

Allied Position

The situation of the Allies at Ypres was distinctly weak (Edmonds: 1932). Although possessing greater numbers, heavy guns and means of artillery observation was weaker; there were two far from first-class French divisions interpolated between the British and the Belgians. There were no arrangements for unity of command of the three different contingents, and the two junctions were ill-chosen: that of the French and British at a shoulder of the salient, and that of the French and Belgians at the canal, where the two forces were on opposite sides of the water. The Germans could hardly select a better sector for attack.

Description of First Gas Attack: The Battle of Gravenstafel, 22–24 April

Late in the afternoon of 22 April 1915, over the battle-scarred terrain around the medieval Belgian city of Ypres, a sound of large-calibre guns was heard. At 17.24, three flares rose from an observation balloon over the German lines and burst against the eastern sky. German artillery commenced a fierce bombardment that landed to the rear of the French and British lines in the Ypres sector. At 6.00 an eerie silence fell over the area.

Peering across the battlefield, the men of two French Divisions, the 87th Territorial and the 45th Algerian, and those on a point of vantage saw two greenish-yellow clouds on either side of Langemarck, in front of the German line. There was no warning of the attack. Jets of white smoke were seen to rise from numerous points in the German front line, and these quickly united to form thick white clouds in front of which could be distinguished a haze of greenish-blue vapour. The clouds began to drift across the terrain at a height of up to 6ft. As they drifted they spread laterally, settling into every depression in the landscape, moving before a light wind, becoming a bluish-white mist spilling into the French trenches, silently enveloping the occupants in a misty, deadly embrace.

Soon a peculiar smell was noticed, accompanied by smarting of the eyes and tingling of the nose and throat. Chlorine, the gas employed, has a powerful irritant action on the respiratory organs and all mucous membranes exposed to it, causing spasms of the glottis, a burning sensation in the eyes, nose and throat, followed by bronchitis and oedema of the lungs.

To the north and south-west of the now mist-enshrouded French positions, British and Canadian troops looked into the haze and, to their amazement, saw soldiers emerging from the cloud, 'running wildly, and in confusion' towards positions to the rear. Moments later French soldiers staggered by, 'blinded coughing, chests heaving, faces an ugly purple colour, lips speechless with agony'. One by one, the guns of the French artillery batteries in the sector stopped firing, and the two French Divisions collapsed.

The Canadian Division held the sector immediately to the right of the French position and their left flank was affected by the gas, whilst they had to swing back to conform with the retirement of the French.

The Ypres front now had a gap over four miles wide containing hundreds of men in a 'comatose or dying condition'.

After half an hour, German troops, equipped with cotton wadding tied over their faces, cautiously advanced into the breach created by the discharge of gas, advancing eventually to occupy the ground up to the Yser canal between Steenstraate and Het Saas.

On 24 April, two days later, during which time the British and French brought reinforcements into the area, the Germans discharged more chlorine gas. The trenches held by the Canadians were in many places only 200 yards from the enemy; they faced the attack unprotected, and many died where they stood rather than yield ground.

On 1, 6 and 10 May 1915, a fresh series of cloud gas attacks was made south of the Menin Road against Hill 60 sector where the fighting was severe.

The war diary for the 2nd Battalion Cheshire Regiment records that:

By the 8th May the battalion were at Verlorenhoek, where a heavy bombardment of the trenches, which began in the morning, 'carried on until the line was broken by a fierce infantry attack made with overwhelming numbers'. This was followed by another gas attack which was 'freely used by the enemy'. Using the gas enabled the Germans to surrounded the positions and with very few exceptions, the whole of the 2nd Cheshire Battalion Officers were killed or taken prisoner, with 17 Other ranks killed; 4 Officers were wounded and 200 ranks; 11 Officers were missing and 182 Other Ranks.

On 24 May 1915, a cloud gas of 'considerable magnitude' was made from the Menin Road to Sanctuary Wood, followed in the day by a serious infantry attack. Lachrymator shells were employed on an extensive scale for the first time during the last of these attacks.

The Germans made no further gas cloud attacks on the British front for seven months.

It is practically impossible to form any accurate idea of the number of casualties and deaths directly attributable to gas in this series of cloud attacks. A large number of men were killed outright by gas in the field, but deaths due to this cause are included in the casualty lists under the general heading 'killed in action' (MacPherson et al: 1923).

The use of chemical weapons by the Germans continued throughout the war and resulted in the development and use of gas by the British at the Battle of Loos. When the British commenced to make warfare gas there was only one plant for producing liquid chlorine, with a maximum output of one ton a day; by the end of 1915, the British had produced 860 tons of this gas and by 1918, 15,500 tons, half representing chlorine in liquid form and the remainder being phosgene, chloropicrin and lachrymator substances.

The Battle of Loos: 25 September–13 October 1915

Men from Chapel Street:

Cheshire Regiment (84th Brigade): 2nd Battalion
Arthur Garner, service number 10419, Machine Gun Corps. Died at Loos 3/10/15.

Devonshire Regiment (20th Brigade): 8th Battalion:
Frank Wyatt, service number 34061.

Grenadier Guards (2nd Guards): 3rd Battalion
Company Sergeant-Major Joe Norton, service number 10330.

King's (Liverpool) Regiment Indian Sirkind Brigade: 4th Battalion
John Ratchford, service number 10773.

Royal Irish Rifles (25th Brigade): 1st Battalion
Edward Lowe, service number 10990.

South Wales Borderers (3rd Brigade): 1st Battalion
Joseph Lowe, service number 19157.

Welsh Regiment (3rd Brigade): 2nd Battalion
Peter Morley, service number 53568.

In September 1915, an Anglo British and French action was planned to break the German line. Thousands of guns were to be massed, which would hopefully destroy the German trenches. Twelve infantry divisions were to launch the attack. Sir Douglas Haig with the First British Army would attack between La Bassee Canal and Lens, with the French forcing their way through the lines south of Lens.

It was arranged that the First Corps, consisting of the 2nd, 7th and 9th Divisions, under Lieutenant-General Hubert Gough, should attack the line between La Bassee Canal and Vermelles, while the Fourth Corps (1st, 15th and 47th Divisions), under Lieutenant-General Sir H. Rawlinson, attack from Vermelles to Grenay, the Hulluch–Vermelles road forming a boundary between the two Corps.

Sir John French Despatch of the character of the front to be attacked by the British Army:

> Opposite the front of the main line of attack the distance between the enemy's trenches and our own varied from about 100 yards to 500 yards. The country over which the advance took place is open and overgrown with long grass and self-grown crops. From the canal southward our trenches and those of the enemy ran, roughly, parallel up an almost imperceptible rise to the south-west. From the Vermelles-Hulloch road southward the advantage of height is on the enemy's side as far as the Bethune-Lens road. There the two lines of trenches cross a spur in which the rise culminates, and thence the command lies on the side of the British trenches. Due east of the intersection of spur and trenches and a short mile away stands Loos. Less than a mile farther south-east is Hill 70, which is the summit of the gentle rise in the ground.

> Other notable tactical points in our front were:

> 'Fosse 8' (a thousand yards south of Auchy), which is a coal-mine with a high and strongly defended slag heap.

> 'The Hohenzollern Redoubt' – A strong work thrust out nearly 500 yards in front of the German lines and close to our own. It is connected with their front line by three communication trenches abutting into the defences of Fosse 8.

> Cite St Elie – A strongly defended mining village lying 1500 yards south of Haisnes.

> 'The Quarries' – Lying half-way to the German Trenches west of Cite St Elie.

> Hulluch – A village strung out along a small stream, lying less than half a mile south-east of Cite St Elie and 3000 yards north-east of Loos.

> Half a mile north of Hill 70 is 'Puits 14 bis', another coal-mine, possessing great possibilities for defence when taken in conjunction with a strong redoubt situated on the north-east side of Hill 70.

The salient features of the Battle of Loos

Planning and Execution

Field-Marshall French had expected the battle to last a week, and favoured a limited attack with the reserves employed when success was achieved. Haig's aim was to win the battle in one day, using the reserves after a hole had been cut in the German line. The problems of the positioning of XI Corps and release of them was crucial to the outcome of the battle. The aftermath of this resulted in the resignation of the French and the promotion of Haig into his position.

Smoke Cloud and Gas Attack

Artificial smoke-clouds were used by the British (Grenadier Guards), to mask the advance of the infantry. Trench mortar bombs and artillery shells were filled with phosphorus, which gave off an intense cloud of white smoke on explosion.

On the morning of 25 September, the Royal Engineers released 140 tons of chlorine gas from 5,000 cylinders. However, crosswinds caused the gas to blow back into British trenches, resulting in 7 deaths and 2,600 injuries; 600 German soldiers were gassed.

Symptoms of Gas Poisoning:

The first effect of inhalation is a burning pain in the throat and eyes, accompanied by a sensation of suffocation and severe chest pain. Retching and vomiting is common; the lips and mouth are dry and the tongue is covered by a thick dry fur. Severe headaches follow with weakness in the legs; if the patient gives way to this and lies down, he is likely to inhale more chlorine; unconsciousness usually occurs, his face assumes a pale greenish-yellow colour. If a man lives long enough to be admitted to a clearing station, and he is conscious, his face is violet red and his ears and fingernails blue; skin is cold and temperature subnormal. Broncho-pneumonia develops possible pleurisy, empyema and gangrene of the lung. Essentially, the men drowned in their own body fluid (Hurst: 1917).

The gas attacks of the Battle of Loos strike at the imagination. Ian Kikuchi (IWM) states that there is something insidious about gas: 'Gas, which moves like a vapour, brings to mind ghosts, phantoms and other things associated with death.' He further suggests that the gas masks themselves play a role in this: 'to protect yourself from the gas you have to make yourself look and sound frightening.'

Extracts from the War Diaries

The Guards Division

The attack began at 6.30 a.m. after four days continuous bombardment by our massed guns. Gas was employed (by the British) but unfortunately the wind was unfavourable, and it moved so slowly that it retarded the advance. Further, the wire in some places had hardly been touched, and consequently the Second Division was held up from the start.

By mid-day the First Corps had secured the whole of the German front from the Hohenzollern Redoubt southwards and had pushed forward to the second line at three points. But in this achievement it suffered heavy casualties, and was left too weak to do more than hold on to the position it had gained.

In the Fourth Corps the First Division swept forward, carried the first two lines of German trenches, and reached the outskirts of Hulluch, where it waited for reinforcements, but as these did not arrive it had to fall back on the Lens–La Bassee road. It pushed through not only to Loos, but even over Hill 70, and the 44th Brigade in this division actually reached the outskirts of Cite St. Laurent.

25 & 26 September.

It was bitterly cold on the night of the 25th, which was spent by the 3rd Battalion in the old British front trench north-west of Loos. Some of the platoons got into an old remnant of a trench and some had to down outside. The men had to constantly get up and run about to warm themselves and then try and snatch more rest. In the morning the battalion started off in the direction of Loos. At first it marched in fours, but on coming into the shell area assumed artillery formation, and went across the open. While ascending the slope it was not fired upon, but when it came down the hill towards Loos shrapnel burst all around it. The battalion relieved the Scots Guards and got into what had formerly been the German third-line trenches. Both Officers and men were filled with admiration at the intricate dug-outs they found; twenty to thirty feet down in the chalk, great trouble had been extended on this part of the line and the German Officers had been accustomed to live almost in luxury. The 3rd Battalion were ordered to dig communication trenches and repair the parapet. Soon the 3rd Batt. Men were soaked to the skin in the pouring rain, and an icy cold wind added to their discomfort, as they had no prospect that night of getting either dry or warm.

27 & 28 September.

The 3rd Battalion was now prolonging the line of the Scots Guards to the right, and holding from the south-west corner of Loos and these positions remained unchanged during the 28th September.

Early in the morning of 28 September, the 4th Battalion were in position at the Loos–Hulluch Road. Fifty men of this battalion were on Hill 70 in addition to thirty of the 3rd Battalion. Some engineers had got out to them and erected barbed wire entanglements. There was a continual procession of maimed and wounded men crawling back to this 'little oasis', who were sniped by the enemy, in the exposed spot.

Diary 4th Battalion Grenadier Guards

8.30 p.m. Lt. W. and a handful of men in a trench.

Saw a party of Germans crawl and advance toward some of the wounded who were unable to move. Feeling sure they intended to take the wounded prisoners, where their injuries would be dressed, orders were given not to fire. The Germans crept on slowly, but on reaching the wounded, they proceeded to bayonet them. It was hardly necessary for Lt. W. to give the orders to fire, as the men with the machine-guns had seen this dastardly act, and the two machine-guns soon wiped out the whole party of Germans. Our wounded men were finally rescued by the Scots Guards.

September 29 & 30.

Shelled by the enemy, who knew the range of the trench precisely. A gallant attempt was made to take Chalk Pit but the attack failed. The Brigade was relieved on the night of the 30th by the Berkshire Regiment. The relief did not finish until past 2 a.m., when the battalion much exhausted after three days' fighting, marched slowly back through Noyelles and Sailly-la-Bourse to Verquigneul, which was reached about 6 a.m.

Throughout the Sunday the fighting was very severe, and it was only with the very greatest difficulty that we held on to Loos. The First Corps was also being strongly counter attacked, and the quarries changed hands several times. All day the Crown Prince of Bavaria, who was in command of the army facing the British divisions, was engaged in bringing up reserves from other parts, and by next day he had strengthened his whole line. The German line ran from Auchy – La Bassee over comparatively flat country to the Vermelles – Hulluch road, where the ground became undulating and culminated in Hill 70.

The Success at Chalk Pit and Puits 14 bis was shortened by tremendous machine gun fire and the position could not be held. This made it difficult for the other brigades to move forward. To relieve the strain on troops more reinforcements were sent in. In going forward this brigade took Hill 70, but it too found it impossible to keep what it had won. The enemy's trenches were marked on the map as being on the crest of the hill, but in reality they were on the reverse slope, and had never been touched by shell-fire. The net result of this attack was the establishment of the British front line running northward from the south-eastern end of Loos and parallel to the Lens–La Bassee road.

The 3rd Battalion Grenadier Guards casualties killed, wounded, and missing amounted to 229.

The 1st Guards Brigade was to advance in the direction of the Bois Hugo and straighten the line, so that it would run parallel to the Lens–La Bassee road. It was to take and hold Chalk Pit and Puits 14 bis and the 3rd Brigade was to advance to Hill 70. This depended on the success on the 2nd Brigade. The 1st Guards Brigade was to assist the brigades by fire as far as possible and collected as many smoke bombs and smoke candles as possible; and at zero hour formed a most effective smokescreen, which drew off the fire of a great many German guns from the other attackers.

The 3rd Brigade 2nd Welsh Regiment was successful in capturing German prisoners in a Support Trench and met their objectives.

The 8th Devonshires advanced into the cloud of gas and smoke. The Germans attempted to break up gas cloud by shelling it which caused numerous casualties. British Artillery had failed to cut the German wire which remained partly intact.

Subsequent Operations

3–13 October
Cheshire Regiment 2nd Battalion

This battle centred around the Hohenzollern Redoubt, a work which protected the Dump, a huge spoilbank from which the Germans had observation over the Rutoire plain as far as Noeux-les-Mines. The 2nd Battalion were ordered into the trenches on 20 September, while three disorganised brigades were moving out. When they at last reached their allotted position, they found the Germans in the trenches on the right and in the continuation of it. However, in the face of repeated orders to withdraw, our men, the Northumberland fusiliers and the Welsh delivered repeated bomb and bayonet attacks.

The fighting was pure trench warfare, close and desperate hand to hand fighting, mainly with bombs, for which the Germans were better equipped than our people. The trenches were permanently congested. The breakdown of the means for removing the wounded made the communication trenches impassable, and the progress of the fighting and local situation were often completely unknown even at Battalion Headquarters. Orders were sometimes issued from Divisional Head Quarters for a position to be attacked which had already been taken at immense sacrifice, and lost again before the orders had arrived! (Crookenden: 1938).

Observational Accounts
Communique from Rawlinson to the King's Advisor (28 September):
From what I can ascertain, some of the divisions did actually reach the enemy's trenches, for their bodies can now be seen on the barbed wire.

Extracts from War Diaries

Battalion in trenches at Hohenzollern Redoubt
27th & 29th September. Battalion embussed in 37 buses for Bethune. Marched to Sailly-La-Bourse then to Annequin in heavy rain.

30th September.
9–5.30 Battalion practised in throwing bombs and grenades. Battalion proceeded to trenches via Vermelles.

1st October.
7 a.m. Heavy fire from Trench Mortars and Aerial Torpedos. Two 2/Lieuts. From No. 1 company killed. Bombing Officer wounded. Enemy gained a footing between a company of the Northumberland Fusiliers S.W. of Redoubt.

12 noon. 2/Lt. commanding No. 2 coy. killed. Actg. Adjutant sent forward to command Coy no. 2.

8 p.m. No. 3 Company brought forward from Support Trench to take part in an attack with No. 4 Company on the CHORD, a strong trench running north to south across the Hohenzollern Redoubt. Attack partially succeeded. 2nd Lieut. No. 4 Company was wounded.

South Wales Borderers 1st Battalion
8th October. **Loos**.

The morning was quiet and about 12.45 p.m. the Germans commenced bombardment on our whole front. About 3.50 p.m. the enemy's fire lifted and his infantry attacked. The attacked however failed being unable to reach the

Glosters–Munster parapet. The reserve battalion were not called on. We were slightly shelled with very few casualties. One Officer admitted to Hospital. We have all companies in front line and H.R. in Chalk Pit.

The Battle of Loos symbolised the evolvement of war – war for a new century. For the first time, the British deployed gas, and joined the chemical arms race. At short notice, a whole new army of over 100,000 volunteers was rapidly mobilised. The Royal Flying Corps which had been attached to the Army was emerging as a distinct fighting force. Using 161 planes, and four observational kite balloons for intelligence gathering and artillery spotting, the squadrons carried out vital target identification sorties and used wireless to enable the Royal Artillery to use artillery ammunition effectively. The Battle of Loos would be the first time in history an aerial tactical bombing operation was carried out.

The Battle of Loos also defined a change in military planning. The purpose of battles was now seen with a new vision. The general assumption had been that battles were fought for large land gains, for the holding of positions and for limiting loss of life (certainly on one's own side). But this had now changed: the Battle of Loos was lost, but some in the command structure saw this as a success, especially Kitchener; they took the view that if heavy casualties were incurred by the enemy, the primary aim had been accomplished. Ponsonby (1920) states: 'It is obviously more valuable to put out of action 50,000 Germans and gain half a mile than to gain five miles and only inflict a loss of 10,000.'

This positional shift in thinking was used in justifying the huge number of British casualties, which stood at: main attack 48,367, with 10,880 more in the subsidiary attack; a total of 59,247 officers, NCOs and other ranks (almost a fifth of all casualties on the Western Front); this includes 2,600 gas attack casualties. The loss of three Major-Generals alongside a great number of officers, and their accumulated knowledge and military expertise, would be of great detriment to the British Army, in the Great War and subsequently in World War Two. By comparison, official estimates state the German casualty rate for the Battle of Loos was less than half this figure, standing at: 20,000 with 600 gas casualties.

As recriminations and blame, resignations and promotions were apportioned; it became obvious that more men would be needed to fall in line, to replace those of the New Army, for whom Loos had been their first and last battleground. Modern warfare demanded a large army. As Kitchener had warned, this was not going to be a short war – the next major offensive on the Western Front would be the Somme in July 1916. In January 1916, conscription for single men aged 18–41 was introduced and a few months later, for married men under the National Registration Act. The total number of men raised was 2,277,623.

The Battle of the Somme

Introduction: The Somme Offensive, 1916

Based on Regimental Histories of the Guards Division and Cheshire Regiment

In the summer of 1916, it was realised that spasmodic attacks on the German trenches were not gaining any meaningful success. The idea of 'breaking through' was abandoned and plans were laid for an offensive in the Somme area. This was to be a joint operation for the British and French with the objectives of relieving Verdun, to stop further transfer of troops from the German Western front to act against the Russians, and to wear down the resistance of the enemy on the Western Front. The plan met with approval, as it was felt that war was changing and becoming more modern, manpower had seen a dilatation with some fifty divisions in the field, and the productivity of ammunition supplies was increasing.

Preparations were on an elaborate scale, and during the months which preceded the attack, the troops wore themselves out in digging assembly and communication trenches, cable trenches and dugouts; in collecting vast dumps of ammunition, war stores of all kinds; and in building miles of railways and trench tramways. During this time, the 'line' had to be held, and importantly, tactical training of the new armies had to be carried on.

Tactical Advantage

The Germans were holding the life-preserving high ground, which our lack of tactical skill had allowed them to seize all the way down the front line to Switzerland.

The vital advantage that observation offers had been absent in the focus of pre-war training, which meant that for most battles of the war, the tactical objective was the 'observation' line. The ridge in dispute formed the watershed between the Somme on the west and the rivers flowing towards Belgium on the east and north. The German position was on the plateau. Its forward edge overlooked the Ancre and the Somme. In order to secure the observation forward, it was necessary to secure the line Morval–Thiepval, where the ground sloped down towards the north-east.

The German defences were arranged in three main systems, one only partially constructed, each consisting of several lines of well-made trenches, well provided with bombproof shelters and dugouts to a depth which gave complete protection from the heaviest shell. The German trench system differed from the British conception of trench lines at that time. German trenches resembled a network rather than lines, the trenches being connected backwards and forwards with communication trenches, made like fire trenches by means of which 'switch' lines could be made to localise attacks which had penetrated the front line. The dugouts were sophisticated in their construction: shelters 30–40ft below ground and connected by elaborate passages, bombproof and protected in front by wire entanglements, many of which lay in two belts 40 yards broad and built of iron stakes interlaced with barbed wire. The Germans could sit out the heaviest bombardment, ready for the first slacking of fire to rush up the numerous exits and man whatever parapets or shell holes the bombardment had left in the original trench. In and between the enemy trench systems, every topographical feature, every knoll, village and wood had been converted into a fortress, houses with cellars were filled with machine guns and trench mortars. Weapons were sited, not only to sweep the approaches and their wire, but their own trenches in case they should be lost.

Armaments
The official account states:

> The material means available for attack in July, 1916, were notably inferior to those developed in the following spring. The number of guns and Howitzers was, in particular, inadequate to cope with so deep and wide an objective presenting so many targets. Their fire was necessarily so dispersed that many strongpoints and machine gun posts were never touched. There was an entire lack of gas shell (which was to become the most potent factor in preparing an assault) except for the almost negligible quantity fired by our Allies' 75.-m.m. batteries. In quality, too, both the artillery weapons and ammunition were indifferent ... Some of the ammunition was not only defective but dangerous.

This troops themselves witnessed the quantity of 'dud' shells the army had fired. But this compared in a small way to the quantity of ammunition supplied. During 1916, the weekly output of Mills' bombs rose to 1,400,000, and during the year 127,000 tons of high explosive and 50 million filled shells were provided.

Tactical Manoeuvres
Crookenden (p.65) suggests that the tactical methods of the infantry were at fault and the very bravery of the troops caused unnecessary losses. He furthers that had the men been quicker across no man's land, and less calm, less well disciplined and less overloaded with stores, bombs and ammunition, the Germans might have been overrun before they could get their small arms to work. He analyses the first day on the Somme and sees it as a race for the parapet between the attackers

and their trenches and the defenders from their dugouts, explaining that this was meant by the man who said, 'The battle of Somme was lost in three minutes.'

By 1 July, the XIII Corps had taken Montauan. The XV Corps had taken Mametz, and isolated Fricourt. The III Corps had captured and held the German front line between Fricourt and La Boiselle. The X Corps had captured the nose of the Leipzig salient, but only held one other point in the German front line north of Thiepval. The VIII Corps failed to hold its capture of the German trenches on the front Beaumont Hamel to Serre. On the extreme left, in VII Corps, the 56th Division failed to maintain its successful penetration of the whole of the German first system.

Though a breakthrough was not made on the first day, the wider strategical results hoped from the battle were achieved. Verdun was relieved, the transfer of German troops to the East was stopped, and the German morale was wiped out.

Battle Preparation

The battle began on 24 June with terrific artillery bombardment of the German positions, from Montauban, where we joined the French, to Serre, and at Gommerecourt – 1,513 guns plastered the enemy trenches, cut his wire, destroyed his earthworks and hopefully wrecked morale. Patrols reported the enemy's wire well cut and his trenches unrecognisable. It was, consequently, anticipated that the advance would be almost unopposed, at least as far as the first trench system. But the German dugouts and high-couraged, well-disciplined occupants had not been taken into account.

Only on the right, with the help of the French heavy artillery, was the victory complete. Elsewhere, as the general advance began at 7.30 a.m. on 1 July, a storm of machine gun, shrapnel and rifle fire swept our ranks and barely half the men survived to reach the German front line, where they killed, wounded or captured every German in it. Here the advance stopped. This was where the New Army Battalions were baptised with fire. Casualties for the first day were some 57,470. This had the effect that subsequent operations were planned on a less ambitious scale. In the early days of July, insufficient time was given for reconnaissance, for the issue of orders, for the arrangements for covering fire and, even, the movement of troops.

The first phase of the battle was unsuccessful. However, in the south, the troops had secured Mametz, Montauban, Fricourt, Contalmaison, and Trones Wood. The main plateau between Delville Wood and Bezentine-le-Petit was secured between the 14–17 July.

The second phase was a longer struggle, lasting from July 18 and culminating on 15 September. This saw success at Pozieres, Delville Wood, Guillemont, Falfemont Farm, Leuze Wood and the fall of Ginchy. Morval and Thiepval remained in German hands.

The third phase saw Flers, High Wood, Martinpuich, Courcelette and the Quadrilateral fall one after the other. On 25 September, Morval, Lesboeufs and Gueudecourt were secured by the British Army, with the French taking Combles. In October, Thiepval was taken, Eaucourt l'Abbaye and Le Sars and in November, as the outcome of an advance, both sides of the Ancre, St Pierre Divion, Beaucourt and Beaumont-Hamel.

The Battle of the Somme successfully met its objectives against the Germans, who had amassed more than half their army on this part of their front. The British took 38,000 prisoners, including 800 officers and substantial military hardware. The battle was a brilliant victory for the British Army, due in part to the new British secret weapon of the tank. The victory would tactically change the way battles would be fought and interpreted. Previously, battles had only lasted a few days with beaten armies showing immediate retreat. Strategically, the Germans did not realise that their position had become untenable for six months, and that retirement from the field was advisable.

Men from Chapel Street fought in all the battles of the Somme and its subsidiary actions. Many of the men fought in a continuum of battles, only to lose their lives before the end of November 1916. Many of the Chapel Street soldiers who survived the Battle of the Somme would go on to lose their lives in the same area in 1918.

Order of Battle for the Battle of the Somme 1 July–16 November 1916

Battle of Albert: 1–13 July 1916
Capture of Montauban
Capture of Mametz
Capture of Fricourt
Capture of Contalmaison
Capture of La Boisselle
Fourth Army (Rawlinson): III Corps: 1st Division; 8th Division; 12th (Eastern) Division; 19th (Western) Division, which captured La Boisselle; 23rd Division, which captured Contalmaison; 34th Division; VIII Corps: 4th Division; 29th Division; 31st Division; 48th (South Midland) Division; X Corps: 12th (Eastern) Division; 25th Division; 32nd Division; 36th (Ulster) Division; 49th (West Riding) Division; XIII Corps: 3rd Division; 9th (Scottish) Division; 18th (Eastern) Division; 30th Division, which captured Montauban; 35th Division; XV Corps: 7th Division, which captured Mamets; 17th (Northern) Division, which captured Fricourt; 21st Division; 33rd Division; 38th (Welsh) Division, remembered for Mametz Wood.
Reserve Army (Gough): Took over VIII and X Corps on 4 July.
Subsidiary Attack at Gommecourt Salient: 1 July
Third Army (Allenby): VII Corps: 37th Division; 46th (North Midland) Division; 56th (1st London) Division.

Battle of Bazentin Ridge: 14–17 July 1916
Capture of Longueval
Capture of Trones Wood

Capture of Ovillers

Fourth Army (Rawlinson): 2nd Indian Cavalry Division; II Corps: 1st Division; 23rd Division; 34th Division; XIII Corps: 3rd Division; 9th (Scottish Division); 18th (Eastern) Division; XV Corps: 7th Division; 21st Division; 33rd Division. Reserve Army (Gough): X Corps: 25th Division; 48th (South Midland) Division; 49th (West Riding) Division.

Subsidiary Attack at Fromelles: 19 July–20 July 1916

First Army (Monro): XI Corps: 61st (2nd South Midland) Division; 5th Australian Division.

Battle of High Wood 20–25 July 1916

Fourth Army (Rawlinson): XIII Corps: 19th (Western) Division; XV Corps: 5th Division; 7th Division; 33rd Division; 51st (Highland) Division.

Battle of Delville Wood: 15 July–3 September 1916

Fourth Army (Rawlinson): XIII Corps: 2nd Division; 3rd Division; 9th (Scottish) Division; 24th Division; 53rd Brigade of 18th (Eastern) Division.
XIV Corps (Relieved XIII Corps at night 16–17 August): 20th (Light) Division; 24th Division; XV Corps: 7th Division; 14th (Light) Division.

Battle of Pozieres: 23 July–3 September 1916

Fighting for Mouquet Farm

Fourth Army (Rawlinson): III Corps: 1st Division; 15th (Scottish) Division; 19th (Western) Division; 23rd Division; 34th Division.
Reserve Army (Gough): II Corps: 12th Eastern Division; 25th Division; 48th (South Midland) Division; 49th (West Riding) Division.
I ANZAC Corps: 1st Australian Division; 2nd Australian Division; 4th Australian Division.

Battle of Guillemont: 3–6 September 1916

Fourth Army (Rawlinson): XIV Corps: 5th Division; 16th (Irish) Division; 20th (Light) Division; XV Corps: 7th Division; 24th Division; 55th (West Lancashire) Division.

Battle of Ginchy: 9 September 1916

Fourth Army (Rawlinson): XIV Corps: 16th (Irish) Division; 56th (1st London) Division; XV Corps: 55th (West Lancashire) Division.

Battle of Flers-Courcelette: 15–22 September 1916

Capture of Martinpuich

Fourth Army (Rawlinson): 1st Cavalry Division; 2nd Indian Cavalry Division; III Corps: 1st Division; 15th (Scottish) Division, which captured Martinpuich; 23rd Division; 47th (2nd London) Division; 50th (Northumbrian) Division; 103rd Brigade of 34th Division; XIV Corps: Guards Division; 5th Division; 6th

Division; 20th (Light) Division; 56th (1st London) Division; XV Corps: 14th (Light) Division; 21st Division; 1st Division; 55th (West Lancashire) Division; New Zealand Division.
Reserve Army (Gough)
II Corps: 11th (Northern) Division; 49th (West Riding) Division.
Canadian Corps (Byng): 1st Canadian Division; 2nd Canadian Division; 3rd Canadian Division.

Battle of Morval: 25–28 September 1916

Capture of Combles
Capture of Lesboeufs
Capture of Gueudecourt
Fourth Army (Rawlinson): III Corps: 1st Division; 23rd Division; 50th (Northumbrian) Division; XIV Corps: Guards Division, which captured Lesboeufs; 5th Division; 6th Division, which also captured Lesboeufs; 20th (Light) Division; 56th (1st London) Division, which captured Combles; XV Corps: 21st Division, which captured Guedecourt; 55th (West Lancashire) Division; New Zealand Division.

Battle of Thiepval: 26–28 September 1916

Reserve Army (Gough): II Corps: 11th (Northern) Division; 18th (Eastern) Division; V Corps: 39th Division.
Canadian Corps (Byng): 1st Canadian Division; 2nd Canadian Division; 3rd Canadian Division.

Battle of Transloy: 1–18 October 1916

Capture of Eaucourt l'Abbaye
Capture of Le Sars
Attacks on the Butte de Warlencourt
Fourth Army (Rawlinson): III Corps: 9th (Scottish Division; 15th (Scottish) Division; 23rd Division, which captured Le Sars; 47th (2nd London) Division, which captured Eaucourt L'Abbaye; 50th (Northumbrian) Division; XIV Corps: Guards Division; 4th Division; 6th Division; 20th (Light) Division; 56th (1st London) Division; XV Corps: 12th (Eastern) Division; 21st Division; 30th Division; 41st Division; 55th (West Lancashire) Division; New Zealand Division; 88th Brigade of 29th Division.
Reserve Army (Gough): Canadian Corps (Byng): 1st Canadian division; 2nd Canadian Division; 3rd Canadian Division; 4th Canadian Division.

Battle of Ancre Heights: 1 October–11 November 1916

Capture of Schwaben Redoubt
Capture of Stuff Redoubt
Capture of Regina Trench
Reserve Army (Gough): II Corps: 18th (Eastern) Division, which captured the Schwaben Redoubt; 19th (Western) Division; 25th Division, which captured

Stuff Redoubt; 39th Division, which also captured Schwaben Redoubt; 4th Canadian Division. All except 19th (Western) Division played a part in the capture of Regina Trench: V Corps: 39th Division.
Canadian Corps (Byng): 1st Canadian Division; 2nd Canadian Division; 3rd Canadian Division; 4th Canadian Division.

Battle of the Ancre: 13–18 November 1916
Capture of Beaumont Hamel
Fourth Army (Rawlinson): III Corps: 48th (South Midland) Division.
Fifth Army (Gough): II Corps: 18th (Eastern) Division; 19th (Western) Division; 39th Division; 4th Canadian Division; V Corps: 2nd Division; 3rd Division; 37th Division; 51st (Highland) Division, which captured Beaumont Hamel; 63rd (Royal Naval) Division; XIII Corps: 31st Division; 120th Brigade of 40th Division.

First Phase Battle of the Somme
The Battle of Albert, 1–13 July

Men from Chapel Street
Edward Lowe, 1st Battalion Royal Irish Rifles
Ernest Brownhill, 1st Battalion South Wales Borderers
Peter Morley, 2nd Battalion Welsh Regiment
Frank Wyatt, 8th Battalion Devonshire Regiment
John Ratchford, 4th Battalion King's Liverpool Regiment
James Bell Houlden, 5th Battalion Cheshire Regiment
John Kirkham, 5th Battalion Cheshire Regiment
Peter Gormley, 9th Battalion Cheshire Regiment
John Green, 9th Battalion Cheshire Regiment
Dennis Hanley, 9th Battalion Cheshire Regiment
James Hanley, 9th Battalion Cheshire Regiment
William Johnson, 9th Battalion Cheshire Regiment
Joseph Wyatt, 9th Battalion Cheshire Regiment
Martin Donnelly, 10th Battalion Cheshire Regiment
James Inions, 10th Battalion Cheshire Regiment
James King, 11th Battalion Cheshire Regiment

The Battle of Albert was a joint Anglo–French offensive which began with artillery bombardment on 24 June followed by an infantry attack on 1 July on the south bank from Foucaucourt to the Somme, and from the Somme north, to Gommecourt. The southern operation was successful with the French Sixth Army and the British Fourth Army inflicting a massive defeat on the German Second Army; however, the northern objective was not realised, from the Albert–Bapaume road to Gommecourt it was an unmitigated disaster. It was here that the British incurred some 60,000 casualties. In a change of agreed strategy, Haig abandoned the offensive north of the road, to reinforce the success in the south. In the south, the Allies pressed forward to the German second line in preparation for a general attack on 14 July.

Adapted from the Cheshire Regimental History:
The 9th Battalion:

John Green; Peter Gormley; James Hanley; William Johnson; Joseph Wyatt. Dennis Hanley died 4/7/16 (Missing no known grave: Thiepval Memorial)

On 1 July, the 9th Battalion was in reserve to the attack on La Boisselle. After the failure of the first original attack the 58th Brigade was ordered to attack at night, at 10.30 p.m. With the CO (Commanding Officer, Colonel Worgan) at Brigade HQ, the battalion was directed to the old British front line, from Locknager to Inch Str. On receiving his orders, the CO hurried to front but could find no trace of the battalion. The trenches were not only very much knocked about, and full of dead and wounded, but were also being heavily shelled. Eventually he found the Captain of 'D' Company, who explained that the battalion had been delayed by finding the communication trenches full of wounded. The Colonel told him to stay put, while he went to ascertain the situation and find the remainder.

From wounded men, he learnt that some sixty unwounded were holding the crater where a 600lb mine had been fired just before zero on 1 July, and some 200 more, with two or three officers, holding a part of the German front line – all belonging to the 34th Division. Realising the importance of holding our gains, he sent 'D' Company to reinforce the crater. On further search, he found a Lieut. with portions of two companies and he sent him also to the German trenches alongside the crater. It was now 9.40 p.m., too late to carry out the original plan of attack, especially as the remainder of the battalion could not be found. So, after reporting personally at Brigade HQ, Colonel Worgan returned to the front line and ordered consolidation to be put in hand at speed.

The scene beggars description. Every shell-hole held a killed or wounded man. The whole area was littered with all the debris of a battle, with equipment, clothing, timber, stores and dud shells.

At 2.30 a.m. on 2 July, a telephone message from Brigade HQ ordered the CO to prepare to attack at once. Although the battalion was very scattered and not easy to get hold of, the Colonel had them assembled in the old German trenches ready to attack in twenty minutes. But the trenches were found to be too crowded and some men were withdrawn. It was not until 4 a.m. that definite orders came. The battalion was to attack La Boisselle and to bomb through it, clearing out all dugouts. It was pitch dark, deathly quiet, no shelling, no machine-gun bursts and no Verey-lights.

At 4.30 a.m., the battalion went over the top under its own covering fire, and charged across the open for the German support trench. Some of the men used a Russian sap to get forward, till it was blocked with wounded. A deep, wide and unexpected communication trench held up the advance. Bombers were sent right and left to clear a way forward. It was terribly difficult to keep direction after dark and among this maze of trenches. One officer killed and one wounded.

At 8.30 on 3 July, the advance had gone as far as the strength of the battalion warranted, some 300 yards short of La Boisselle. Consolidation was put in hand, and only then did the Lieut. have his wounds dressed. At the end of the day, Lieut. W. was the only officer left with the CO.

On 4 July at 2.45 a.m. the battalion received further orders to continue the attack in conjunction with the 57th Brigade on the left, and the 9th Welsh on the right. By 3.45, no touch had been gained by either flank, so our men started bombing along saps towards the Germans. To have attacked over the top, without troops on the flanks, would have been impossible. The ground was swept by German machine-gun fire, with four rows of uncut wire protecting their front.

During this attack, a small party was detached to bomb a post, but the party was driven off and one man was left wounded and prisoner. He was taken down a dugout where there were twenty-five Germans. He remained until a commotion overhead and the explosion of a bomb at the end of the dugout told him that the British were advancing again. He was quick to act. He seized a bomb in one hand and a revolver in the other, and under this threat his captors more or less cheerfully consented to becoming the captives! His comrades found him in charge of twenty-five Germans when they started mopping-up.

These bombing parties progressed till stronger parties of German bombers attacked and drove them back. It was at this point that the Captain, who had been kept back to replace casualties, organised and inspirited the defence. The position was held until 3.30 a.m. when the battalion was relieved.

The 11th Battalion:

James King died 3/7/16 (Missing no known grave: Thiepval Memorial)

The 11th Battalion also saw action on 1 July in conditions as bad as the 9th Battalion. It attacked Thiepval from the direction of Authuille.

From the outset, things started to go wrong: the battalion's Brigadier had taken care to get all the arrangements 'cut and dried' as the short notice allowed. But late in the evening, the Corps Commander, who earlier had heard and approved the whole plan, sent for the Divisional Commander. It seems it took the latter an hour to go, and an hour to return with a new plan.

The plan was received at Brigade HQ on 3 July at 12.30 a.m. Zero was to have been at 3.00 a.m., which led to the Brigadier protesting. The resulting consequence was that Corps HQ agreed to a three-hour postponement of infantry, but not of the artillery attack! The 11th Battalion, under Colonel Aspinall, struggled through heavily shelled communication trenches, packed with wounded moving out, on stretchers and walking, and were hours late.

They received no fresh orders, could not identify the rendezvous, objectives, nor find other troops. Practically every battery telephone wire was cut. The orders for the barrage for the new attack had to be carried by runners, who, in the darkness and congested state of the trenches, could only travel slowly. Most of the batteries did not see their orders till half way through the preliminary bombardment for the 3 a.m. attack. For the later attack, only half the necessary ammunition was available. It is easy to understand now why the artillery was so poor. The gunners were as desperate about their inability to help the infantry as the latter were at not receiving support. But without notice, without reconnaissance, without ammunition, what could the artillery do?

Whilst new orders were being drafted, Brigade HQ was shelled and forty indispensable personnel staff became casualties.

An advance was made with little artillery support, and the battalion joined the 8th Border Regiment in their movement.

They were met by a withering fire of machine guns, under which they walked forward till the battalion 'simply melted away'. Colonel Aspinall was killed and every Company Commander was a casualty. The Adjutant Captain of the Suffolk Regiment, with energy and bravery, got the survivors back to the starting line.

The Regimental history states that on the morning of 4 July, no organised body of men existed. Men were gathered on an ad hoc basis from no man's land. Sixty men reached the enemy front line and established themselves there, but they were withdrawn after dark.

At roll call on 6 July, of 20 officers and 657 men who went into the attack, only 6 officers and 50 men remained: a loss of 622 men. James King was amongst this number.

They spent a miserable night in pouring rain. A draft arrived, and with these reinforcements, another attack was made on 8 July.

The battalion advanced in two parties, one led by the CO of the South Lancashire Regiment, who was soon knocked out by a shell splinter. The companies he was leading soon went astray. Eventually, the Adjutant having found that one of the trenches from which the attack was to start was held by the enemy, tried to arrange to attack this first. He was given command of the 8th South Lancashire Regiment, his own two companies, and the 78th Trench Mortar Battery, and told to attack. Again there was no artillery support and the attack failed.

During this fighting, about sixty men joined the Highland Light Infantry in Leipzig trench, but all who reached the enemy line were either killed or captured.

Crookenden (p.71) was very scathing of the order to attack, when the planned original attack, which had the advantage of adequate preparation and military skill, had failed. He questions how these attacks could succeed without reconnaissance or artillery support. In a clear case of the truism of the phrase 'lions being led by donkeys', he condemns them being ordered at all, stating: 'how little the higher commanders and their staffs were alive [sic] to the true state of affairs'.

'A' Company 11th Battalion, Cheshire in a German trench, 1 July 1916.
(Wikimedia Commons)

The 5th Battalion

James Bell Houlden 'A' Company (King's Medal, Queen's Medal South Africa
Campaign 1898–1902) aged 49 years; John Kirkham.

On 1 July, on the whole front of attack only one Cheshire Company went over
with the first wave at zero, 7.30 a.m.

This was the 'A' Company of the 5th Battalion (Pioneers of the 56th London
Division), attacking Gommecourt on the extreme north flank of the British
Army. The company was split up among the attacking Battalions of the 169th
Brigade, with the attack concentrating on constructing strong points.

This attack had a wide no man's land to cross, no less than 800 yards. It would
have been double this, but for a fine piece of work by the 5th Battalion some days
earlier in making a new jumping-off trench.

'A' Company lost all its officers and 130 men. 'A' Company was recruited in
Altrincham.

'B' Company had the task of removing barricades and making trench bridges
as the attack progressed, and carried out all its tasks. The total number casualties were 3 officers and 43 men killed, 5 officers and 154 NCOs and men were
wounded.

'C' Company had a similar task with the 168th Brigade, but orders miscarried and the company remained inactive.

Crookenden defines a Pioneer Battalion as one that has a dual role to play, namely, it must be capable of taking the part of Infantry of the Line as well as being capable of carrying out engineering duties, either by itself or in conjunction with the Royal Engineers. Its chief work is that of field engineering, and it is only in an emergency that it is called upon to act as infantry. He explains that the work carried out is almost entirely battle zone work, and that its great objective in all offensives is to help towards the successful exploitation of an attack, which largely depends on the speed and skill with which communications (roads, bridges, tracks and tramways) are repaired or constructed. The movement of reserves, the advance of artillery, the supply of ammunition for the guns, the getting forward of supplies of food, water and ammunition to the infantry as well as reliefs and the evacuation of the wounded are dependent on the restoration of communications, and tracks and routes constructed.

He explains that its object is not to 'make' roads of communications, but to facilitate the means of progress temporarily passable as quickly as possible, leaving the permanent improvement to troops in the rear. He highlights the importance of road reconnaissance, which demands speed and accuracy. He states that it is vital to the successful organisation of engineering operations and is one of the tasks which were frequently allotted to Pioneer Officers. He furthers that these duties, especially trench construction, repair and wiring, were very arduous. Due to their being in the battle zone, they almost always had to be carried out at night. This involved long and trying marches up to the site of work and back, frequently under shell fire, as the approach areas were always the subject of the enemy's artillery attention in the evenings. He states that finding their way and setting out the work in pitch darkness, when the site was only described as a map reference, demanded a high standard of training and skill on the part of officers and Non-Commissioned Officers (NCOs).

He concludes by saying that the heavy loss in officers of the 5th Battalion shows how dangerous pioneer work was.

The 10th Battalion

Martin Donnelly; John Inions

The 10th Battalion was in the trenches from 2–15 July. The later part of this time was in front of Ovillers, where they had a 'very sticky time', but making no attack until 12 July.

Extracts from War Diaries

2nd Battalion Welsh Regiment
Lesbrebis

3 July. 2 Lieuts. and 2 other rank accidently wounded and 4 other rank accidently killed by bomb explosion.

10th Battalion Cheshire Regiment
Trenches

3 July. We arrived in the early hours of the morning and were accommodated in reserve trenches in Avely Wood, which was extremely muddy and not at all comfortable. After spending the day resting we commenced to relieve the 19th Lancashire Fusiliers at 8.30 p.m. in the front line trenches.

11th Battalion Cheshire Regiment
Thiepval

3 July. The trenches were exceedingly badly knocked about, affording little cover from fire and in a great many places little cover from view.

8th (Service) Battalion Devonshire Regiment

4 July. Consolidation, burying the dead and clearing the battlefield continued, a number of Devon Regiment are buried in a cemetery (consecrated) in Mansel Copse.

1st Battalion Royal Irish Rifles ration party in communication trench 1 July 1916. (Imperial War Museum)

Battle of Bazentin Ridge, 14–17 July

Men from Chapel Street

Peter Morley, 2nd Battalion Welsh Regiment
Ernest Brownhill, 1st Battalion South Wales Borderers
Joseph Margiotta, 1st Battalion Highland Infantry, Gordon Highlanders
John Ratchford, 4th Battalion The King's (Liverpool) Regiment
Joseph Arnold; Martin Donnelly; John Inions, 10th Battalion Cheshire Regiment
Frank Wyatt, 8th Battalion Devonshire Regiment

The Cheshire Regimental History reveals that the whole of the 25th Division were used in this battle. Three thousand men were assembled in the dark and formed up, astonishingly only 500 yards from the enemy, 'without confusion, and undiscovered'. The attack started at 5.30 a.m., soon after orders were received.

The attack started under very heavy fire, which meant crawling. The slope to the German trenches was swept by small-arm fire and the soldiers appeared immediately, causing a German counter-attack which was made on the right flank. This attack reached the starting trench and had to be bombed out. The attack on the left nearly reached the German trench, but was mowed down by machine-gun fire and withdrew with heavy losses. Attempts were made to bomb up a trench leading towards the Germans but these were hampered by shell fire, making the trench untenable.

On 14 July, the 10th Battalion (Cheshire Regiment) was nearly destroyed by shell fire. And under a full moon with no artillery support, the battalion made two attacks, one at 11.00 p.m. and one at 2.50 a.m. (on 15 July), with the 8th Battalion Loyal North Lancashire Regiment carrying material.

In the first of the attacks, a good many men reached the enemy trenches, but it was not in sufficient order or numbers to maintain their position. It is noted that the loss of officers was severe. The second attack was made mainly by bomb, with the Loyal North Lancs and Lancashire Fusiliers combining numbers and nearly reaching the objective. However, it was beginning to get light and machine-gun fire was becoming more effective. The decision was made to withdraw 100 men back to the starting trench. These 'heroic efforts' made the capture of Ovillers possible. Crookenden criticises the lack of artillery support and wonders 'how anyone expected these attacks to succeed'. His goes on to complain that the New Armies seem to have been trained almost too mechanically, or they would hardly have gone on in such conditions.

Casualty figures for the Cheshire Regiment for the period of 3–15 July were: 5 officers killed, 3 officers missing and 7 wounded, 38 NCOs and men were killed, 72 missing, 276 wounded. Most of the casualties occurred on the 14 and 15 July.

Extracts from War Diaries

10th Battalion Cheshire Regiment
La Boiselle

14 July. At 11.p.m. we attacked the Trenches S of Ovillers in force assisted by 8th Bn. Loyal North Lancashire Regiment. We actually got into the enemy trenches in places, only to be driven back by intense machine gun fire. By 2 a.m. we had reorganised & with the assistance of the 11th Bn. Lancashire Fusiliers, we again attacked at the point of the bayonet, but were again driven back by machine gun fire, & suffered very heavy casualties. A certain amount of ground was gained by 'C' Company (assisted by the Lancashire Fusiliers) in bombing up a trench on the right flank of the attack, but very stubborn resistance was met with. 40 yards was gained & a block made.

15 July. The Battalion was relieved during the afternoon by the 2nd Royal Irish Rifles, and we bivouacked just outside Albert. Everyone was very tired & felt the strain of the last few days.

4th Battalion King's Liverpool Regiment
Meaulte

14 July. Moved 5 p.m. to old German front line S. of Fricourt.

15 July. Moved 5 a.m. in reserve just W. of Besantin-Le-Petit Wood – dug in. 1st Middlesex attacked German lateral line between High Wood & Martinpuich – heavy shelling – Relieved 4/Suffolks & 1 Company of 1st Middlesex in front line 11 p.m. Our line from cross roads N. of Besantin to 400 yards S. 2 ½ Coys front line. 1 ½ in reserve. We left. 3 men killed (Officers) 25 men wounded & 1 missing.

Front Line 16 July. Dull – rain – dug in new line cross roads to cemetery & occupied it – shelling enemy's lines – 1 Officer Died of Wounds. 1 man Killed & 5 Wounded.

17 July. Fine. 1st Middlesex Coy. Commanders round trenches 3 p.m. This relief cancelled. Relieved by 2nd R.W.F. 5 men Killed. 15 Wounded. & 2 shell-shock.

18 July. Relief completed 3 a.m. Moved to bivouac in valley E. of Caterpillar Wood – dug in – dull day. Moved in to support (enemy counter-attacked) dug in Flatiron Copse to Sabot Copse. 2 Officers and 17 men wounded. R.S.M. slightly. Returned to bivouac 8 p.m. 1 man to base under age. 1 man to R.F.A. base.

19 July. Fine. CO & Coy. Commander reconnoitred ground in vicinity of Besantin le. P. Wood & village. Coy. Commander round trenches 3 p.m. Relieved 2nd R.W.F. & 20 R.F. in front line. Relief complete 20.15 p.m. 4 Coys. in front line from Cross roads N. of Besantin le.P. to quarry. Bombardment during night & 22 men wounded.

1st Battalion Gordon Highlanders

12 July. Showery. Bn marched at 8.15 p.m. to Montauban Alley Brigade in reserve for attack on Longueval position (German 2nd Line defences)

Montauban Alley:

14 July. Thick haze, followed later by some showers. Attack on German 2nd Line position commenced at 3.25 a.m. German 2nd Line captured. At 10 a.m. Bn moved forward to Caterpillar Valley where they dug in. Heavily shelled by 6' gun in the afternoon. 7 casualties.

Caterpillar Valley:

15 July. Day fine – cool in the evening. Officers reconnoitre position in front from High Wood to Longueval. Op & Lt Corp & 3 men established in Front Line. 2 casualties from 6' gun.

17 July. Showery. Patrol went out at 2 a.m. under 2 Officers. Sgt. And. of the patrol wounded and missing. Orders received to attack Longeuval village next morning.

Between Bazentin-Le-Petit & High Wood

Men from Chapel Street
Cheshire Regiment:
1st Battalion Cheshire Regiment: Sergeant James Arnold; John Booth; Thomas Booth Thomas Corfield; John Davies; Hugh Hennerley; Peter Hughes.
9th Battalion Cheshire Regiment: Peter Gormley; James Hanley; William Johnson; Joseph Wyatt.
8th Battalion Devonshire Regiment: Frank Wyatt.

20 August. From the time the Battalion arrived at the Quarry, hostile shelling was persistent and heavy, until about the fourth day after when it gradually diminished in volume.

21 August. During the evening of the 20th and the morning of the 21st the enemy were seen in considerable numbers in the North West of High Wood. They were several times dispersed by our own Lewis Guns. In the afternoon our patrols advanced from the forward sap-head NW of High Wood and the sap head was pushed slightly further forward.

22 August. Hostile artillery again kept up heavy barrage especially across the main communication trench, almost all day and night. During the whole period in the line A Coy. was in an advanced sap, C Coy. was in the front line, B Coy. in support and D Coy. in reserve. During the shelling the three companies in rear suffered rather severely from heavy shells. On this date a hostile aeroplane was brought down to the East of High Wood by our own aeroplanes. Two of our scouts went 250 yards from our saphead, located a new German work and brought back most valuable information which led to the correction of our trench map, and ultimately of our own artillery fire. This patrol reported a party of Germans with field bayonets in the Switch Line.

23 August. The hostile shelling continued almost without a break until afternoon …

Waterlot Farm

Men from Chapel Street
1st Battalion Cheshire Regiment:
Sergeant James Arnold; John Booth; Thomas Booth Thomas Corfield; John Davies; Hugh Hennerley; Peter Hughes.

Cheshire Regimental History

About the middle of July the Somme Offensive had reached a critical stage. The Salient with its apex at Delville Wood was too narrow an area in which to deploy large bodies and, being open to bombardment on both sides, invited a German counter-attack. It was this moment that the 16th Battalion (Bantams) was sent into line. On their way up they passed the First Battalion of the Regiment who cheered them on with the 'Quickstep'. (Bantam battalions such as 15th and 16th Cheshires were raised from men below the British Army's minimum regulation height of 5ft 3in (160cm), many enlisted from coal-mining areas and were physically strong.)

War Diary for 1st Battalion Cheshire Regiment

16 September.
12.30 a.m. Brigade Operation Order A6013 received, giving definite orders to move.
4 a.m. Battln left Morlancourt for Citadel arriving there about 6.00 a.m. Brigade in same camp as formerly. Fine but cold. Commanding Officer attended conference at Bde Hdqes. (Brigade Headquarters).
12 noon. Received half an hour's notice to move.
6.50 Battalion moved to Waterlot Farm to reserve 20th Division via Peronne Road – Maricourt-Bricqueterie-Trones Wood Battalion in positions in slit trenches and Headquarters in cellar in Farm by midnight.
Waterlot Farm
17 September. Tea from cookers in Trones Wood and rations issued. Fine morning. Bosche shelled Delville Wood on our left. Commanding Officer went to Brigade and found we might have to move up tomorrow. Commanding Officer and Company Officers reconnoitred way up to trenches. 3 new officers of 1st Bedfordshire Regt arrived.

Second Phase Battle of the Somme

The Fourth Army's next plan of attack was the German second defensive position from the Somme past Guillement and Ginchy, north-west along the crest of the ridge to Pozieres on the Albert-Bapaume road.

The objectives for the attack were the villages of Bazentin le Petit, Bazentin le Grande and Longueval adjacent to Delville Wood, with High Wood on the ridge beyond.

The plan was that following on from a five-minute artillery barrage, four divisions would make an attack on a front of some 6,000 yards. A creeping barrage and attacking waves would push through no man's land, leaving only a short distance to cross.

With most of the objectives captured and the German defence in the south of the Albert–Bapaume road under great strain, the attack did not follow through due to communication failures, casualties (some 25,000) and general disorganisation.

Battle of Delville Wood, 14 July–5 September

Men from Chapel Street

Frank Wyatt, 8th Battalion Devonshire Regiment

The Battle of Delville Wood was an operation to secure the British right flank, while the centre advanced to capture the higher lying areas of High Wood and Pozieres. After the Battle of Albert, the offensive had evolved to the capture of fortified villages, woods and other terrain that offered observation for artillery fire, jumping-off points for more attacks and other tactical advantages.

War Diary 8th Battalion Devonshire Regiment

The Regiment moved from Bazentin Le Grand Wood to White Trench, where it rested until 19 July. From there it moved to the assembly position south of High Wood. Later in the evening, the battalion was joined by the Warwick Regiment and marched the next few days to Dernacourt, Mericourt until reaching Ailly Sur Somme where it bivouacked and trained.

In this period, the 5th Division was attacking the German line between Delville Wood and High Wood in order to capture Longueval. Attacks were made on 20 and 23 July.

The official *History of the Great War* records that on 26 July, General Rawlinson had visited General Fayolle, the commander of the French Sixth Army, to arrange details of the next Franco–British attack.

They were joined later in the day by Sir Douglas Haig, who arrived at Dury to confer with Generals Fayolle and Foch. General Foch said that he intended to attack along the whole front south of the Somme, from Lihons to Barleux, as soon as he was ready, but he required three days' bombardment which would begin as soon as the weather had cleared sufficiently: north of the river, he only waited for a clear day which would favour observation during the actual attack.

The British Commander-in-Chief told General Foch that he wish Guillemont to be captured as soon as possible – not necessarily as part of a

Franco–British attack, although the attack on Falfemount Farm-Maurepas must be one operation.

As a result of this interview, General Rawlinson arranged with General Foch next day that on 30 July an assault should be launched on the whole front: from the Somme to Maurepas, Falfemont Farm and Guillemont before the French reached their objectives, which were more distant. This decision appeared to satisfy all requirements, for General Fayolle was reluctant to push forward his left until Guillemont was in British hands.

Battle of Pozieres, 23 July–7 August

Men from Chapel Street
Ernest Brownhill, 1st Battalion South Wales Borderers
Peter Morley, 2nd Battalion Welsh Regiment

Cheshire Regiment
9th Battalion Cheshire Regiment: Peter Gormley; James Hanley; William Johnson; Joseph Wyatt.
10th Battalion: Joseph Arnold; Martin Donnelly; John Inions.

The village of Pozieres was captured by the 1st Australian Division of the Reserve Army and was the only success of an Allied operation after the failures of 22/23 July, when a general attack with the French in the south resulted in a series of separate attacks due to communication failures, supply failures and poor weather. The period 23 July–7 August was marked by a series of German bombardments and counterattacks which ended with the Reserve Army taking the plateau north and east of the village. The battle was concentrated around the area of Mouquet Farm. The 10th, 11th and 13th Cheshires fought in the area during August without taking part in the set-piece attack.

Battle of Guillemont, 3–6 September

Men from Chapel Street
Edward Birmingham, 9th Battalion Royal Dublin Fusiliers
Frank Wyatt, 8th Battalion Devonshire Regiment

1st Battalion Cheshire Regiment
Sergeant James Arnold; Joseph Arnold; John Booth; Thomas Booth; John Davies; Hugh Hennerley; Peter Hughes.

On the first day of the battle, the village of Guillemont was captured by the Fourth Army. Guillemont itself was on the right flank of the British sector near the boundary with the French Sixth Army. German defences ringed the British salient at Delville Wood to the north and had the advantage of observation over the French Sixth Army to the south towards the Somme River. The Germans held numerous fortified villages and farms north from Maurepas at Combles, Guillemont, Falfemont Farm, Delville Wood and High Wood.

In a big offensive, a combined attack by French and British troops was planned with the objectives being Combles, Ginchy, Fleurs and Le Sars. The main objective was to widen the salient towards the north, in the hope that Guillemont would fall. Fighting around Guillemont had already been going on for a month.

The Taking of Falfemont Farm

For the Cheshires, the fighting was concentrated around Falfemont Farm. The junction with the French was in the valley running from Hardecourt to Combles. The French left was completely overlooked by the high ground between Combles and Guillemont, still in German hands. On this high ground was Falfemont Farm, which the French insisted on being captured before they began their advance. Tanks were to be employed further north and it was hoped that the cavalry might break through to Bapaume.

The 13th Brigade was detailed to make this attack three hours before the main zero hour on 3 September. The 1st Battalion was moved into Chimpanzee trench immediately north-west of Hardecourt on 1 September and was detailed as immediate reserve under the orders of the 13th Brigade. The battalion was heavily gassed when it moved across the valley south-west of Hardecourt, but suffered no casualties.

Unfortunately, this preliminary attack by the 13th Brigade failed, due to the French not providing the artillery support it had undertaken to supply. This meant that the 1st Battalion was now immediately ordered to reinforce the 13th Brigade front line. As the battalion left Chimpanzee trench (the war diary gives the number of men as 280) to the front line they had to cross the forward slopes of the hill north-east of Hardecourt, in full view of the enemy and under heavy shell fire. A barrage of 5.9s was playing on the valley south of Angle Wood. The companies were ordered to move independently, adopting the most suitable formation. The companies were split into 'A' and 'C' Companies moving on the trenches occupied by the 13th Brigade immediately north-east of Angle Wood, and 'B' and 'D' went into trenches west and north-west of Angle Wood.

When the 1st Battalion arrived, they found the trenches crowded with men with heavy shelling underway. As chaos was brought to order in the trenches, the 1st Battalion took over the front line and the men of the 13th Brigade were being brought back to the reserve slope of the hill north-east of Angle Wood. During the night, the brigade was withdrawn and reinforcements brought in from the Norfolk Regiment on the right and the Bedfordshire Regiment on the left. Though Falfemont Farm remained in German hands, the main attack had been fairly successful with Guillemont being taken. The French had command of the high ground north of Maurepas.

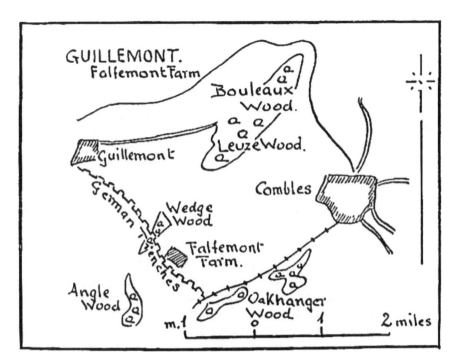

Sketch map of Falfemont Farm. (Chester Military Museum)

On 4 July, orders were issued by the 15th Brigade for an attack on Falfemont Farm by the Norfolks on the right, the 1st Cheshires in the centre and the Bedfords on the left. The attack was to take place in the afternoon at 3.00 p.m. The plan was for the two Companies of 'A' and 'C' to move on the right and left and attack the Farm along with the trenches immediately to the north of it. 'B' and 'D' Companies were to move forward in support and occupy the trenches 'A' and 'C' had assaulted. The Norfolks on the right were to attack the Farm and the Bedfords were to attack the German trenches immediately south of Wedge Wood.

The attack by the Norfolks and 'A' Company failed owing to heavy machine-gun fire, and a large number of Cheshires were killed. On the left, the Bedfords and 'C' Company were successful in their objective and entered the German trenches to the north of the Farm. 'C' Company, assisted by the Bedfords, raised a bombing party which gained a footing in Falfemont Farm, and by dark the objective was realised and the Farm was won. The Cheshires and Bedfords held the high ground from Falfemont Farm to Leuze Wood.

The cost of the battle had been high, with many popular officers losing their lives, some six were wounded and five WOs missing. Only 280 men remained untouched. The Germans had also lost heavily, with whole machine gun detachments being killed at their posts.

The next day, 5 July, passed quietly except for some shelling, and by the evening the French were seen advancing up the valley to Combles, which would not be taken for another three weeks.

Extracts from War Diaries

Cheshire Regiment

Trenches.

1 September. 10.00 a.m. Contact Aeroplane flew over lines. Signals put out. The situation in the trenches throughout the day was quiet, and in spite of the fact that the advanced trenches had no communication trenches leading to them, parties carrying water & were able to get up in the open and not worried by sniping.

Shelling was not heavy, but Battalion HQ which were at the corner of Duncan Alley and Maltz Horn Trench B5 d 70/90 were shelled intermittently throughout the day.

In the early morning a report was received that some field guns on Trench 75 were falling short in a trench occupied by our 'B' Company. Casualties during the day were not very heavy but amounted to about 23 other ranks.

During the morning OC 'B' Company sent out a patrol to German gun pits about 150 yards N. to N.W. of strong point at B 1 a 90/05, and found that one was unoccupied and another contained 10 Germans and a machine gun.

1 September. 2.30 a.m. Relief of the 14th Warwicks by us was completed at this hour, though the information that the relief was complete was not received until 6.30 a.m., owing to the fact that the orderly lost his way. The enemy used a considerable number of lachrymatory shells (tear gas), near Battalion Headquarters which made the valley unpleasant.

5 September. The Battalion about 280 strong left Chimpanzee Trench, calling at Billion Farm and came down to camp at the Citadel.

7 September. Battalion in camp at Citadel. Inspection of feet etc. Muster Roll Call. Battalion strength including all transport 442. Men very worn out and in need of a rest. Divisional Commander came round and congratulated Commanding Officer on success. Congratulatory messages received from C.in C. (Colonel in Chief). Army and Corps Commanders. Cool but fine day. 'A' Company bathed. Battalion rested as much as possible. We shall probably have to go in again to hold the line. CO (Commanding Officer) in bed with temperature.

9th Royal Dublin Fusiliers

Front line.

6 September. To reinforce the 8RDF (Royal Dublin Fusiliers). Also experienced considerable casualties. 1 Officer died of wounds 3 wounded. The 8RDF had 1 Off. killed 1 died of wounds and 4 wounded. O.R. (Other Ranks) 13 killed 62 wounded 2 missing.

7 September. We advanced our line 300 yards. Some enemy shelling. Shelled Leuze Wood & attacked it but we did hold it.

Dummy Trench.

8 September. Resting today orders to move up for attack of Guinchy (Ginchy).

Battle of Ginchy, 9 September

Men from Chapel Street

16th (Irish) Division 48th Brigade:
Edward Birmingham, 9th Battalion Royal Dublin Fusiliers

Adapted from *The Battles of the Somme*, Phillip Gibbs

The Irish sprang up and went forward cheering. They shouted, 'Go on, Munsters!' Go on, Dublins!' and old Celtic cries. 'Now the, Irish Rifles!' It was at the Battle of Ginchy that Irishmen from the north and the south, Protestant and Catholic put aside political and religious differences and came together as one fighting unit against the German side of the 185th Division, the 19th Bavarian Division and the machine-gun company of the 88th Division.

The attack began just before 5 o'clock after a heavy bombardment with a creeping barrage from the south in four waves in open order, without about 50 yards between each wave, and on the left troops reached their first halting-place in the village, right across the first German trenches and dugouts, in eight minutes after starting-time a record time of 600 yards.

On the right the Irish were checked by three machine guns well placed, which swept the ground with waves of bullets. Many men dropped. Others fell deliberately with their faces to the earth so that the bullets might skim above their prone bodies. At the same time the Irish officers and men were being sniped at by German marksmen who had crept out into shell-craters. It became imperative that the machine guns were taken out.

It was here that a brilliant little piece of tactics was done by the troops on the left of the right wing, who swung round and attacked the machine-gun position from the west and north, in an encircling movement so that the German teams had to run out of the loop with their weapons to some broken trenches 300 yards away, where they again fired until knocked out by some trench-mortars attached to one of the Irish battalions. This enabled the right wing to advance and join the left, and they then advanced together through the villages, with the Irish Rifles remaining to hold the captured ground, and the Dublins charging ahead.

In the centre of the village among all the dugouts and tunnels was the ruin of the old farm where the enemy had another machine gun which they served with bursts of fire. They came on with the infantry, ranging their little engines to the farm, and aiming with such skill the machine gun was put out of action by a short storm of high explosives.

The men were still suffering from snipers and ordinary riflemen hidden in all kinds of places in the northern half of the village, where there were concreted and tunnelled chambers with loop-holes level with the ground, through which they shot. 'The Irish were reckless of all this and swept over the place fiercely searching out their enemies. In shell-craters and bits of upheaved earth and down in the dugouts there was hand-to-hand fighting of the grimmest kind. The Bavarians struggled savagely, using bombs and rifles, and fighting even with the bayonet until they were killed with the same weapon.'

It was all very quick. Within ten minutes of reaching the line halfway through the village the leading Dublins had got to the northern end of it and sent out advance parties 200 yards beyond. There was now just one major problem which could have led to disaster: the Irish had expected that their left flank would be supported by other troops attacking between Ginchy and Delville Wood, but owing to the difficulty of the ground and because of the rapidity of the advance, this had not happened. This left the victors of Ginchy with an exposed flank to the north-west of the village.

Gibbs recounts that a young sapper from Dublin, realising the situation, took command of a body of men and dug a defensive flank and established strong posts as a protection against a counter-attack. The situation was equally perilous as the troops engaged in an enterprise on that side had not yet made good their ground. The achievement of the Irish Brigade was outstanding – a hostile front of 900 yards to the depth of nearly a mile with no supporting troops on either flank.

Gibbs's account recalls the greatness of the capture of Ginchy, stating 'the valour of those Irish boys who were not cowed by that sight of death very close to them and all about them, and those who went straight on to the winning-posts like Irish race-horses'.

War Diary, Royal Dublin Fusiliers

Front Line.

9th September. 48th Bde. Formed up opposite Guinchy with left [?] Bde. Moving from Waterlot Farm the 47th Irish Brigade on right 49th detailed to hold Guinchy but two battalions used as reinforcements to 48th. 48th formed up two battalions in front in four waves. 7 RIR (7th Royal Irish Rifles) on left and 1 RMF. on right. 9 RDF (9th Royal Dublin Fusiliers) behind 7 RIR (7th Royal Irish Rifles) and 8 RDF (8th Royal Dublin Fusiliers) behind IRMF. First objectives was taken quickly by 7 RIR (7th Royal Irish Rifles) and IRMF and final objective by the 9 8 RDF (Royal Dublin Fusiliers) reinforced by Royal Inn Fusiliers. Attached is account of taking of Guincy.

10 September. The Battalions assembled at Bernafay Cross Roads during the early morning where the field kitchens awaited them with hot food. The Bttn. moved to Carnay where they had dinners and moved on to Happy Valley for the night.

Third Phase Battle of the Somme
Battle of Flers-Courcelette, 15–22 September

Men from Chapel Street
Peter Morley, 2nd Battalion Welsh Regiment died 22/9/16
Ernest Brownhill, 1st Battalion South Wales Borderers

<u>Guards Division 2nd Brigade</u>
Company Sergeant-Major Joseph Norton, 3rd Battalion Grenadier Guards

<u>1st Battalion Cheshire Regiment</u>
Sergeant James Arnold; John Booth; Thomas Booth Thomas Corfield; John Davies; Hugh Hennerley; Peter Hughes

The Regimental War Diary for the 3rd Battalion Grenadier Guards states that it was not until the beginning of September that the Guards Division arrived in the Somme area.

This was the third and final offensive mounted by the British Army, which attacked an intermediate line and the German third line to take Morval, Lesboeufs and Guedecourt, which was combined with a French Attack on Fregicourt and Rancourt to encircle Combles and a supporting attack on the south bank of the Somme. Parts of the line had to be straightened and 'pockets' of Germans cleared away before the general attack of 15 September.

The war diary for the 3rd Battalion Grenadier Guards for the period of 1–12 September states that they were at Morlancourt for training. During their stay, there was a three-day period of brigade training in which the assault was practised. The reason given for the training was that it was necessary to move all supporting troops simultaneously with those detailed for the actual assault in order to avoid enemies' barrage.

The following Battle Order gives in precise detail how the objectives would be reached.

Battle Orders, 12 September 1916

The Guards Division Order, No. 76

The Fourth Army will attack the enemy's defences between Combles Ravine and Martinpuich on Z day with the object of seizing Morval, Lesboeufs, Gueudecourt, and Flers, and to break through the enemy's system of defence.

The French are undertaking an offensive simultaneously on the South and the Reserve Army on the North.

The attack will be pushed with the utmost vigour all along the line until the most distant objectives are reached. The failure of one unit on the flank is to not to prevent other units pushing on to their final objective, as it is by such means that those units who have failed will be assisted to advance.

Preliminary Bombardment.-(a) Commencing on the 12th September a bombardment and wire-cutting on the hostile defensive system will take place from 6 a.m. to 6.30 daily. (b) The preliminary bombardment will be similar to that of previous days, there being no increase of fire previous to zero. (c) At 6.30 each evening from the 12th September inclusive night firing will commence, and continue till 6 a.m. lethal shells being used.

(a) The Sixth Division is to attack on the right and the Fourteenth Division on the left. (b) The 2nd Guards Brigade will attack on the right of the Division, the 1st Guards Brigade on the left. The 3rd Guards Brigade will be in Divisional Reserve.

Forming-up Areas.- Forming-up areas are shown on attached maps. The 1st and 2nd Guards Brigades will allot a forming-up area for the 75th and 76th Field Companies R.E. respectively in their forming-up areas.

Instructions as to movements of troops to their forming-up areas will be issued separately.

The objectives allotted to the Guards Division and neighbouring divisions are shown on (attached map).

First objective is marked Green.

Second	"	"	Brown.
Third	"	"	Blue.
Fourth	"	"	Red.

(a) 50 per cent Field Artillery covering the Division will be used for creeping barrage, and 50 per cent for stationary barrage. (b) Details of the stationary barrages will be issued later. In all cases the stationary barrage will lift back when the creeping barrage reaches it. (c) At zero the creeping barrage will open 100 yards in front of our front trenches, and will advance at the rate of 50 yards per minute until it is 200 yards beyond the first objective, when it will become stationary. At zero + 1 hour the creeping barrage will become intense on the line 200 yards in front of the first objective, and will creep forward at the rate of 50 yards per minute in front of that portion of the 1st Guards Brigade which is in advance to the second objective. (d) At zero- + 1 hour and 10 minutes the creeping barrage will become intense on a line of 200 yards in front of the first objective as far north as T.86.4.6,, thence on a line 200 yards in front of the second objective, and will advance at the rate of 30 yards per minute until it has passed 200 yards beyond the third objective, when it will become stationary.

This barrage is to cover the advance of the tanks. There will be no creeping barrage in front of infantry during their advance to third objective, which commences at zero +2 hours. At zero + 3 hours and 30 minutes the creeping barrage will become intense on a line of 200 yards in front of the third objective and will advance at the rate of 30 yards per minute until it has passed 200 yards beyond fourth objective, when it will become stationary. This barrage is to cover the advance of the tanks. There will be no creeping barrage in front of the infantry during the advance of the fourth objective, which commences at zero + 4 hours and 30 minutes. (f) In the attack on the first and second objectives gaps of 100 yards will be left in the creeping barrage for the routes of the tanks.

The flow of troops to the 2nd Guards Brigade and 1st Guards Brigade must be maintained so as to ensure a strong attack being pressed against each successive objective. Sufficient men will be left in each line captured to clear it of the enemy. No troops of the 2nd and 1st Guards Brigades will be detailed to remain behind in objectives after they have passed for purposes of consolidation.

The task of the two leading Brigades is to press the attack through to their ultimate objectives with every means at their disposal.

The 3rd Guards Brigade will advance at zero + 1 hour and 30 minutes until its leading troops reach the south-western outskirts of Ginchy, where the Brigade will halt and await orders.

Special instructions as to action of Reserve Brigade will be issued.

Tanks will be employed to operate with the attack; instructions as to their movements are attached. (Remainder of orders related to R.E.R.A., Aircraft and Transport.)

C. Heywood Lieut.-Col.,

General Guards Division.

The Regimental History makes the crucial point that so great was the danger of battalions being 'practically annihilated' in an attack, that orders had been issued for a certain nucleus of officers and NCOs to be left with the Transport, whenever a battalion went into action, so as to make sure of a sufficient number surviving to carry on the work. On this occasion the Second in Command, the junior Captains of companies, the Battalion and Company Sergeant-Majors and Quartermaster-Sergeants in each battalion were left behind.

Explanation of Tactical Manoeuvres

The Brigade was formed up in nine waves (a wave being a carrying party) at 50 yards distance and at zero time all waves advanced together under cover of: (1) A standing barrage on the enemies' front line; (2) a creeping barrage starting 100 yards in front of the assault and moving forward at 50 yards per minute. When the creeping barrage reached the standing barrage, both lifted to 200 yards beyond the German front line. The leading waves passed over the front line and formed behind the barrage. Standing barrage was then put down on the second line. The front trench was cleared by the rear waves.

Between 9–13 September the battalion moved into camp at 'Happy Valley'. There was very little in the way of accommodation. The weather was fine and training continued, following by a march to Carnoy and bivouacking, there was still little cover for the men.

The following day, 14 September, sees a very full day of organisation of equipment and supplies: distribution takes place of bombs, sandbags, tools, (five shovels to three spades), S.A.A. and flares for use with contact patrol aeroplanes. The men's packs, greatcoats and surplus kits, and the officers' kits were sent to the Divisional Store near Meaulte.

At 9.00 p.m. The battalion marched off by companies to take up position. It was a fine clear night with a moon and the companies moved up via Trones Wood, Guillemont, and Ginchy. The assaulting place of the Brigade was clear of the village as the enemy had proved to be very quick in putting down a barrage on it. The right of the Brigade rested about 100 yards from Ginchy telegraph and the frontage occupied was about 500 yards. The battalion was the right front battalion and was formed up in four waves, all men in single rank and companies in columns of half companies with a 50-yard distance between platoons. The 1st Bn. Coldstream Guards was on the left, the 1st Bn. Scots Guards was immediately in rear of us.

The battalion reached the assaulting point without difficulty or interruption, only one man being slightly wounded. On the other hand there were no assaulting parallels dug and the battalion had to dig some kind of assaulting trenches by linking up shell holes. Further owing to the necessity of being clear of Ginchy village the Brigade was not in immediate touch with the 1st Guards Brigade which was on the left and slightly in rear of us.

The Battle

15 September 1916

Zero hour was timed for 6.20 a.m. The men were in position at 3.00 a.m. After a short sleep between 3.00–5.45 a.m. they were given sandwiches and an issue of rum. 'Complete silence reigned, except for the sound of the tanks making their way slowly to their places,' the tanks were attached to the Division and were at the rear of the battalion. The diary continues:

We were in immediate touch with 6th Division on our right. At 6.00 a.m. our heavy artillery fired about 40 rounds in quick succession. This of course woke up the enemy, who put down his usual barrage on Ginchy village (particularly the NE corner), where it was expected and started shelling Leuze Wood. There were no troops there. Orders were passed down at 6.15 to fix bayonets and get ready, and five minutes later the attack started.

The first objective or Green line lay over the ridge about 600 yards away. The ground in and around Ginchy was a battered mass of irregular ridges and shell holes, which overlapped and stretched away into the early morning mist. The difficulty lay in the fact that there were no absolutely no landmarks to go by. No one except the Irish Guards had seen the ground before, as it had been impossible to send officers up during the heavy fighting of the last days.

The diary states the difficulties lay in the fact that although it should have been a simple matter to pick out Lesboeufs road and the church of Lesboeufs, which would have served as a guide, the actual ground was a desert of shell holes, with the enemy's shells falling all round, making it impossible to distinguish anything.

As the 3rd battalion started off, it met with unexpected intermediate lines. These were in fact no more than connected shell holes but served to shelter a number of Germans who 'fought with the utmost bravery'. The guns had not bombarded them, and the creeping barrage had passed over too quickly to do much harm. The diary notes that though the men holding them were all shot or bayoneted and the delay caused slight, it did have the effect of breaking the regularity of the formation and telescoping up the men in the rear.

It was during this time that CSM Joe Norton took action for which he was awarded the Distinguished Conduct Medal (DCM), for a 'gallant exploit'. A contemporary newspaper reported:

> The situation turned ugly, when Sergeant-Major J. Norton who was lying astride the wire gathered some men together and led a bayonet attack against a German bombing party. This momentarily relieved the situation and with great courage he killed or captured sixty Germans.

The diary states that almost at the outset Captain Mackenzie was hit, and fell as he led the attack. He was mortally wounded but got up and struggled on, until he fell, and raised himself up on one knee and cheered the company on. He was carried down on a stretcher but never recovered and died in the ambulance on the way to the casualty clearing station.

At the same time, Lieutenant Raymond Asquith[i] was shot through the chest and killed as led the first half of No. 4 Company. It is noted in the regimental history that he 'had endeared himself to both officers and men in an extraordinary degree since joining the regiment at the beginning of the war, and his preference of his service with his Battalion to the good staff appointment which he had just given up had won him the admiration of all ranks'.

As the battle progressed, serious casualties were incurred by the 3rd battalion's officers, with numerous officers killed, fatally wounded or wounded. The diary evidence reads:

> While these intermediate lines were being cleared, an extremely heavy machine-gun fire was opened from the right flank, where the Sixth Division had been held up from the start. The tanks which were to have flattened out the wire and helped the advance never appeared, and so it came about that, from the moment it crossed over the Ginchy ridge and came into view of the enemy's lines, the 2nd Guards Brigade was committed to a hard and continuous fighting in a position of much more difficulty.

Added to this, the Brigade itself had become mixed up, and although still all together it now advanced as a brigade rather than four battalions. This lead to

---

[i] Mr Asquith was the son of the then Prime Minister H.H. Asquith.

surmounting problems: whenever the leading wave met with any check, those in the rear, who were impatient to get at the enemy, closed in on them; this led to companies as well as battalions becoming intermingled. As an inevitable result of this quick advance, the right flank of the Brigade became completely exposed. The Commanding Officer Lieut-Colonel Sergison-Brooke took the decision to throw out a company as a defensive flank to within 200 yards of the enemy's flanking trench, to keep down the fire, whilst the rest of the 3rd Battalion Grenadier Guards pressed on to the main assault.

It had been arranged that after the first objective had been captured the artillery should bombard the second objective and prepare it for attack. There was now some uncertainty as to whether the advance should continue or not. However, despite mounting casualties they did push on and with the 1st Battalion Scots Guards, they reached the first objective – securing it to the specified time. The regimental history notes that in some parts between the right and left columns of the assault, and on the extreme right, the wire had been untouched. As soon as any man gained a foothold in the trench he immediately proceeded to clear the way by bombing.

The diaries note that though the Germans had fought with a great tenacity in the intermediate lines, the garrison of the first objective offered comparatively little resistance, and surrendered in large numbers. The men by this time were out of breath due to the pace and the fact that that they were carrying a good weight. The pause in the first objective was used to recover and sort out the prisoners, who were grouped together and sent back in batches. It is noted that in part of the line the German machine gunners turned their guns on them, but the prisoners ran as fast as they could back through the lines.

During this time No. 1 Company was attempting to keep in touch with the Sixth Division. As the Battalion advanced, Capt. Wolrige-Gordon started firing down the enemy's trench where the machine guns were holding it up. This caused confusion amongst the Germans as they couldn't understand where the fire was coming from. Once they had ascertained this, their snipers 'got to work' and accounted for many men before the captain could join the rest of the Battalion.

In the meantime, three battalions of the Coldstream advanced, carrying all before them. However, as the Regimental History notes, this was also not without complication:

> When men in line are going forward with no reliable landmarks to guide them, small incidents, quite insignificant in themselves will often cause a slight change of direction without their being aware of it. On starting off the 1st Battalion Coldstream met with little resistance, and in its endeavour to rush the foremost German trenches the left flank of the Battalion moved ahead faster than our creeping barrage. Quickly realising what had happened, the men checked the pace and hung back for a little, while the right flank of the Battalion pressed on. The check was momentary, but caused the whole Battalion to swing slightly to the left.

This led the 2nd and 3rd Battalions Coldstream in the 1st Guards Brigade also to also ease off slightly to the left, and, as often happens, the slight deviation was exaggerated as the advance continued, and soon all the Coldstream battalions were moving in a northerly instead of a north-easterly direction. A switch trench running at an angle into the German main line gave them the impression that they were going in the right direction, as it seemed to square with their advance.

The 2nd Battalion Irish Guards swung with the 1st Battalion Coldstream, but the 1st Battalion Scots Guards followed the 3rd Battalion Grenadiers. While this was happening the 2nd Battalion Grenadiers from the 1st Guards Brigade, having completely lost sight of the 2nd and 3rd Battalions Coldstream as it passed through the enemy's barrage, continued to advance according to its orders, and eventually forced its way to the first, where to its surprise it found itself between the 3rd Battalion Grenadiers and the 1st Irish Battalion Irish Guards.

Despite all of the confusion, the Division had swept everything in front of it. Some of the German trenches however, still remained untouched and in order for progress to be made these had to be dealt with. When the 1st Battalion Coldstream began their swing to the left, a gap was made between the two front battalions of the 2nd Guards Brigade, which widened out as the advance progressed. Observing this, Captain Lyttelton pushed up 100 men of the 3rd Battalion Grenadiers to fill the intermediate space. But as this gap gradually extended smoke and dust made it impossible to see where they were going, these 100 men were able to keep in touch with the 1st Battalion Coldstream only, and became detached from the rest of the Battalion.

The Regimental History highlights the fact that progress towards the first objective was made very difficult by the failure of the 6th Division to take the Quadrilateral. It states that as soon as the attacking lines showed themselves they were met by a sweeping fire from the enemy's machine guns on the right flank, and were mown down. After the first objective had been entered and the Coldstream Guards were organising an attack upon the second objective, it was discovered that the whole of the first objective was not entirely secured. To counter this, an attack was immediately made on the portion of the line still occupied by the enemy.

After losing the commander of the 1st Battalion Coldstream, orders were given to bomb down the trench with a party of the 2nd Irish Guards. But hardly had this started when the Germans came running down the trench holding up their hands. The diary, in a startling revelation, details that they were being pursued by another bombing party, not the 3rd Battalion Grenadiers as might have been expected, but the 2nd Battalion Grenadiers.

With the first objective now secured, the advance for the second objective took place. On the extreme right no further ground could be gained, but further towards the centre the 3rd Battalion Grenadiers reached a position they assumed to be the second objective, but this in fact was incorrect — according to the report from the aeroplanes, it was in fact halfway between the first and second objectives. During this advance, six officers were killed, reported missing or wounded.

Speculation surrounded whether Lesboeufs could have been taken: but with the sight of Germans retiring in haste to Bapaume, patrols were organised to press on to Lesboeufs, as there was a determination to keep the Germans in front and on the move. Twenty or so men were collected to reconnoitre towards Lesboeufs and the 3rd Battalion Grenadier Guards brought the whole party up to about 120 men. This party pushed on, and met with no opposition for about 800 yards. At this stage, they found themselves in an unoccupied trench running along the bottom of a gulley, with standing crops in front of them. They could have pushed on to Lesboeufs, but owing to their small numbers and, as they expressed it, the 'draughtiness of their flanks', they decided to hold on to where they were and send back for reinforcements. The official history reveals that orders were accordingly despatched to the Brigade Headquarters, and were marked, 'To be read by all officers on the way.'

This daring attempt to capture more ground from the enemy was quite a feasible operation, but it did depend on reinforcements reaching them before the Germans returned. A decision was taken to hold the trench until an adequate force arrived, and with every precaution taken against surprise, Lewis guns were placed on each flank. From 1 p.m. onwards, 'this gallant little band waited and waited for the reinforcements which never arrived'. Ponsonby (p.105) states:

> the Germans finding the British attack had spent itself, began to return in small bodies and by 5 p.m. a whole battalion was seen advancing. The position of the party was becoming more perilous. Gradually the Germans were moving round each flank, and even getting to their rear.
>
> By 6 p.m. they were still doggedly holding on to their trench, being fired on by all sides, when suddenly a company of the enemy, 250 strong, charged them in front. The surprise was complete, as the standing crops hid the Germans till the last moment. With 250 of the enemy rushing a trench occupied by less than 100 British troops it might have been thought all the men would be killed or taken as prisoners.

But the men who had followed their respective captains were 'naturally stout fighters', and when the order to retire was given, actually contrived to disengage themselves and get away, after killing a good number of the enemy. Even the Captain of the 3rd Battalion Grenadier Guards, in an extraordinary last stand, threw his empty revolver at the Germans, who, thinking it was a Mills bomb, ducked, which gave him time to scramble out of the trench and escape.

Had the Germans stayed where they were and fired at the retreating party, Ponsonby (p.106) notes they might have inflicted considerable losses, but they came running on, firing from the shoulder, which allowed the party to rejoin the main British line with few casualties. When the men were safe, the pursuers were greeted with a deadly fire from our trenches that numbers of them were killed, and the rest scattered in all directions.

General Ponsonby pressed for the 3rd Guards Brigade to be sent up, but the reports which reached General Fielding from the air that the troops were not in the positions ascribed to them, and as the situation on both flanks of the Division had been unsatisfactory, and the Germans were reported to be massing between Morval and Lesboeufs, he considered it would be impossible to throw forward all his reserves. However, the 4th Battalion Grenadiers was ordered to reinforce the 2nd Guards Brigade, and to strengthen the right flank.

All that night the right flank of the 2nd Guards Brigade was being bombed, and at one point the men were standing back to back and firing both ways. The next day, 16 September, the 2nd Guards Brigade was relieved by the 61st Infantry Brigade, who continued the attack, and secured the next objective. On 20 September, the 3rd Battalion moved into bivouacs at Carnoy, where it remained until the second attack of the Guards Division on 25 September. The 2nd Guards Division was then in reserve and owing to the complete success of the attack; its services were not required. The 3rd Battalion Grenadiers was in Corps Reserve during the attack, but returned to the Brigade in the evening.

Casualties
Officers Killed or Died of Wounds: 4. Wounded: 10. Missing: 4.
Other Ranks Killed: 31. Wounded: 155. Missing: 209.

Below is an example of training, preparations and fatigues that was typical of military duty in between battles of the war:

Battalion Diary Entries

17–19th September 1916. Re-organising took place. Owing to having left 20 per cent of the officers, C. S. Majors and a percentage of senior NCOs this was not so difficult as might have been expected. The casualties among specialists, especially signallers and Lewis gunners, in particular, had however been severe. Weather very wet and camp and roads got into a very bad state.

Once at Carnoy training resumed.

Two drafts joined the battalion: 198 men on the 20th and 133 on the 21st also, supplies of musketry, bombing, and smoke helmets.

The diary also notes that:

1 O.R. was killed and 10 wounded on 23rd whilst carrying ammunition to the forward dump. On the 25th the battalion was in Corps Reserve, with the Guards Brigade in reserve.

From 1st October to 11th October inclusive except Sunday, the battalion went into training with additional instruction in the following: (a) Trench Routine. (b) Open Fighting. (c) Protection. (d) Dimensions & correct designations of all types of trenches such as saps, parallels etc. (e) Regimental History. (f) Customs and discipline of the Regiment by means of short lectures.

Musketry and Bayonet Fighting were to be done in gas helmet order by all ranks (especially young Officers and drafts). Helmets were to be worn for at least 20 minutes. (There was also training in Bombing and Physical Drill). In musketry attention was to be paid to the following:-

(i)The Firing Position (ii) Aiming (aiming discs) (iii) Rapid Loading (dummies) (iv) Control by fire Unit Commander (v) Descriptive Points (clock method) (vi) Special Practice for Snipers and Lewis Gunners.

The battalion diary states that:

Officers and NCOs will be examined in all the Military Subjects in which they should be proficient. Leave will not be granted to those who are not proficient. The instruction of specialists (Stretcher-bearers, Signallers and Lewis Gunners) will proceed independently.

The Battle of Morval, 25–28 September

Men from Chapel Street
1st Battalion Cheshire Regiment
Sergeant James Arnold; Joseph Arnold; John Booth; Thomas Booth; John Davies; Hugh Hennerley; Peter Hughes.

Ernest Brownhill, 1st Battalion South Wales Borderers
Guards Division 2nd Brigade
Company Sergeant-Major Joseph Norton, 3rd Battalion Grenadier Guards

Adapted from the Cheshire Regimental History
A general attack was to be made by the British and French Armies for 25 September. The main British attack was to be made north-east towards Bapaume to potentially make an opening for the Cavalry. The French were to attack Sailly-Saillisel. On the right of the British attack was the 5th Division, which had already seen hard fighting and suffered heavy casualties. The 1st Cheshire Regiment had only had ten days to refit since the strenuous fighting near Falfemont Farm. Although this fact was recognised by the High Command, it was felt that as extensive an attack as possible should be made. It was decided that the 5th Division on the right, with the 6th and Guards Divisions should

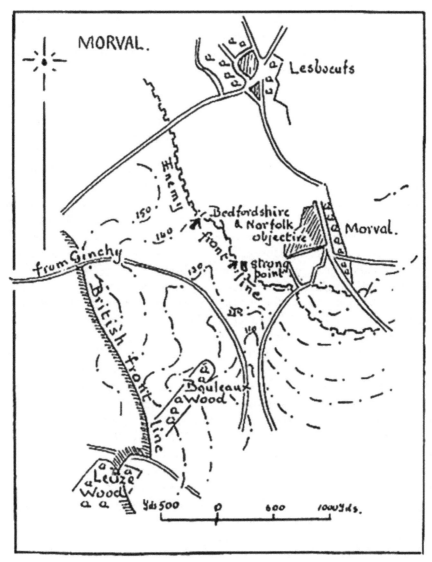

Sketch map of Morval. (Chester Military Museum)

attack the line Morval–Lesboeufs. The advantages gained would be good observation for any future advance and would assist the French to pinch out Combles
which would be surrounded on three sides.

The attack was to be in three stages. The first objective was the German front
line, at the bottom of the valley between Ginchy and Morval. This task was allotted
to the Bedforshire Regiment. The second objective was the German support line,
halfway up the slope to Morval. This task was given to the Norfolk Regiment. The
third objective was to be captured by the 1st Cheshire Regiment on the eastern
edge of Morval. The final objective was allotted to the Royal Warwicks, with a line
from which observation could be obtained on Sailly-Saillisel and Le Transloy.

The attacks were to take place at fixed intervals. The time between the attacks was to be occupied by getting battalions into position to go forward with the barrage. Three tanks were to follow the attack to assist in mopping up the German trenches south-west of Morval.

Assembly trenches had to be sited and dug at night. They were extremely well made and the labour that went into them was well spent.

At 12.55 p.m., the Norfolks captured their objective; the Bedfords and then the Cheshire, under a creeping barrage, reached the western edge of Morval at 2.42. They pushed through the village and reached the eastern exits at 2.55 and pushed out parties to secure their flanks and begin consolidation. The Royal Warwicks passed through this line to their final objective.

Contrary to expectation the attack on Morval and Lesboeufs had gone without a hitch and the line advanced some 2,000 yards, but what was regarded as the main attack in the north had not progressed as anticipated. The Cavalry were ordered back into reserve. Opposite Morval, the German line had been completely disorganised. Bodies of men could be seen hurrying back towards the Sailly-Saillisel–Le Transloy road, and a battery was observed galloping out of action from a position about a mile north-east of Morval. Had the Cavalry been available for action on this front, there was little doubt that Le Transloy could have been reached and possibly Bapaume. As it was, Le Transloy was not captured until a month later.

As a result of the capture of Morval on the north, and of Saillisel to the east by the French, Combles fell without the necessity for a direct attack on the town.

The whole operation was a great feat of arms, well planned, well executed and well supported by artillery. Mutual cooperation which had been lacking in the earlier Somme battles contributed to the success of the advance.

The 5th Battalion, which was the Pioneer Battalion of the division (the only men of the Cheshire Regiment to go over the top on the first day of the Somme) also played a vital part in the operations. They dug a trench on 19 September to protect the left flank of the Morval position, consolidating the ground won by the 56th Division in Bouleaux Wood, from which a view of the valley between Morval and Combles could be gained.

The following message of congratulations was received:

The heavy fighting in Delville Wood and Longueval, the attack and capture of Falfemont Farm line and Leuze Wood, and finally the storming of Morval, are feats seldom equalled in the annals of the British Army. They constitute a record of unvarying success which it has been the lot of few Divisions to attain, and the gallantry, valour, and endurance of all ranks have been wholly admirable.
    RAWLINSON.

This was the last battle of the 1st Battalion Cheshire Regiment on the Somme. They had taken part in three separate operations, and their losses in killed, wounded and missing had been about 20 officers and over 1,000 soldiers. After each action, they had received large reinforcements, many men having no connection with the county, but all had united to maintain the reputation of the Regiment.

War Diary 1st Battalion Cheshire Regiment

Headquarters were detained owing to some wounded of the Argyle and Sutherland Highlanders not being removed, and while the Commanding Officer, Adjutant, Medical Officer and 2nd Lieut. were arranging their removal, the enemy bombarded the Sunken road with gas shells, necessitating the use of box respirators.

Oxford Copse–Citadel, Bray:

> 27 September. Battalion returned, after relief to Oxford Copse arriving about 2.30 a.m. The total casualties during the operations: 4 Officers – slightly – 140 ORs. The Battalion moved to Citadel, arriving in camp at 8 p.m.
> 28 September. Battalion in camp at Citadel which was bombed last night, necessitating all lights and fires being put out.

Battle of Thiepval Ridge, 26–28 September

<u>Men from Chapel Street</u>
Cheshire Regiment 1/6 Battalion: Patrick Egan; Edward Caine

To assist the main attack on the Thiepval Ridge on 26 September, the 118th Brigade made a feint attack in the area north of Hamel. The 6th Battalion raided many the enemy trenches in conjunction with this attack. Under cover of a barrage, they crossed no man's land at 9.00 p.m. and rushed the enemy's trenches. Fierce fighting ensued with the covering party on the enemy parapet keeping the enemy at bay in face of heavy machine-gun fire, while another party attempted to clear the enemy trenches. All trenches were found to be blocked with knife rests and loose wire. All of the German garrison were killed or driven off, and a difficult withdrawal was made. The battalion lost twelve men.

Le Transloy, 1–18 October

<u>Men from Chapel Street</u>
Edward Lowe, Royal Irish Rifles

<u>Cheshire Regiment 5th Battalion</u>
James Bell Houlden; John Kirkham

Operations were undertaken during October to secure a line from which the main Le Transloy system would be attacked at a later date. The first objective was to drive the Germans from the west crest of the ridge, with the second objective to secure a position on the eastern crest giving observation over Le Transloy.

Mud and Beyond the Great Divide

The French had the definite tactical objective in the high ground above Sailly-Saillisel, which enfiladed the British line. The Allies' experience was very different. The Somme mud was a continuous bedevilment: directly the line halted, the mutual bombardment would resume and the ground would be churned up; mud would reappear filling the shell holes and slaking the terrain. As they advanced they took their mud with them. Unless there was a breakthrough of such a depth as to penetrate beyond the shelled area, there was no escape from it. Men were wading into bogs and plunging and floundering to clamber out on to firm ground. Men were literally bogged down with the weight of their equipment, progress was limited. War in open countryside compounded the problem and rain was another factor. Crookenden (p.89) likens the experience to a state of mirage, where each successive advance 'must inevitably recede further and further away'. In late autumn, distances had to be reckoned in mud rather than in time. Mud became an obstacle to movement, which few of the higher staff, he states, ever appreciated at its proper value.

Trench foot was a resulting fungal infection of the feet caused when exposed to damp, cold conditions and poor hygiene. Trench foot can occur in temperatures up to 16°C and within as little as thirteen hours. It can be prevented by keeping the feet clean, warm and dry. Preventive measures during the war included regular foot inspections, using whale oil, laying wooden duckboards to cover the ground in the trenches and the increased practice of troop rotation, which kept soldiers from prolonged time at the front.

Adapted from the Rifle Brigade History

The immediate problem was to get within striking distance of Le Transloy.

> The tanks were already useless on the treacherous ground. The men employed in the assault stumbled exhausted into their assembly positions, and, at zero, slithered and slipped, staggering under the weight of their equipment, through sludge and water in their effort to keep up with the barrage. The dash of the September battles was irrevocably gone. But the winter was fast approaching, and it seemed to be worth any sacrifice to get out of the awful mud before it came. None but the Fourth Army came to within striking distance of the Le Transloy line, and they would break through once again on a wide front and find themselves in open country.

5th Battalion

1.45 p.m. One company of the 5th Battalion was with the 168th Brigade on the right, and one with the 169th Brigade on the left. The battle raged for forty-eight hours with very little progress. The 5th Battalion had a very strenuous five weeks in September, and during the period of this battle they were digging trenches and constructing strong points. The most famous of these works was a trench called Gropi (Groves' Pioneers) about 1,000 yards long, in front of Bouleaux Wood. The

Corps Commander considered it a perfect example of a battle trench. It was dug in one night, within about 100 yards of the Germans.

The British front line now ran just east of Morval–Les Boeufs–Guedecourt.

Battle of the Ancre Heights, 1 October–11 November

Men from Chapel Street
Cheshire Regiment
9th Battalion Cheshire Regiment: Peter Gormley; James Hanley; William Johnson; Joseph Wyatt.
10th Battalion: Joseph Arnold; Martin Donnelly; John Inions.
1/6th Battalion: Edward Caine; Patrick Egan.

Extracted from the Regimental History of the Cheshire Regiment

This battle was undertaken to gain the ridge running from just south-west of Martinpuich to the high ground north of Thiepval, which was crowned by the Schwaben and Stuff redoubts. The capture of this ridge would give the advantage of observation over the Ancre Valley and Grandcourt. Thiepval had been captured, but not the top of the ridge.

On 9 October, the 10th Battalion made a single-handed attack on the Stuff redoubt. The attack started on the southern portion of the redoubt, which the Cheshires held, and was intended to capture the remainder. The 10th Battalion moved up by platoons and relieved the troops holding the front line by 10.15 a.m. on 9 October. After a hot meal and by 12.35 a.m., as an intense artillery fire opened on the enemy trenches, every man was in his place. The barrage was rather 'over' the enemy trench, and under its cover the battalion formed up in no man's land, advancing and keeping good direction and not bunching.

The advance of the first wave was very rapid so that the men were in the German trenches before their soldiers had time to man the parapet and get their machine guns to work. On the right, the enemy put up a poor fight, and on the left a bombing party rushed a strong point where there were several dugouts, from which many Germans were emerging. A melee ensued. Many Germans were killed in the open or in dugouts. Five German officers and 100 prisoners were captured. Fierce bombing and a determined bayonet charge took place before the enemy block, some way up the two communication trenches leading away from the redoubt, were captured: these were the second objectives.

A block was then made here to protect the left flank, but was twice destroyed by our own artillery fire. The third wave assisted in the capture of the second objective. The situation was now quite desperate: all communication with the Artillery (ours) had been cut, and increasing German pressure with bomb and rifle drove back the position by 50 yards. As the shelling was severe and relentless on the communication and support trenches, the supply of bombs and ammunition was precarious.

Around 4.30 p.m., the Germans brought up a *mindenwerfer* (a mine launcher for short range mortars – the weapons were used by engineers to clear obstacles such as barbed wire and bunkers, which long-range artillery could not accurately target). Under cover of its fire and of heavy artillery barrage, they made a counter-attack which was successfully driven off. In the evening the situation quietened, but later another counter-attack was put down. Throughout this confrontation the 1st Wilshire Regiment was invaluable in carrying bombs and stores.

Extracts from Diary of Colonel A. C. Johnston, Commander 10th Battalion

8th October. The weather seems to be dead against us; pouring with rain. Attack postponed and relieved in the trenches by 8th Loyal North Lancashire Regiment. It is extraordinarily bad luck; everything was ready, the men turned up to it and quite ready to go over. The battalion returned to dug-outs near Orvillers where the men were able to be warm and comfortable. The Colonel reveals that at 8 p.m. he received a message to say they had to do the attack at 12.35 p.m. the next day. This meant 'trudging all the way up there in the mud next morning, doing a relief, making final arrangement without much margin if anything were to go wrong, and then doing the attack'.

Going over the top
9th October. Started out from dug-outs at 8 a.m. and relieved the 8th N. Lancs, without a hitch by 10.30 a.m. The men had a hot meal at 11 a.m. The Colonel tells how he went round the trenches, had a talk to the men, and gave final instructions to the officers. By 12.20 p.m. everything was ready, and all the men were in their places.

The Colonel reports 'that our "heavies" shelled one or two trench junctions behind the German front line in the morning, but otherwise it had been quiet'. At 12.35 p.m., an intense barrage was put on to the German front line, on to their communication trenches leading backwards, and to neighbouring trenches on the battalion's flanks:

> Stoke mortars (this was a new weapon developed in 1915), conformed to the artillery barrage. Heavy artillery shelled German dug-outs and places where the enemy was known to keep his supports. Our machine-guns covered our flanks, and swept the German communication trenches with overhead fire. At the same moment, our fellows climbed out of our trenches and formed up in No-man's land.

The Colonel states that he was a bit anxious as the barrage, instead of being on the German front line, was over it, and it was his judgement that: 'there was really no reason why the Germans should not man their parapet'. He counted six or more German sentries standing up and firing at 'our fellows', but the firing was wild, and he states that none of 'our chaps' were hit.

> The men were splendid. There was no faltering. They went straight over without bunching or losing direction, and were in the German trench before they could get their machine guns into action. It turned out that the trench had not been damaged by our bombardment. Aeroplane observers, who watched the attack from above, reported that it was the best carried out attack they had seen, and people who watched it through their telescopes from behind, all remarked how well the men went over, and said that it was quite a model of how an attack should be done. On the right, the enemy put up their hands at once, but on the left where fortunately I had thickened our line in anticipation of some trouble, there was quite a lively 'mix-up', and some 40 Germans were killed at this point alone, besides those bombed, burnt and buried at the bottom of their dug-outs. The whole of the Stuff Redoubt was in our hands, and, so far, at trifling cost.

The diary goes on to state that that after three minutes (our) barrage began to roll back, and the third wave passed over the first objective, and kept close to the barrage assaulting the next line that had to be taken. Further fighting ensued, with more Germans captured, and big dugouts crowded with the enemy were bombed. A block was made across Stump Road but it was in this area that the Germans were in great strength and a tremendous fight took place which lasted for two hours.

The Colonel states that as long as they had a good supply of rifle grenades, they were able to keep the Germans back, but points out that with their egg bombs and stick bombs, his men could be out-thrown – this caused a pull-back of some 50 yards.

The Colonel experienced continuing difficulties, this time due to heavy German barrage causing a great deal of confusion and difficulty getting bombs, ammunition and sandbags into the captured trenches. Communications to the rear were cut beyond repair, and smoke and flashes made visual signalling impossible. With understated irony, the Colonel records in his diary that he had only one officer above the rank of 2nd Lieutenant, who had only a few days' experience in the trenches, he states that: 'fortunately he was not wounded until 7p.m.'

At 3.00p.m., the Colonel made a tour of the trenches to buck up morale and states that it was a lively walk!

The German shelling became more severe, which increased in its ferocity at 5.00 p.m. This was a prelude to a counter-attack, and it was expected that this would be on the right. The fourth company were sent up (reference: Point 80); and as the Colonel surmised, the counter-attack took place up and along Stump Road. Three officers were 'knocked out'. The attack was repulsed with rifle and Lewis gun fire. The enemy put down another stiff barrage at 6 p.m. and attempted another counter-attack. This time, however, the artillery was able to assist and the counter-attack was nipped in the bud. Due to the lack of communication, the battalion had to see the first counter-attack through entirely by themselves. 'There were many casualties and eventually the advanced barricades had to be abandoned, owing to the fire of our Gunners which we could not get them to lengthen.'

The diary entry further states that about 7 p.m. things had begun to quieten down, but that they still had trouble from a *minenwerfer* in front of the right and there was shelling throughout the night. By dawn, the Cheshires were firmly established in the trenches, and the Colonel notes that the Germans had apparently for the present, 'given us best'.

The casualty figures were: 1 officer killed, 8 officers wounded, 137 NCOs and men killed, wounded or missing.

The Colonel records:

> ... but I do not know that that was very heavy when one considers how much we had done. We had captured the whole redoubt and the trenches beyond it, and killed certainly 70 or 80 Germans, exclusive of those killed or burnt in their dug-outs, or of casualties from our shelling. We had taken 120 prisoners, and the men behaved splendidly throughout, and there were many acts of great gallantry.
>
> 10th October ... It was great to see the men coming back with a grin from ear to ear, with German helmets and other souvenirs hanging all over them.
>
> The Worcesters 1st Battalion, gave the 10th Battalion a rousing cheer on its way back to rest.

Further Diary Entries:
6th Battalion.

> The 6th Battalion took part in an attack on the Schwaben Redoubt on the 6th October by the 37 Division. The battalion was in reserve, but two platoons reinforced the Cambridgeshire Regiment and lost 3 Officers and 14 NCOs and men.

Attack on Regina Trench, 21–22 October
10th Battalion
The 25th and 39th Divisions attacked Regina Trench. This attack was carried out under a barrage starting between 12 noon and 6 p.m. The troops had by now gained confidence in barrages and moved close under it. The enemy's wire had been effectively cut and was no longer an obstacle. The 10th Battalion was also 'carrying' and had one company garrisoning Stuff Redoubt.

13th Battalion
The only one of our Battalions in the front line. It advanced in three waves and took its objectives without much difficulty, though the casualties were severe. 12 officers and 198 men.

11th Battalion
The battalion was split up, one company was attached to the 8th Border Regiment, one was carrying for the two assaulting Brigades, and two companies were 'holding' Hessian trench. Some of the men of the 11th Battalion, attached to the 8th Borders, overran the objective and got ahead of the barrage. In consequence, a gap occurred

at the point of junction of the Brigades, and here the enemy held out for some time. In the end, the enemy post was taken and its defenders all killed or captured; a large dugout holding 150 men was afterwards found at this point.

9th Battalion
Colonel Johnston is critical of the omission of the 9th Battalion's action (for which they shared in the Battle honour) in their Battalion diary and the Brigade War Diary, except for an observation of their being 'thigh deep' in mud. He is scathing of their Brigade-Major, who he states: 'hardly records any movements except his own, in the Brigade War Diary'.

Battle of the Ancre, 13–18 November

Men from Chapel Street
Cheshire Regiment:
9th Battalion Cheshire Regiment: Peter Gormley; James Hanley; William Johnson; Joseph Wyatt.
1/6th Battalion Cheshire Regiment: Edward Caine; Patrick Egan.

Extracts from the Regimental History of the Cheshire Regiment

The official history records that the attacks in this battle were made in more favourable conditions than those on the right flank near Le Transloy.

The Butte de Warlencourt marked the limit of progress on the right flank. From there, the line ran through Stuff trench and Regina trench north of Thiepval, to St Pierre Divion and from there it ran north. It was a position unchanged since 1st July.

The greater part of the front now looked down on an enemy in low lying and water-logged valleys.

> To make movement at all possible, duck-board tracks were laid from Thiepval to the assembly area. The trenches had been so shot about and damaged by weather that even in daylight it was hard to locate one's position or even to say whether one was in a trench or not. Fifteen yards a minute was the fastest that could be calculated on. Evacuation of wounded was almost impossible. Men had to sit down and pull their legs out of the mud.

The Fifth Army was to attack Grandcourt–St Pierre Divion–Beaumont Hamel. The 6th Battalion was formed up in the Schwaben redoubt ready to advance in four lines, part of the main attack. Zero was fixed for 5.45 a.m.

The weather was again a factor and the darkness was accentuated by a thick fog which lasted until 9 a.m. This caused confusion on the left of the attack, which moved forward under an excellent barrage. The 6th Battalion down the Strassburg Line was interrupted by a loss of direction, and they and the Black Watch were

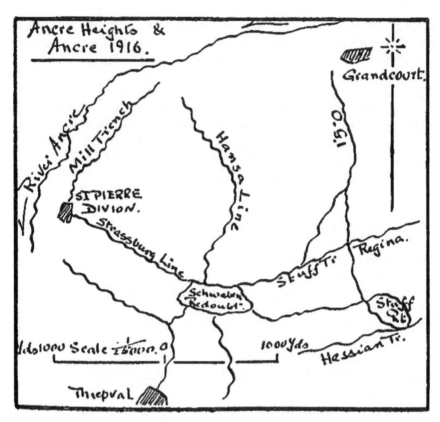

Sketch map of Ancre Heights and Ancre. (Chester Military Museum)

attributed with the objective being missed. However, after reorganisation they captured their objective – Mill trench, along the banks of the Ancre – by 8.30 a.m.

Three officers were killed during the battle (including the captain who led the leading wave), and total casualties amounted to 167. North of the Ancre, although Serre again resisted all attacks, Beaumont Hamel was captured.

War Diary 9th Battalion Cheshire Regiment

12 November. The Regimental Band played at the camp in the afternoon. Brigade working parties were found. The mist is not too thick. The Bn. moved into the line as already detailed. On the way into the line the Bn. was shelled. One Officer killed 'B' Coy had 4 killed and 6 wounded. During the whole night the enemy shelled at intervals, principally Hessian Trench. The line held was from R21b 9.7. to R.21.a.9.51/2.

14 November. The enemy were shelling at intervals throughout the day and night HQ dug-out and most of the Coy. HQ dug-outs came in for special attention. The thanks of the 5th Army Commander was received.

15 November. The enemy shelled front line and Hessian Trench several times during the day. The enemy's fire appears to come from Loupart Wood principally. One of our listening posts fired on a German patrol of 10 men barrage and saw two fall. The enemy appear to be decidedly nervous and he put up frequent 4.2 barrages during the day. Lt. E. was badly wounded in the head and legs.

16 November. The enemy continued the shelling of our trenches. Retaliation being called for the enemy quietened down, our heavies doing good work. A report from the C.C.S. stated that Lt. E. had succumbed to his wounds. The Bn. was relieved by the 7 Bn.

17 November. The day was spent in rest and cleaning up. The weather was bright and cold. The casualties of the Bn. during this last tour in the trenches amounted to, 1 Officer Died of Wounds, 1 Officer Wounded, 19 Other Ranks, Killed in Action, 44 Other Ranks Wounded. The Bn. was under orders to Wellington Huts but this did not take place.

Gravel Pit

18 November. The Bn. moved up to the Gravel Pit in Divisional Reserve in accordance with operation orders issued on the 15th inst and which had not been postponed on account of bad weather. This morning it was snowing which later tuned to rain.

2.30 p.m. The Bde. also put at our disposal a Tank and 10 Worcesters for mopping up purposes, but these two items did not eventuate.

Trenches

18 November. Bombed a dug-out and secured a machine gun. The enemy counter-attacked with bombs and this party had eventually to make their way back and withdrew to Stuff + Bulgar Trenches where they met men of the 10th Worcesters. This party returned with 1 prisoner and a M. Gun. The M. Gun had to be abandoned in a shell hole our men being too exhausted to carry it. Here they remained having placed themselves under the orders of the O.C. 10 Worcesters. Another party of 2 Officers + 40 men got right up to the Ancre where they got in touch with the above mentioned party.

This was the Battle of the Somme, 1916.

Men from Chapel Street continued to fight and die in the area throughout the war. There were follow-on battles in the Somme sector in 1918. The battles were entitled: The First Battles of the Somme, between 21 March–5 April, and 4 July, 1918; followed by the Second Battles of the Somme, 1918 between 8 August and 3 September. The British naming of all battles during the First World War was the responsibility of the British Battles Nomenclature Committee.

Paradoxically, 'Somme' is an old Celtic word for 'tranquillity'.

The Balkans Southern Front: Mediterranean Expeditionary Force (MEF) Gallipoli Campaign

Introduction

The Gallipoli Campaign, or Dardanelles Campaign, took place on the Gallipoli Peninsula between 25 April 1915 and 9 January 1916.

Location

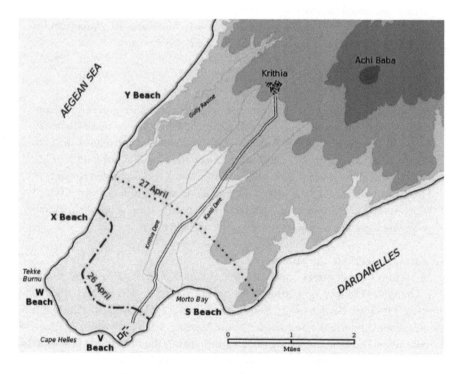

Cape Helles and beach landing area. (Wikimedia Commons)

The Gallipoli Peninsula is located on the European part of Turkey, with the Aegean Sea to the west and the Dardanelles Strait to the east. The peninsula runs for about 60km in a south-westerly direction into the Aegean Sea, between the Hellespont and the Gulf of Saros. The Dardanelles are the narrow straits of water giving access to the Sea of Marmara, which provides a sea route to the Russian Empire.

Military Advantages
Controlling the straits would give the Allies several possible advantages:
* The Royal Navy could attack Constantinople, capital of Germany's ally, Turkey.
* The navy could attack Turkish industry, which was mainly based around the Sea of Marmara.
* Greece and Bulgaria might join the war on the side of the Allies against Turkey.
* British and French merchant ships could send vital arms, equipment and other supplies to their ally, Russia. In January 1915, the Russian commander, Duke Nicholas, was asking for Allied help because the Germans were pushing his forces backwards.

The Campaign
The Allies included the armies of Australia, New Zealand, Newfoundland, India, France and Russia supported by the Labour Corps of Egypt, Malta and the Oriental Expeditionary Force, set against the armed force of the Ottoman Empire and its allies.

British forces involved at Gallipoli
29th Division (landed 25 April 1915)
Australian and New Zealand Corps (landed 2 April 1915)
Royal Naval Division (landed 25 April 1915)
42nd (East Lancashire) Division (landed May 1915)
52nd (Lowland) Division (landed June 1915)
13th (Western) Division (landed 6–26 July 1915)
10th (Irish) Division (landed 6–7 August 1915)
11th (Northern) Division (landed 6–7 August 1915)
53rd (Welsh) Division (landed 9 August 1915)
54th (East Anglian) Division (landed 10 August 1915)
(www.longlongtrail.co.uk)

The Major Battles and Events
The Naval bombardment of the Straits Forts (19 February–16 March)
The Naval attempt to force the Straits (18 March)
The Landings at Cape Helles and Anzac Cove (25 April)
The First Battle of Krithia (28 April)
The Turkish night counter-attack (2 May)
The Second Battle of Krithia (6 May)

The Third Battle of Krithia (4 June)
The Battle of Gully Ravine (28 June)
The Landings at Suvla Bay and the Anzac attack on Chunuk Bair (6–10 August)
The Battle of Scimitar Hill and attack on Hill 60 (21–22 August)
Evacuation of Anzac and Suvla (19–20 December)
Evacuation of Cape Helles (8–9 January 1916)

Men from Chapel Street
Royal Marine Light Infantry (Royal Naval Division)
George Clarke; Charles Clarke (Probable Service).

42nd (East Lancashire) Infantry Division [Territorial Force]
Lancashire Fusiliers, 125th Brigade: 7th Battalion (1/7th)
John O'Connor, service number 2266; William Hughes, service number 52884.

Manchester Regiment, 127th Brigade: 6th Battalion (1/6th)
Corporal Michael O'Connor, service number 62628.

Manchester regiment, 127th Brigade: 7th Battalion (1/7th)
James Murray, service number 295087.

(The 6th and 7th Battalion recruited from the suburbs of Manchester and Cheshire.)

13th (Western) Division (40th Brigade)
8th (Service) Battalion Cheshire Regiment
William Groark, service number 11267, died 18/8/15; James Ratchford, service number 10455; William Ratchford, service number 11235; James Riley, service number 11222.

The following accounts describe the experiences of a population deracinated into war in the Mediterranean. They are taken from the Divisional Diary of the 42nd (East Lancashire) Regiment, the Battalion War Diaries and General Hamilton's personal diary.

They give an insightful and graphic account of the landing at Cape Helles and the difficulties encountered; the climate, geography and topography of the peninsula; the planning of operations, decision-making processes and consequences; the battles and outcomes; and the inevitable evacuation of the peninsula.

Cape Helles – Gallipoli Peninsula

After a naval bombardment on 15 February, which served as a threat and a warning to the enemy, a naval attempt was made on 18 March to force the Straits, which failed disastrously, though it attained one objective – it relieved the pressure on the Russians.

The large Turkish forces withdrawn from the Caucasus were now deployed to defend Gallipoli and the Straits. The previously undefended peninsula was now converted into an impregnable position against attack. Artillery was mounted to cover every approach, and barbed wire entanglements were concealed in the shallows and placed on shore.

On 25 April the 29th Division landed at various beaches of the southern extremity of the peninsula, around Cape Tekke, Cape Helles and the village of Sedd-el-Bahr. The Anzacs (Australian and New Zealand Army Corps) landed on the Western shore a dozen miles to the north, just beyond the headland at Gaba Tepe.

Landings, Battles and Preparations

Hamilton records in his diary how he wrote a long cable to Kitchener, formally asking leave to call upon Maxwell to send him the East Lancs. Division, and was exultant when Kitchener responded with the cable reply that, 'I feel sure you had better have the Territorial Division.' Hamilton's diary recorded that: 'the best buck up for the Army will be the news that the lads from Manchester are on their way to help us.'

On 5–6 May, the Lancashire Fusilier Brigade, with No. 2 Section Signal Company and the 2nd Transport and Supply Company, disembarked at 'W' and 'V' Beaches, across the blood-drenched hulk of the *River Clyde*, and were temporarily attached to the 29th Division. Vehicles and animals were slung into the lighters (landing craft), the A.S.C. (Army Service Corps) mules had been supplied by the 49th Reserve Park a few hours before embarking at Alexandria, and were unknown to the drivers who brought them safely ashore. As the cable-wagons could not be landed, each man of the Signal Section took as much equipment as he could carry.

The men set foot ashore close to the spot which became world-famous as 'Lancashire Landing' a few days earlier, by the 1st Battalion Lancashire Fusiliers. In his first despatch, Sir Ian Hamilton wrote, 'So strong, were the defences of "W" Beach that the Turks may well have considered them impregnable; and it is my firm conviction that no finer feat of arms has ever been achieved by the British soldier – or any other soldier – than the storming of these trenches from open boats, by the 1st Lancashire Fusiliers.'

Hamilton describes 'W' Beach as:

An ant's nest in revolution, with five hundred of our fighting men running to and fro between cliffs and sea carrying stones to improve the pier. On to the pier picket boat, launches, dinghies, barges, all converge through the heavy swell with shout and curses, and hair-breath escapes. Other half-naked soldiers are sweating, hauling, unloading, loading, road-making, dragging mules up a cliff, pushing mules down a cliff: hundreds more are bathing, and through this pandemonium pass the quiet stretcher bearing pale, blood stained burdens.

Lancashire Fusiliers boat Gallipoli, May 1915. (Wikimedia Commons)

He observed that the Turks had, so far, left it pretty well alone. In the afternoon, Hamilton went ashore and inspected the Lancashire Brigade of the East Lancs., noting that they 'are a very fine lot of Officers and men'.

Within a few hours of landing the Territorial Brigade was in action, in what became known as the 2nd Battle of Krithea. The first battalion to disembark, the 6th Lancashire Fusiliers, took over trenches from K.O.S.B. (King's Own Scottish Borderers) at dusk, on the extreme left of the British line, between Gully Ravine and the Aegean Sea. The remainder of the Brigade marched during the night, reaching a point above Gully Beach at daybreak on 6 May.

A general advance of the whole line, stretching right across the peninsula, from a point about three miles north of Tekke Burnu on the left to a point about one mile north of De Tott's Battery on the right, was ordered for 10 a.m. The 6th L. F. gained more than 400 yards before being held up by heavy fire from rifles and machine guns. This was the greatest advance made by any unit that day, and the ground won was held. The 7th were in support of the 6th. One company of the 8th reinforced the extreme left, another company supported the left of the 88th Brigade on the right of Gully Ravine. This ravine, about 50 yards wide, with steep cliffs 40–60ft high, formed a dangerous gap in the line, and during the night its bed was occupied by another company of the 8th. Under cover of night the trenches, having been cleared of dead and dying, were deepened and improved.

The attempt to continue the advance next morning was not successful. The 5th L. F. deployed and passed through the 6th in the front line, the rest of the Brigade being in support, to press home the attack. The Brigade's objective was a point about a mile to the north of the furthest point reached by British troops throughout the campaign. Some parties of the 5th gained a little ground, but they were enfiladed, the intensity of the fire drove them back, and the line remained unaltered. A renewal of the attack in the afternoon, when the brigade was reinforced by two battalions of the 87th Brigade, also failed. At sundown the brigade was relieved, and the Lancashire Fusiliers rested on the cliffs until the following evening when they were moved to a less exposed bivouac further inland, among the trees near Morto Bay. The Territorials had been thrust at once into the fighting line because they were badly needed, they were severely tested and 'stood it well'. When they landed, the position of the depleted 29th Division was precarious. The men were exhausted, with the limit of human endurance almost reached. It was vital that an advance was made and less exposed positions secured, if they were not to be driven into the sea by force of numbers. The arrival of the Territorial Brigade had enabled the worn-out Regulars to attain this object. The No. 2 Section Signal Company had done good work. For two days their tasks had been done in the open, under continuous fire, all lines having been laid on the surface by hand.

Hamilton records in his diary that, 'The beautiful Battalions of the 125th are wasted skeletons now; shadows of what they had been.'

By some blunder or misunderstanding on the part of the Naval Authorities, most of the transporters conveying the reminder of the Division were sent northwards up the coast to Gaba Tepe, instead of to Cape Helles. The first to arrive, the *Derflinger* with the 5th and 6th Manchesters on board, was chased by a destroyer and brought back with all speed to Helles, where these two battalions disembarked on the evening of 6 May at 'W' and 'V' beaches. The 7th and 8th Manchesters landed on the same beaches on the following day under shell fire, which caused several casualties. The Manchester Brigade assembled on the cliffs between the beaches before moving inland to the rendezvous known as Shrapnel Valley. The other transports, including the *Crispin* with Headquarters on board, arrived off Gaba Tepe on 8 May and anchored there for the night.

Landings on open beaches exposed the Allies to chance firing from the Turkish front, and presented a visible target to batteries at Kum Kale on the Asiatic shore. At Cape Helles, the transports anchored at varying distances from the shore, and the troops were transferred to steam-tugs and trawlers, each carrying about 500 men to the makeshift piers of 'trestles' or old barges, or to the jetty formed by the stranded *River Clyde* on 'V' Beach. Horses and mules were slung overboard and loaded into lighters. The ground swell increased the difficulties and dangers.

Men scrambled into the tugs and many began to realise that they were now confronting the biggest thing that had yet entered into their lives. 'They joked and chaffed one another, and smoked their pipes, as if crossing to the Isle of Man', while the thunder of the heavy guns echoed against the cliffs. The men were not yet 'heroes', and few of them had yet been tested by fire: to steady their nerves and conceal from their comrades – and themselves – the anxieties and doubts that would not be denied, they made fun of the ordeal that lay before them.

Each boatload was welcomed by a Landing Officer, whose role was to move men and baggage clear of his 'pier' and beach in order to make room for the next batch and prevent the short stretch of foreshore from becoming hopelessly blocked. The strip of firm sand at the water's edge soon changed to loose sand and shingle, which sloped gradually to the foot of the cliffs, about 150–200 yards from highwater mark.

Heaven and Helles

The cliffs rose abruptly to the height of 50–60ft, except in the centre of the bays, where higher ground was reached by rough winding tracks. From the top of the cliffs a view of Achi Baba was obtained, a sight that was at first of interest, but soon gave way to detestation. The top was no place to linger, as the Turks in front and in Asia had good visibility of any occupants. Low scrub and grass covered it; beyond, the ground dipped slightly before it began to rise nearly 600ft to the summit of Achi Baba, about 6 miles to the north-east. The only trees near the Helles beaches were small groups of windswept firs and a few limes, but further inland, near the nullahs (streams), and far away on the right, in the French area around Morto Bay, more foliage could be seen.

There were many wild flowers, including pink citrus, wild thyme and wild roses, lilies, tulips, cornflowers and here and there vivid red patches of poppies relieved the general impression of green. It was over the carpet of flowers that the stretcher-bearers with red crescent flags would bear away their wounded and bury their dead. Hamilton stated that it was by his order that the Turks were being left a free hand to carry out this pious duty.

By July, Hamilton's attitude had changed. In refusing the request from the Commandant of the Ottoman Forces for a five-hour truce to bury thousands of dead, he notes in his diary: 'Our Intelligence are clear that the reason the Turks make this request is that they cannot get their men to charge over the corpses of their comrades.' Hamilton poignantly states that on the grounds of humanity and health, he should like the poor chaps to be decently buried, but finds himself saying no, rationalising that: 'Dead Turks are better than barbed wire.'

The peninsula had an abundance of tortoises, lizards, tarantulas, scorpions and frogs. At a later date some ammunition was wasted on the flocks of migrating cranes and storks, until shooting at them was forbidden. The number of birds which lived and nested on the peninsula, undeterred and indifferent to the noise and carnage was remarkable. Linnets, goldfinches, turtle doves, magpies, jackdaws;

during the summer many rollers were seen, they were called 'parrots' for the brilliance of their plumage. The winter brought English birds, robins and dunnocks, starlings and chaffinches, to remind men of home. Birds of prey abounded, from the griffon vulture to the kestrel. Levantine shearwaters, known to the Turks as 'the souls of the damned' – a name which gained significance as the months passed – flew in flocks round the cape.

For nearly 2 miles inland this ground formed a narrow, congested bivouac for troops newly landed or in reserve, and a rest camp for those which had suffered heavily. Corps Headquarters, ordnance, supplies, hospital tents, transport vehicles and long lines of picketed horses and mules covered large expanses. At first, men lay in twos and threes in small natural hollows, in coffin-shaped holes hastily dug to the depth of 2–3ft, or in shallow trenches which provided some little cover for men lying down. Later, oilsheets were used to cover these trenches as a protection from the sun by day and the cold by night. The difference in temperature was keenly felt by men who had passed the preceding seven months in Egypt. On the first night ashore, officers and men unable to sleep because of the cold, stamped backwards and forwards until tired, then huddled together until forced to take violent exercise again.

Firewood was very scarce as there were few trees or bushes, but it had to be obtained somehow for the trench fires over which the men brewed their tea and cooked their food. It was not uncommon to see casefuls of tins of bully-beef tipped out on the roadside, so that the wooden case could be split for fuel. Rifle butts which lay beside their dead owners met the same fate.

There was very little protection from shell fire on the peninsula, due to the nature of the ground, the position of the Allied armies between the guns of Achi Baba and the batteries of the Asiatic shore. There was an entire absence of material for revetting trenches and constructing shelters and dugouts, and wood and other small material could only be brought from Egypt or Mudros in small quantities, that which seldom made its way beyond the beaches; sandbags became as precious as drinking water; defences could not be worked on as there was no time and no men available. The cliffs provided shelter from the shell fire from the north, but none from 'Asiatic Annie', the heavy gun (or guns) which shelled 'W' and 'V' Beaches continuously, from various points along Erenkoi Bay east of Kum Kale, inflicting casualties and much damage. Into this too-crowded, unprotected area the Turk consistently pitched his high-explosive shells, and the ear-splitting crash and 'coal-box' effect greeted the Territorials on arrival and gave them their first impression of warfare.

Had the enemy at this period been in possession of more and better ammunition, the position would have been untenable. Owing to the shortage in the early days, solitary wagons and pack-animals could be moved about freely by day behind the lines, within view and range (with open sights) of the guns of Achi Baba; as the Turk rarely wasted a shell on the chance of destroying a man or horse, by extending to a distance of 400 yards, even a battalion transport could often go forward and backward unmolested by day. The incessant rifle fire at night made the area immediately behind the front lines more dangerous than by day.

Before the Division landed there had been little attempt at sanitation; there were not nearly enough men for fighting purposes, and no one had time to worry about such things until too late. The flies had then arrived.

On 11 May, the East Lancashire Division was ordered to take over the whole of the British front line, except for the portion held by the Indian Brigade.

But though there was a lull in the fighting after 8 May, the shelling of the trenches, rest camps, cliffs and beaches never ceased for long. Even bathing parties suffered from the shelling, and the Turkish rifles blazed away day and night without cessation, causing much loss to working parties and men in bivouacs far behind the front line, and even in the RAMC (Royal Army Medical Corps) tents below the cliffs. At night, the continuous 'plop' of bullets striking the water could be heard from the cliffs of Gully Beach. There were casualties from hidden machine guns; and the courage, enterprise and skill of the Turkish snipers were the cause of many fatal wounds. Owing to the shallowness of the average trench, it was difficult for even the most careful and experienced to keep under cover, and most injuries received at this time were head wounds.

The Field Ambulances had great difficulty on landing. Dressing stations had to be made in clefts in the cliffs, with tarpaulin sheets stretched from boulder to boulder for shelter. The shortage of appliances and equipment during the first few weeks was a serious handicap. The Field Ambulances had not been able to provide bearers to evacuate from First-Aid Posts, and the battalion stretcher-bearers carried the wounded a distance of 3 miles to the beach.

Practically everything required for the army in Gallipoli had to be brought from the base at Mudros, the harbour of the Island of Lemnos nearly 40 miles away. Water, rations, ammunition, equipment and material of all sorts were transferred from the ships to flat-bottomed lighters and landed, frequently in rough weather, and generally under fire from the Asiatic coast.

A Divisional Supply dump was established on the top of the cliffs above 'W' Beach. The rations were manhandled from the beaches to this dump, where they were issued to the Regimental Quartermasters and divided between companies. The loads consisted of full boxes and half-filled boxes of bully-beef tins, tins of biscuits, jars of rum, sacks of loaves, whole cheeses, tins of jam, bags of tea and sugar, sides of bacon and on mail days, bags of letters and parcels. The Turks had a good idea of the routes to be taken. Casualties among the ASC (Army Service Corps) and trench ration parties were frequent, especially at night. Mules and horses carried the loads; mules were steadier on rough tracks than horses and could carry an equal weight. The journeys of the ration-parties, from Battalion Headquarters to Company Headquarters, was no less exciting than those of the Battalion transport parties. Bearing heavy boxes or bags on heads or shoulder they crossed from trench to trench in the open, tripping over wire, stumbling into holes, dodging rifle fire and too often falling victims to the sniper. Another danger was from the Turkish snipers who hid in the scrub – mostly camouflaged, and generally in advance of their trench system. Fir Tree Wood was a happy hunting ground for the snipers, some of whom remained in their hiding places during our advance, in order to pick men off at short range during the night. The

Territorials received valuable tips from the Regulars on the best method of dealing with snipers.

During this period, the men not in the front lines were kept busy unloading supplies at the beaches and transporting them to the dumps, road-making, trench and well digging and performing many other fatigues. The digging, deepening and repairing and strengthening of trenches was a never-ending task, which had to be performed under fire from artillery, machine guns and snipers. The soil was mainly a stiff yellow loam, which stood well unrevetted until the rain came, when it was transformed into peculiarly bad mud.

On 25 May there was a memorable cloudburst on Achi Baba, and in a few moments the nullahs were in spate, the trenches flooded, and thousands of men soaked to the skin. It was unforeseen and could not be provided against, and the hardship inflicted on the troops was very great. The Lancashire Fusiliers Brigade Headquarters was under 4ft of water for several hours, and the Signal Office was washed away. For a time, the Krithia Nullah was impassable, and many dead Turks were carried down.

Towards the end of the month, the submarine menace developed into a very real danger. The battleship *Triumph* was torpedoed on 25 May as she lay at anchor off Anzac. She sank in ten minutes, with a loss of ten officers and sixty-eight men. Two days later the *Majestic*, Rear-Admiral Nicholson's flagship, lying off Cape Helles, was sunk by the same German submarine. This disaster was witnessed by many of the Territorials on the beaches and cliffs. As other British and French battleships were attacked by submarines about the same time, it became clear that naval co-operation must be dispensed with, as ships at anchor offered too easy a target for torpedoes. The consequences of this meant that all the large ships were sent back to the safety of Mudros, and the 'regatta-like' gathering at the mouth of the Dardanelles melted away.

This was promptly seized on by the Turk, who used the opportunity for propaganda purposes. An ingeniously worded pamphlet, printed in English, French and Hindustani, and dropped from aeroplanes, stated that all the battleships and transports had been destroyed, that the Germans had gained control of the seas, and that no further supplies need be expected. 'Don't take our word for it, but see for yourselves. Last week you saw a large fleet of all kinds of vessels off Cape Helles. Look for it to-day. You have fought bravely; give yourselves up now to an enemy who respects your valour and will treat you well.'

On 25 May the designation of the Division also changed, and as the 42nd (East Lancashire) Division, it took precedence in numerical order over all other Territorial divisions. The Lancashire Fusilier Brigade became the 125th Infantry Brigade; the East Lancashire Brigade the 126th; and the Manchester Brigade the 127th.

By the beginning of June, it was realised that very little had been gained. After five weeks of toil and struggle, valour and self-sacrifice, unsurpassed in history, no more had been achieved than the securing of a mere foothold on the peninsula. There was a significant manpower shortage – not enough drafts to fill the gaps in the ranks, and of reinforcements of sufficient strength, to allow even a breathing space to the overworked, worn-out remnants of the heroic 29th Division.

The Russian collapse in Courland, Galicia and Poland took away all hope of support from the north and east, and set free Turkish divisions in the Caucasus and Asia Minor for the defence of Gallipoli, and Bulgaria was about to join the side of her former enemy against her former friends.

Submarine activity became a very real menace to communications, and had deprived them of the support of the heavy naval guns, and there was a shortage of shells of high explosive. The daily allowance was limited to three rounds per gun, and at times to one round, compared to the French 75s which fired continuously.

The casualties of the M.E.F. numbered 38,000. The difficulties had been under-estimated, and the preparations inadequate, and as the present position at Helles was an impossible one it was necessary to move forward and, by repeated assaults, to push the enemy's lines farther and farther from the landing-places.

Preparation for the 3rd Battle of Krithia

Lieutenant-General Hunter-Weston, commanding the 8th Army Corps, held a conference at the Corps Headquarters on 27 May, to settle details of an advance along the whole front in order to bring the first-line trenches within assaulting distance of the Turkish trenches. By evening the movement was reported com-pleted, and the troops were digging themselves in. Casualties had been few, but by the morning it was realised that in the darkness mistakes had been made and the new line was, in places, 50–150 yards in rear of the positions indicated. A fresh advance to rectify this was successfully carried out by the 127th Brigade, but this time the casualty list was much heavier.

On 3 June, orders for the attack were issued. The first objective of the 8th Army Corps (of which the 42nd Division formed the centre, and the Indian Brigade on their left, and the R. N. on their right) was the main line of Turkish trenches, about 200 yards from the first line. The second objective was the enemy's third line. The French objective was the line of the Kereves Dere Nullah.

At 8 a.m. on 4 June, the heavy guns and howitzers would open the bombard-ment of certain strong positions. At 11.50 a.m., an intense bombardment of the enemy trenches would begin. At 11.20, all guns except those on the approach lines would cease fire, and the infantry would cheer, raise their bayonets above the parapet, as though about to assault with the object of inducing the Turk to occupy his front trenches, which would be heavily bombarded by all guns and howitzers, the machine guns firing in bursts as targets presented themselves. At noon, the first line of infantry would advance, without firing, to the assault of the first objective, the batteries lifting to range on the trenches further back. At 12.15 the second line would advance, pass through the first line, and attack the second objective.

Divisional conferences were held at the Headquarters of the 125th Brigade, and General Douglas issued and explained his orders and disposed the troops under his command as follows: First wave – two battalions of the 127th Brigade consisting of a half a battalion each of the 7th, 5th, 8th and 6th Manchesters, from right to left in the order named. The objective for this line was the front line of the Turkish trenches. A half-battalion of the 5th Lancashire Fusiliers was to follow in support on the left flank. The second wave consisted of the 127th Brigade.

Their orders were to rush through the front line of Turkish trenches and gain the second objective, which was less than a mile from Krithia. A half-battalion of the 6th L. F., as a working party, and the 1st Field Company, R. E. were to follow the other half-battalion and the 2nd Field Company were to follow the second wave, to consolidate the lines gained. All the above troops were under the command of Brigadier-General Noel Lee. The remaining half-battalion of the 5th L. F. was to form the garrison of the line of trenches held as the firing-line before the attack.

The 9th Manchesters were to occupy the second line, which was strengthened by redoubts. The 7th and 8th Lancashire Fusiliers were to be in Divisional Reserve. The 9th Manchesters was the only battalion of the 126th Brigade acting with the Division, the 4th and 5th East Lancashires and the 10th Manchesters being still split up among the skeleton battalions of the 29th Division.

The 3rd Battle of Krithia

The bombardment that opened at 8 a.m. on 4 June was the heaviest and most prolonged that the peninsulas had witnessed. At 11 a.m. every available gun both on land and sea was firing, including six batteries of four guns each of the famous 75s generously lent by the French Commander. These were firing high-explosive shells. The whole Turkish line was enveloped in smoke, and it seemed impossible that any positions could withstand its fury.

The village of Krithia and the whole of the hillside appeared to be a mass of flame and dust. The plan was to cease fire on the front trenches at 11.20 a.m., which had the effect intended. The enemy prepared to meet the expected assault. A hail of bullets swept over the trenches of the 127th Brigade, and a few moments later the renewal of the bombardment caught the Turks as they were manning the trenches or hastening through the communication trenches to reinforce their thinly held front line.

The last half hour of waiting was a severe test of nerves and it was a relief when noon arrived. The operations at the end of May, the digging in no man's land to push the line closer to the enemy, while the Turk knew perfectly well what was intended and had been able, by the light of a waxing moon, to thin out the working parties, had been highly dangerous and trying to the nerves. The losses had been 'deplorable', but the will to overcome the difficulties had given officers, NCOs and men confidence in one another. Each platoon, each company, knew that it would not let the others down when the big event should come off.

At 12.00 promptly, the leading wave of the 127th Brigade went over the top for the first time, and advanced steadily and in good order. They were met by devastating rifle and machine-gun fire, but those who escaped the bullets pressed on in a steady line and by bitter hand-to-hand fighting made good their first objective. In places, the wire was untouched by the bombardment, and men died cutting it so that their comrades might pass through.

The second wave followed at the appointed time. Within five minutes, the Turkish front-line trenches had been captured, and the second in half an hour, and during the afternoon the fourth line of the Turkish trenches had been penetrated.

Sappers accompanying the successive waves found disconnected buried mines, and assisted in the construction of new trenches and the reversal of captured ones. On the left, the 29th Division had seized their first objective, but their further advance was checked, as the barbed wire on their left remained undamaged, and the Indian Brigade was held up by this obstacle.

The professional soldiers of this division paid generous tribute to the amateurs of the 4th and 5th East Lancashires and 10th Manchesters, who fought with such spirit and determination within their ranks.

On the right, however, initial success was soon followed by a reverse which had disastrous consequences. The R. N. Division had gone forward with a considerable measure of success. The French had rushed a formidable redoubt, called 'the Haricot' after its shape, but unfortunately their colonial troops gave way before a furious bombardment and counter-attack, and the Haricot was once more in Turkish possession. With their right flank exposed to the concentrated fire of innumerable machine guns, the Naval Division, cruelly reduced in numbers – one brigade losing sixty officers – were compelled to fall back to their original line, leaving the right flank of the 42nd Division in the air, the gap being 300 yards from front to rear.

The Turks were quick to take advantage of the situation. Also, they were amply supplied with bombs, whereas at this date our men had none – a serious handicap in close fighting. Turkish bombing parties began to eat their way into this flank, which was also enfiladed by rifle and machine-gun fire, and in spite of the most determined opposition of the Manchesters, of the Lancashire Fusiliers who were in support, and a party of Engineers, the position became critical.

In the meantime, the 7th Lancashire Fusiliers had been moved up to the old fire trenches when these were vacated by the second wave, and at 2.45 p.m. two companies of the 8th L. F. were sent to fill the gap between the right of the 127th Brigade and the R. N. Division. At 3.35 p.m. it was seen that the enemy was massing troops in a nullah on this flank, seriously threatening the foremost line. The French Commander had, however, promised to make a fresh attack on the Haricot at 4 p.m., and it was hoped that this, by enabling the R. N. Division to advance, would relieve the pressure.

However, they were unable to make the attack, and the position of the 7th Manchesters became untenable. The Divisional Commander, after consulting the Corps Commander, at 6.30 p.m. ordered the withdrawal of the foremost line to the main Turkish trench. The retirement was made with the greatest reluctance; the few remaining officers had great difficulty in making the men realise that the order to withdraw must be obeyed. The idea of giving up the ground they had won was almost unbearable, for the four Manchester battalions had resolved to hold on to their gains, whatever the cost might be. 'C' Company of the 6th Manchesters had penetrated to a considerable distance beyond the bifurcation of the nullahs, but, being enfiladed from the higher ground on the right, found it impossible to retire. Its commander, Captain H. B. Pilkington, was mortally wounded in the head, but, propped up in the trench, he continued to direct and encourage his men. The company was practically wiped out.

The cost had been very great. Of the 770 men of the 6th Manchesters, only 160 answered roll call that night (Corporal Michael O'Connor was one of this number). A company of the 8th Manchesters, which at noon leapt out of the trenches 200 strong, could only muster 18, with other units reporting similar figures. Early in the afternoon Brigadier-General Noel Lee had received a shell wound in the throat, from which he died on 21 June in hospital in Malta. When he fell, Lieutenant-Colonel Heys, 8th Manchesters, assumed command, until an hour later, when he was compelled to return to his battalion, as hardly any officers were left; he was killed soon after he rejoined. The last remaining officer of this Battalion, Captain Oldfield, was killed shortly after he had organised the withdrawal of the battalion. Lieutenant-Colonel Lord Rochdale, 6th Lancashire Fusiliers, assumed temporary command of the 127th Brigade, until 21 June. The 7th Manchesters had also lost their Commanding Officer Major Staveacre, who had succeeded to the command of the battalion on 28 May, when Lieutenant-Colonel Gresham was invalided to Malta.

Much difficulty was experienced in getting the wounded down the crowded and battered trenches and communication ways. It was a rough journey for wounded men from either of these posts to the General Clearing Station on 'W' Beach; only hand carriage was available for those who could not walk, and though they were not fired upon deliberately, there were many casualties among the bearers. The wounded could not be attended to quickly enough to prevent a line of stretcher cases, waiting to be dressed, forming outside the stations.

The Territorials had proved themselves in the Division's first pitched battle, with credit and distinction. Though the assaulting waves had been exposed to converging fire from higher ground on either flank, their attack had been brilliantly successful. At the end of the day, the front had only been advanced about 400 yards, yet the Manchesters had gained 1,000 yards and could have advanced still farther. There was little doubt that the Turkish centre had been pierced, and if the troops on the right had not been compelled to fall back, or there had been reserves to bring forward, they would have seized the ground behind the village of Krithia, the key to the Achi Baba position.

The Division had captured 217 prisoners, including 11 officers.

The next day, 5 June, was mainly given over to the consolidation of the front to meet the expected counter-attack. On the evening of 5 June the first line was still held by the 127th Brigade, but during the night it was relieved by the 125th Brigade.

There were two weak points:

1. A pronounced salient where the right of the 42nd Division linked with the left of the R. N. Division. A strong work was in the process of formation to strengthen this.
2. The ground between the Vineyard and the right branch of the Krithia Nullah had many facilities for bringing enfilade and reverse fire to bear on our line. This became the scene of the hardest fighting.

At 3.45 a.m. on 6 June, the enemy began to shell our line: at 4.25 a.m., strong bodies of Turks were working their way down the Krithia nullahs. At the same time, an attack was delivered on the trenches held by the 8th Manchesters, but this unit had just been reinforced by three platoons of the 7th Lancashire Fusiliers and the attack was easily repulsed.

Some Turks succeeded in getting part of the trench held by the 5th Manchesters, but were driven out again by the combined action of the 5th Manchesters and the 5th Lancashire Fusiliers. At 6.20 a.m., the 88th Brigade, on the left, were obliged to fall back slightly, and this exposed the left flank of the 5th L. F., they were forced to fall back below the bifurcation of the nullahs. Here they were reinforced by a weak company of the 7th Lancashire Fusiliers. Bombing attacks and bayonet charges continued throughout the morning, and reserves were brought into the front lines until the Divisional Reserve constituted only sixty men of the 7th Lancashire Fusiliers.

Casualties were heavy, including two officers of the 8th L. F. The three battalions of the 126th Brigade should have rejoined the Division on the 5th, but they too had been fiercely attacked, and although suffering severely, were upholding the credit of the Lancashire Territorials. As the 29th Division could not spare any of these battalions, the Chatham Battalion of the R. N. Division was attached to the 42nd Division, and held in reserve.

By 1 p.m. the situation had improved, and the number of Turks in and around the nullahs had greatly diminished. The 5th and 7th Lancashire Fusiliers were now ordered to take the offensive; the small redoubt near to the bifurcation of nullahs, which had been captured by the enemy, was attacked and retaken. By the evening of 6 June the enemy's attack, which had been made in great strength and with much bravery, had been repulsed, with the only gain a small indentation by the Krithia Nullah.

For three days, the fight had raged without intermission. Worn out, hungry, thirsty, sleepless men had fought and dug and fought again until the line had been firmly established and held by the physically exhausted remnants.

On 7 June, counter-operations were undertaken after dark with the object of straightening the line from the Vineyard towards the nullah.

The casualties in the 42nd Division during the four weeks, killed, wounded and missing, amounted to 4,184.

In his Official Despatch, General Sir Ian Hamilton made special mention of the part taken by the 42nd Division, in summarising the sequence of events and final outcome he stated that: 'The Manchester Brigade of the 42nd Division advanced magnificently.' In a private letter to the Divisional Commander he expounded that he 'never saw any finer piece of work than that performed by the Manchesters that day'.

Later on the evening of 4 June, the following message was received from the Divisional Commander Lieutenant-General A. G. Hunter-Weston, C.B. D.S.O., to be conveyed to all ranks:

Please express to the 42nd Division, and particularly to 127th Brigade, my appreciation of the magnificent work done by them today. The 127th Brigade attacked with gallantry, and held on to the objective ordered with tenacity. It was a very fine performance. Please convey this to all the troops of the Division when possible, and tell them that I deeply appreciate their gallant conduct and devotion to their duty. The renown they have gained for the Division will not only reach the ears of all in Lancashire, but throughout the British Empire. I feel sure that the same tenacity will be maintained to-night and throughout the Campaign.

General Hamilton, on board HMS *Wolverine*, wrote in his diary:

Chapters could be written about this furious battle fought in a whirlwind of dust and smoke; someday I hope somebody may write them. After the first short spell of shelling our men fixed bayonets and lifted them high above the parapet. The Turks thinking we were going to make an assault, rushed troops into their trenches, until then lightly held. No sooner were our targets fully manned than we shelled them in earnest and went on at it until – on the stroke of mid-day – out dashed our fellows into the open. For the best part of an hour it seemed that we had won a decisive victory.

On the left all the front line Turkish trenches were taken. On the right the French rushed the 'Haricot' – so long a thorn in their flesh; next to them the Anson (Royal Naval Division) lads stormed another big Turkish redoubt in a slap-dash style reminding me of the best work of the old Regular Army; but the boldest and most brilliant exploit of the lot was the charge made by the Manchester Brigade.

In the centre who wrested two lines of trenches from the Turks; and then, carrying right on; on to the lower slopes of Achi Baba, had nothing between them and its summit but the clear, untrenchable hillside. They lay there – the line of our brave lads, plainly visible through a pair of good glasses – there they actually lay! We wanted so it seemed, but a reserve to advance in their support and carry them 'right up to the top. We said – and yet could hardly believe our own words – 'We are through'.

Alas, too previous that remark. Everything began to go wrong. First the French were shelled and bombed out of the 'Haricot'; next the right of the Naval Division became uncovered and they had to give way, losing many times more men in the yielding than in the capture of their ground.

Then came the turn of the Manchesters, left in the lurch, with their right flank hanging in the air. By all the laws of war they ought to have tumbled back anyhow, but by the law of the Manchesters they hung on and declared they could do so for ever. How to help? Men! Men, not so much now to sustain the Manchesters as to force back the Turks who were enfilading them from the 'Haricot', and from that redoubt held for awhile by the R. N. D. on their right.

Not wanting to fall back but realising the state of affairs, Hamilton implored Gouraud (French) to make a push, he promised the Naval Division would retake their redoubt, if he could retake the 'Haricot'. However, this did not materialise and so Hamilton: 'ran myself to Hunter-Weston's Headquarters, so as not to let another moment be lost in pulling out the Manchester Brigade'. Hamilton wrote in his diary:

> The upshot of the whole affair is that is that the enemy still hold a strong line of trenches between us and Achi Baba. Our four hundred prisoners, almost all made by the Manchester Brigade, amongst whom a good number of officers … Three or four hundred yards of ground plus four hundred prisoners are distances and numbers which may mean little in Russia or France, but here, where we only have a mile or two to go, land has value all its own. But, to have to yield up the best half – the vital half – our gains – to have our losses trebled on the top of a cheaply won victory – these are the reverse side of our medal for the 4th June.

The War Diary for the 6th Battalion Manchester Regiment records that on 7 July a letter was received by the Commanding Officer from Major General W. Douglas D.S.O. commanding (1/1 East Lancs) 42nd Division. It reads as follows:

> My Dear Pilkington,
> In regard to our conversation today I am still hoping that you may be able to collect evidence of some of the splendid acts of gallantry by Officers and men of your Battalion during the assault of June 4th.
>   It is most unfortunate, that owing to the many casualties you sustained, many deeds worthy of the Victoria Cross have not been reported. I hope that your men know this. The dash, steadiness, reckless bravery and endurance shown by the 6th Manchesters, and indeed, by the whole Brigade, was equal to the best traditions of the British Army …

By the end of June, Hamilton recorded in his diary that the East Lancs. Division was in a bad way. He stated that one more month of neglect, and it would be ruined. He cabled the War Office informing them that a state of 'wastage' had been reached, especially in the 127th Manchester Brigade, and that even with drafts, if they go on fighting in their present condition and suffer further losses, the remnants will 'not offer sufficiently wide foundation for reconstituting cadres'. He gave the following shortage figures of officers and rank and file in each Brigade including the reinforcements reported as arriving:

> 125th Brigade: 50 officers, 1,852 rank and file.
> 126th Brigade: 31 officers, 1,714 rank and file.
> 127th Brigade: 50 officers, 2,291 rank and file.

In his personal diary, he refers to the East Lancs. as a 'perishing formation', he notes that when a battalion which entered upon a campaign 1,000 strong – all keen and hopeful – gets down to 500, comrades begin to look around at one another and wonder if any will be left. He furthers that when it falls to 300, or less, the unit, in his experience, is 'better drawn out of the line'. He feels their predicament, stating that the bravest men lose heart when, on parade, 'they see with their own eyes that their Company – the finest Company in the Army – has become a platoon – and the famous battalion a Company'.

By 9 July, Hamilton had received a cable stating that there were no men left in England to fill either the 42nd Division or the 52nd. He notes in his diary that the Naval Division must fade away, and laments, 'Poor old Territorials!' He charges, 'Why go on making these assurances to the British Public that we have as many men coming in voluntarily as we can use?'

August saw the ravages of sickness reduce the fighting strength of the Division more than the bullets of the enemy. Dysentery and jaundice were rampant, and an epidemic of septic sores ran through the Division. There had been no break in the hot dry weather. Many of the wells had become defiled, others had run dry and this contributed to the amount of sickness. Insanitary conditions were inseparable from the type of warfare waged in so confined a space, the continuous strain extracted from all, the lack of sleep, the tropical heat, the monotonous and unsuitable food, the lice and above all the plague of flies, with which no sanitary measures and precautions could cope. The country was one huge graveyard in which hundreds of corpses of friends and foe lay unburied, and the air was heavy with the stench.

In October, there was an amalgamation of battalions and a move down to Gully Beach. Although not sad to be leaving Krithia, Achi Baba Nullahs and the Vineyard, the names conjured up other memories of heroic attempt and gallant performance, of courage, self-sacrifice and devotion to duty, cheerfulness in the face of adversity, of enduring friendships, of doggedness and determination, of great pride in the comrades who had fallen, whose graves, marked by biscuit-box crosses, lay thick in the Krithia Nullah. Mention of the names brought back the scenes, the smell of wood fires – and manure incinerators – the Hindus at rest making chupatties, the gullies thronged with men and animals; the linesmen of the Signal Company coolly and efficiently laying lines and repairing wires under shell and machine-gun fire, the crack of rifles; the despatch riders driving furiously over ground that no motorcycle was ever meant to negotiate, animals and men.

A 'rest' was more of a reality in the new area, and it was comparatively safe, but in Gallipoli the word rest had a very different significance from that attached to it at home. It had now become too closely associated with hard work to be really popular. It meant heavy fatigues day and night, much digging, the unloading of lighters and carrying the heavy loads.

But a Beach Fatigue had its compensation, for it was possible at times to bathe if one was not too fastidious to object to coal dust and refuse from lighters, nor to the close companionship of the dead horses and mules that floated around. These were constantly being towed out to sea, but the homing instinct, or the current, brought them back again.

'W' Beach even boasted a canteen (run by enterprising Greeks), and men who had time to spare and were possessed of patience might, after waiting for hours in a queue, come back with a bit of chocolate and a tin of fruit – rare and precious luxuries. One day, would-be purchasers found the military police in possession. The Greeks had been arrested as spies, and were not seen again. In due course, the Division ran its own popular canteen on Gully Beach.

The move to a rest-bivouac at Gully Beach was a 'great improvement upon previous resorts', its attractions read like a holiday advertisement. A sea front, excellent bathing in the Mediterranean, superior accommodation on ledges cut into the cliff face. Inside the ravine, the bends gave complete protection from shell-fire; caves had been dug in the cliff sides one above the other up to 40ft above the gully.

By night, the illuminations in these regular tiers of dugouts, with the black outline of the cliff tips beyond the highest tier of lights standing out distinct against the starlit sky, gave the ravine an effect of glamour and romance that contrasted strangely with the grim reality of the day. 'Doesn't it remind you of Belle Vue?' (Manchester's great tourist attraction) was a comment frequently made by the men.

Battle of Krithia Vineyard, 6–13 August

The primary purpose of the Gallipoli campaign was to obtain possession of the Narrows, in order to secure demand on the Dardanelles and cut off communication with the Asiatic shore. It had been hoped to achieve this by pushing forward from the south, but the original force had been far too small for the purpose.

During May, June and July the Turkish garrison had been greatly increased, and also the supply of guns and shells, and the defences on Achi Baba strengthened, but the British reinforcements and drafts to fill the gaps had been relatively small. There was little prospect of success by a frontal assault from Helles. The Commander-in-Chief decided upon an attempt to reach the Narrows at Maidos, 5 miles across the peninsula from Anzac, the formidable Sari Bair range intervening.

Plan of Attack

A new landing was to be made on 6–7 August at Suvla Bay, a few miles north of Anzac Cove, and it was hoped that the force landing here would seize the northern slopes of the Sari Bair range, while the troops from Anzac would storm the central and southern heights. On 6 August, an attack was to be made from the right of Anzac in order to divert attention from both the landing and the true objective; and a vigorous offensive was ordered at Helles, with the object of containing as large a Turkish force as possible within the southern area and of drawing their reserves from the north.

The line of trenches from the Achi Baba Nullah to the Krithia Nullah (both inclusive) was held by the 125th Brigade on the right and 127th on the left, the 126th being in reserve. The French were on the right of the 125th Brigade and the 29th Division left of the 127th Brigade. The 5th Manchesters, who were acting in conjunction with the 88th Brigade (29th Division) having the objective of the Turkish trench on the right of the Brigade.

The bombardment began at 2.30 p.m. on 6 August, and soon high-explosive shells could be seen bursting in the trench which the 5th had been ordered to take. At 3.50 p.m. they attacked, but on reaching the objective, found they had been enticed into a dummy trench, without cover and exposed to enfilade fire. To prevent the right flank of the 29th Division 'in the air', the first line of the 7th Manchesters was ordered to get into 'touch'. The two lines regained the firing-line having lost 40 out of 200 men.

A few hours later, the Battle of the Vineyard began, the bombardment by the British and French batteries opening at 8.10 a.m., and increasing in intensity at 9.00 when the naval guns joined in. The fire on the trenches south-east of Krithia Nullah was both heavy and accurate but the trenches within the triangle formed by the fork of the nullahs suffered little damage. Half a battalion of the 126th Brigade was attached to the 125th on the right, and another half-battalion to the 127th Brigade on the left. One battalion of the 126th Brigade was to hold the original line. Two batteries of machine guns assisted by bringing a crossfire to bear on the enemy's trenches.

At 9.40 a.m., the troops went forward wearing tin back-plates that could be seen by the artillery spotters. On the right, the Lancashire Fusiliers gained their first objective, but the 5th and the 8th found 'their portion' was merely a shallow trench raked with enfilade fire. Parties of the 6th and 7th reached their objective, but enfilade fire and a superiority of numbers compelled them to fall back. One of the few officers to reach this objective was Major Law of the 7th Lancashire Fusiliers. Soon after 11 a.m., portions of the first objective were taken by a strong Turkish counter-attack, but the Vineyard remained in our hands.

The 5th and the 7th L. F. made a gallant effort to recover what had been lost and were partially successful. At 1.30 p.m. another enemy counter-attack in close formation was caught by (our) guns and brought to a standstill. The Turks suffered severely in counter-attacks upon the Vineyard, and for some hours they gave up their attempt in this quarter, resuming it at night with no more success. The 5th and 8th L. F. reoccupied a portion of their first objective in the evening. Parties of the 4th Lancashires and 10th Manchesters gave great assistance in both attack and defence.

On the left, the Manchesters showed similar dash and determination, but owing to the great difficulties of the ground between and about the nullahs and to the intricacy of the Turkish trench system, which, with nests of machine guns, had escaped our shells, they were unable to hold any of the trenches taken in the initial assault. Their losses were grievous, the attacking lines being mown down by the enemy's machine guns.

The casualties for the two days were: killed: officers 20, other ranks 203; wounded: officers 36, other ranks 770; missing: officers 24, other ranks 511

The result was that a tactical point of some importance had been won and held by the tenacity of the 125th Brigade, and that a large Turkish force had been pinned down when urgently needed in the north. The Turks had been massing troops in front of the Division as they had intended to attack our lines of force, on 6 or 7 August. Sir Ian Hamilton telegraphed to the Corps Commander: 'Your operations have been invaluable, and have given the Northern Corps the greatest possible help by drawing the main Turkish efforts on yourselves. I was sure you were ready for them tonight.'

But though the sacrifice had not been altogether in vain, the advance from Suvla Bay and Anzac had failed.

The conquest of the Dardanelles was seemingly more remote that ever. Yet, for one half-hour, it had seemed so near! On Chunuk Bair, at dawn on 9 August, when companies of the 6th Gurkhas and 6th South Lancashires had stormed the cliffs and driven the Turks headlong before them, victory was in sight; the goal – Maidos and the Narrows – and the Turkish Army in the south would be cut off. Then suddenly a salvo of heavy shells crashed with infernal accuracy into the midst of them, mangling and destroying the exulting victors.

Where the salvo came from will probably never be known with certainty, but there can be little doubt that the shells were British.

The remnants of the 400-strong force could only make for shelter. There was no shelter in front, and the chance had gone, never to return.

The War Diary of the 1/7 Lancashire Fusiliers for 6–13 August gives the following account:

> 4–6th. A quiet time until the 6th, when our left made an attack on the enemy's right. We are to attack tomorrow the enemy's centre.
>
> 7th. The Brigade attacked the enemy's centre. Distribution left to right 6th, 7th, 8th, & 5th Battalions. The first objective was carried, but unfortunately the 5th & 8th Battalions had to retire. Heavy attacks made on the line held by the 6th & 7th throughout the day and night, but we still held on.
>
> 8th. Still holding on in spite of Turk's vigorous attempts to retake.
>
> 9th. Were relieved by the East Lancashire Brigade, commencing about 12 noon. Our men were thoroughly worn out, the strain having been enormous. Out of 410 N.C.O's and men of our Battalion going into action only 139 returned.
>
> 13th. The trenches gained by us were lost on the night of the 12th–13th.

The Battalion Diary for the 6th Manchester Regiment notes the following lesson to be learned from the battle: 'it is a mistake to overpile the trenches with men. Men were ordered up from the Support & even Redoubt line, & the firing line became so thick that it was impossible for officers and NCOs to maintain proper control.'

The diary also records some 100 men were sick, affected by a particular kind of sand colic.

On 15–17 November a violent storm, accompanied by a deluge of rain, drove the sea higher and higher up the shore, swamping bivouacs on the beach. In the Gully conditions were even worse. Bales of hay, sacks of bread and drowned mules were washed down the ravine into the sea. On the night of 26 November, a still fiercer storm raged in the peninsula. At Anzac and Suvla the trenches were quickly waist deep, and the current swept down taking kit, equipment and rations, even men being washed away. In palaces the trenches filled, and the troops must drown or stand on the top, a sure target for the

Turk had he not been in the same predicament. The gale became a hurricane; the crash of thunder, the blinding flashes of lightning, heightened the sense of catastrophe, and the bitter cold made it more unbearable.

Piers and landing stages were destroyed and beaches strewn with wreckage. During 27 November the rain came down steadily; then it veered to the north and brought snow and cruel blizzards. A hard frost followed, and at Anzac and Suvla men were frozen to death; others lost their limbs – some their reason – and cases of frostbite were numerous. In the south, the conditions were less disastrous than further north, but the suffering of the troops was intense. Altogether about 10,000 sick had to be removed from the peninsula as an outcome of the four days' tragedy. When the floods subsided, Gully Ravine was a bed of deep mud.

Lord Kitchener visited the peninsula in the middle of November, and on his return to England had reported in favour of evacuation. On 8 December, General Munro issued orders to evacuate Anzac and Suvla, and on 16 December the withdrawal of 80,000 men, nearly 5,000 animals and 200 guns began. The evacuation was carried out without loss and was one of the finest and most wonderful achievements of the war.

Nearly 14,000 Lancashire territorials had disembarked on the inhospitable shores. The Division that left Gallipoli barely numbered 5,000, though every battalion and unit had received drafts from the second and third lines in England, or from Egypt, and thousands had rejoined from hospital. Those few, thought of what might have been; and of the great-hearted comrades and brothers-in-arms whom they left behind.

Many now lay in the cemetery above Lancashire Landing, a glorious resting place from which, when alive, they had looked out upon the intense blue of the Aegean Sea. Others had been buried where they fell. Soon the lovely blossoms of the rock rose and the gorgeous poppy would be covering their graves.

The 42nd (East Lancashire) Division's Gallipoli Campaign is expressed by Rupert Brooke's allegorical poem 'The Soldier':

If I should die, think only this of me:
That there's some corner of a foreign field
That is forever England. There shall be
In that rich earth a richer dust concealed

Casualties of the 42nd Division at Gallipoli: 395 officers, 8,152 other ranks, killed, wounded, and missing.

Cheshire Regiment: 13th (Western) Division, 40th Brigade

The 8th (Service) Battalion landed at Anzac and was divided among Regiments of the Australian Light Horse Brigade.

Giving a description of conditions faced on arrival, the Regimental History describes the situation as follows:

When they disembarked, the troops did not know whether they were in Europe or Asia. The only order issued was 'Attack the Turks'. Our Battalions on disembarking were slung into the scrub with no more than this order, without reconnaissance, without transport, without ammunition supply, without artillery and without communications. As a military situation, it beggars description.

8th (Service) Battalion War Diary, August 1915

The Battalion embarked and landed at Anzac on Gallipoli Peninsula on 4 August.

Russells Top

On 7 August at 3.a.m., the Battalion moved up to trenches at Russells Top. At 4 a.m., Australian Light Horse Brigade attacked NEK opposite Russells Top. The Battalion now being in support trenches and under orders to support the above attack and to carry it further. The first line of Turkish trenches was not captured, and the attack was stopped. Half the Battalion of the 8th Cheshire Regiment was sent to support Royal Welch Fusiliers who were attacking out of Monash Gully, but this attack could not be pushed home, the other half Battalion Cheshire Regiment manned the fire trenches on Russells Top during the day, and at night was relieved by Australian Light Horse Brigade and this half a Battalion went into support. Half a Battalion was now in support behind Walkers Ridge and the other half Battalion in support in Quinns Post. Not all the machine guns were in action.

On 9 August, the Battalion was ordered to move out to relieve troops who had been attacking heights towards Chunuk Bair. The Battalion assembled and marched to No. 2 Post, along the beach, when orders were received to return. Half the Battalion to the ledge behind Russells Top and half the Battalion to Monash Gully in support of Quinns & Courtneys position. On 14 August, the Battalion took over the firing line from Gloucester Regiment and Wellington Battalion, Australian and New Zealand Brigade on the east ridge of Chailakdere.

On 15–24 August, the Battalion dug trenches and established defences on this ridge, the enemy snipers caused some casualties, and the snipers of the Battalion did good work during this period.

The following orders show the immense detail and planning that went into the evacuation of the Gallipoli Peninsula by the 8th Cheshire Regiment, who had the honour of going to Helles with the 13th Division.

Orders to Evacuate Suvla and Anzac
SECRET

The evacuation consisted of two stages: an Intermediate stage for the embarkation of vehicles, stores and a proportion of personnel and guns, and a Final stage of embarkation of remaining fighting and medical personnel and guns.

In addition to equipment and stores which could not be carried, documents and records were to be evacuated at once, and the systemic arrangement made for the burning of letters and papers which it was not proposed to take away. This was very important and it was impressed upon every officer, NCO and man that nothing which can be of any use to the enemy and which could be sent in or destroyed was to be left behind.

As the Turks were in great need of sandbags, parties were detailed to slashing the sandbags in the parapets, et cetera with clasp knives so as to render them useless, whilst still remaining serviceable up to the time of evacuation.

Extreme vigilance by all was essential during the intermediate and final stages owing to increased possibility of attack by the enemy. Every effort was to be made to keep things normal to prevent the enemy from discovering that the evacuation was proceeding. For instance, tents were to be kept standing and Red Cross flags flying, whilst the personnel became reduced; sniping and counter-sniping were to be kept up at the usual rate, patrolling was to be active, and its empty camps and bivouacs' fires kept burning as usual and men occasionally to be seen to perambulate.

The importance of reconnaissance prior to any movement was also to be impressed on all concerned. Embarkation was to be as follows:

Troops in right and centre subsections:
Either at 'C' Beach, Lala Baba, or South Pier, Lala Baba.
Troops in left subsection:
At West Beach, Suvla.
Troops at Lala Baba:
Either at 'C' Beach, Lala Baba, or South Pier, Lala Baba.

The line of withdrawal from the right and centre subsections was to be by the direct road from Chocolate Hill to Lala Baba along the south side of the Salt Lake.

The line of withdrawal from the left subsection was to be over a footbridge, which was being thrown about 100 yards south of the road bridge over the Ashak Dere to a spot at the north-east corner of Supply Depot, West Beach, marked 'Forming up place', and then to West Beach.

Subsection and other commanders were responsible that the above routes up to the places of embarkation were carefully reconnoitred beforehand, and especially at night, by all officers concerned, and by a proportion of NCOs. This was stressed as a matter of the highest importance, and care was to be taken if done by day, so as not to attract the enemy's attention.

Mines were to be placed in position but were not to be made active until further orders were received.

It was important that each man was in possession of his iron ration during and after the evacuation, and the usual inspection of these articles was to be carried out with special care during this period. Under exceptional circumstances of the evacuation, stretcher-bearers and such men belonging to machine gun detachments would have to carry the guns in withdrawing may be exempted from carrying rifles and ammunition, which could be returned to store. During this intermediate stage arrangements for evacuation of the sick and wounded would be as normal.

It was emphasised by the GOC that the operation about to be embarked upon could be easily carried to a successful conclusion, provided there was rigid discipline and implicit obedience with the intelligent application of orders on the part of all concerned. The closest supervision by officers and NCOs throughout the whole period was necessary. During the actual withdrawal in particular, the troops were to be moved close up and in as compact formations, either in large or small bodies, as the tactical situation permitted. Officers and NCOs were distributed amongst each party, particularly in the rear, to ensure perfect discipline throughout.

The troops to be embarked during the intermediate stage at Lala Baba on the night of 14/15 December were the units of the 13th Cyclist Co., 8th Welsh Regiment (Pioneers), Advanced party HQ 13th Div. Following on from this on 17/18 December would be one battalion of the 39th Infantry Brigade, half the 72nd Field Company Royal Engineers, half the Bearer Division, 40th Field Ambulance at West Beach, 133rd Fortress Company Royal Engineers at Lala Baba.

The final stage was arranged to commence on 18 December. The troops at the disposal of commanders of subsection in the trenches were:

Right subsection:
1 Section 71st Field Co. R.E.
38th Infantry Brigade (less 1 battalion a Lala Baba)
Bearer Division, 39th Field Ambulance
Centre subsections:
1 Section 88th Field Company Royal Engineers
40th Infantry Brigade
Bearer Division, 41st Field Ambulance
Left subsection:
½ -72nd Field Company Royal Engineers
3 Battalions, 39th Infantry Brigade,
½ - Bearer Division, 40th Field Ambulance

On the night of 17/18 December, the strength of the 39th Infantry Brigade in the trenches was to be reduced to 600 of all ranks. If the battalion strength was not sufficiently strong on that night, the figures from one or more of the battalions remaining could attach to and embark with that battalion. Battalions selected to remain to the end were to report to Divisional Headquarters on receipt of orders.

On the night of 18/19 December, the following troops were to embark at Lala Baba:

½ -88th Field Company Royal Engineers, Proportion of 30th Infantry Brigade, Proportion of 40th Infantry Brigade.

The trench strength on the morning of 19 December was to be: 2 Battalions of 38th Infantry Brigade (strength 1,000); 3 Battalions of 40th Infantry Brigade (strength 1,500).

Machine guns, complete with detachments and 7,000 rounds per gun were to be moved at night:

38th Infantry Brigade 6 guns to Lala Baba; 40th Infantry Brigade 6 guns to Salt Lake lines.

The guns of the 40th Infantry brigade with their ammunition was to be left at the well just in rear of the centre of the new Salt Lake lines under charge of a guard.

The 39th Infantry Brigade was to evacuate 7,000 rounds per gun for half its machine guns at night, but to retain half its full number of guns for the present.

The 13th Divisional Operation order No. 7 on 16 December stated that the final withdrawal from Anzac and Suvla would take place simultaneously on 18 and 19 December.

The 40th Infantry Brigade to send one battalion to Lala Baba at 17.45 on 18 December instant and to be quartered there. The troops to embark during the final stage as follows:

Night of 18/19 December:
2 Sections 88th Field Company Royal Engineers
2 battalions 38th Infantry Brigade
1 battalion 40th Infantry Brigade
½ Bearer Division 39th Field Ambulance
½ Bearer Division 41st Field Ambulance
South Pier, Lala Baba.
1 battalion 39th Infantry Brigade West Beach.

Night of 19/20 December:
Div. HQ and Signal Company
71st Field Co. Royal Engineers
88th Field Co. Royal Engineers (loss 2 Sections)
38th Infantry Brigade (loss 2 battalions)
40th Infantry Brigade (less 1 battalion)
½ Bearer Division 39th Field Ambulance
½ Bearer Division 41st Field Ambulance
Tent subdivision, 41st Field Ambulance
Embark South Pier, LALA BABA
72nd Field Company Royal Engineers (loss 2 sections)
39th Infantry Brigade (less 2 battalions)
½ Bearer Division 40th Field Ambulance
Embark West Beach.

As the members of all ranks to stay on the Peninsular for the last day of the final stage are limited to the figures as understated, details from battalions remaining to the end in excess of these numbers were to be evacuated with battalion embarking on night of 18/19 December:

38th Infantry Brigade 1,000
39th Infantry Brigade 1,100
40th Infantry Brigade 1,500

Battalions remaining to be nearly 500 (or 550) strong as possible.

Instructions as to withdrawal of guns and as to embarkation of artillery personnel during the final stage was to be issued direct by G.O.C. 13th Division.

Further orders concerning Bearer Divisions of Field Ambulances or portions of them detailed to embark, such personnel as required with brigades were sent forward at dusk to join brigades, and were to withdraw with them. The remainder of the personnel were to embark which were not required with brigades to move at 17.45 on the night in question to Lala Baba and West Beach respectively.

In cases where it was not possible to keep battalions complete for embarkation, but as far as was practicable, companies were to be embarked complete. The officer commanding each detachment for embarkation was to report to the staff officer of this division superintending the embarkation.

On the night of 18/19 December, the troops for embarkation were to withdraw from the trenches at 17.45. On the night of 19/20 December the present fire trenches were to be held up to 01.30. Machine guns remaining in present fire trenches were to be withdrawn under arrangements made by Brigadier-Generals Commanding, but the last gun in each case was to leave the trenches no later than 22.30 on the night of 19/20 December.

Every endeavour was to be made to maintain the usual appearance of the trenches by regular sniping, fires, et cetera. On both nights, troops from the right and centre subsections to withdraw by the direct road from Chocolate Hill to a forming-up place at the old mule lines just east of Divisional headquarters and then to South Pier. Rifles were to be unloaded at the forming-up place and troops moved in single file to the place of embarkation. Troops from the left subsection were to withdraw by the footbridge over Asmak Dere to forming-up place 'Y', then to West Beach.

On the night of 19/20 December, the half battalion 38th Infantry Brigade was to hold the Lala Baba defences with 1½ companies occupying trench D3 with two machine guns already placed there. On the same night, the battalion 40th Infantry Brigade were to be sent to hold the Salt Lake lines and to occupy those trenches together with six machine guns which were already there.

Troops holding the Lala Baba defences and the Salt Lake lines Infantry Brigades on withdrawal were to be under the direct orders of the GOC 13th Division. Brigade headquarters 38th and 40th on withdrawal were to report at Divisional headquarters at 24.00, an officer would be selected in each case by the Brigadier General Commanding to control the final withdrawal from the fire trenches of the subsection.

As soon as the Lala Baba trenches and Salt Lake lines were occupied, small posts, each under an officer, were to be placed to cover the gaps in the wire entanglements just in front of the Lala Baba defences and Salt Lake lines. Groups were to be pushed forward to challenge any person approaching the lines.

On the night of 19/20 December, troops in the left subsection were to come under the orders of the GOC 11th Division at 17.00, who would be responsible for their embarkation. His headquarters would be at the present 9th Corps headquarters at Suvla.

The CRE was to arrange for mines to be made active along the front of the fire trenches as soon as it was dusk on the night of 18/19 December and along the front of the Salt Lake lines and Lala Baba defences as soon as it was dusk on the night of 18/19 December. He was also to arrange for the approaches from both sides to the gaps in the wire entanglements in the Lala Baba defences and Salt Lake lines to be marked at dusk on the night of 19/20 December with flour, and for R. E. to be with the infantry posts at the gaps in the wire ready to close them when required. He was also to arrange for flying patrols to warn possible stragglers from crossing the mine fields.

During the night of 19/20 December, troops from 2nd Mounted Division and from Anzac would withdraw from Salt Lake lines and Lala Baba defences, the former by Yeomanry and Anzac roads, the latter by Anzac Road and along the sea beach. The troops from Anzac would be Indian troops. Arrangements had been made for officers of the 2nd Mounted Division and Anzac to notify officers in charge of the infantry posts at the gaps in the wire when all the troops were due to come by those roads were withdrawn, so that the gaps in the wire could be closed.

During the withdrawal from the trenches absolute silence, except for necessary orders which were to be given in an undertone, was to be observed. Troops were to be marched in close formation, in bodies of such size as the tactical situation would permit. No smoking was permitted, and no lights were to be shown and due care was to be taken to ensure that any articles carried by the troops did not rattle. Unless permitted by the order of an officer, no firing by troops withdrawing was permitted. Fires were to be left burning as usual. The extreme importance of these instructions was to be impressed on all concerned.

On the night of 18/19 December, the troops were to embark wearing their packs. Packs belonging to troops embarking on the night of 19/20 December were to be sent in under Brigade arrangements, in the case of the 38th and 40th Infantry Brigades to Divisional headquarters, and in the case of the 39th Infantry Brigade to 'forming up' place 'Y', West Beach.

If the troops remaining till the night of 19/20 December brought in their own packs, they were only to be sent in small parties, so as to avoid unduly weakening the garrisons of trenches. Packs in all cases were to be packed as directed in Divisional Routine Order 94.

Troops were to be informed that blankets would probably not be available to replace deficiencies on reaching the destination of the division, which was Mudros and not Imbros as had been previously stated, and it was therefore in their own interests that the packs should not go astray. Camp kettles that were now with units were to be brought in by parties embarking on the night of 18/19 December. After that time, cooking to be done in mess tins which were to be retained by troops remaining to the end.

The Divisional Signal Officer was to make arrangements for signal communication between Divisional headquarters (this was where either where they were situated or at the Battle Post) and the following:

(a) The trenches now occupied in 'B' Section.
(b) The headquarters of the battalion to occupy the Salt Lake trenches.
(c) The headquarters of the half battalion to occupy the Lala Baba defences.
(d) The detachment to hold trench D3.
(e) 'C' Beach.

In withdrawing, the officers for whose benefit telephone lines were provided, were to see that they were disconnected, and that all telephone instruments were safely brought in when they were no longer required.

During the night of 19/20 December, at least 200 yards, the telephone wire on each line was to be cut and removed.

The following ammunition per gun was to be maintained:

Morning 18th

18-pr. 300 rounds per gun. 5" Howr. All ammunition on shore.

Morning 19th

Remainder, if necessary increased to a minimum of 200 rounds per gun. All ammunition on shore.

Infantry when withdrawing from the trenches were now to carry 220 rounds per man.

On each day of the final stage, watches were to be checked through the Signal Company daily at 01.00 and 16.00.

Extreme punctuality in all movements was essential. Acknowledgement was required by wire.

Instructions for Embarkation

GENERAL.

The quickness with which Troops embark from the pier to the lighter and again from the lighter to the Troop carriers is of primary importance. Officers must remember that the time their comrades may have to wait on shore is dependent on the quickness with which they release the lighter for another journey.

EMBARKING from PIER into LIGHTER.

Troops to file on to the lighter in a single file and leading men to be made to descend below decks at once lead as far as they can go. Hesitation on the part of the leading men to descend is a frequent cause of delay. When the lower deck is full (about 250) top deck to be filled.

Lighter load is 400.

An Officer to be in the rear of each company or detachment embarking.

Gangways and passages on to the lighter to be kept clear.

No man to be sent back from Pier for any baggage. Once on the pier all ranks embarking must file straight on with what they are carrying.

EMBARKING from LIGHTER into TRANSPORT.
On arrival at the Transport the Senior Officer on first Lighter to arrive is to assume command.

On arrival of a Lighter at a Transport the Senior Officer on Lighter, is to get the men off as quickly as possible so as to release it for another journey.

The Senior Officer on the first Lighter is to supervise the disembarkation from subsequent Lighters. He is to get in touch with the master of the Transport at once and find out details of accommodation.

Note:- Sufficient copies issued for distribution to Co. Comdrs. Company Commanders) Infantry R.E. (Royal Engineers) and A.S.C. (Army Service Corps).

The question of closing the wire gaps in front of the SALT LAKE lines and LALA BABA defences on the night of 19th/20th is a matter of importance.

The C.R.E. will arrange for this to be done, posting R.E. (Royal Engineers) detachments at the various gaps to ensure that the work is carried out correctly.

The gap in the wire at LALA BABA defences North of LALA BABA to be closed as soon as the detachments of the 13th Division, Field Ambulance of the 53rd Casualty Clearing Station, and R.A.N. Bridging Train have withdrawn to LALA BABA.

The Officer commanding SALT LAKE lines will ascertain from the staff officers 2nd Mounted Division posted on the ANZAC Yeomanry roads respectively when all the 2nd Mounted Division and Indian troops have withdrawn through SALT LAKE lines, and from his own Officer posted on the direct CHOCOLATE HILL road when all the 13th Division troops have withdrawn through these lines. He will then direct the R.E. officer (who will be with him) to close the gaps and he will withdraw the remainder of his troops to the forming up place at LALA BABA for embarkation. The R.E. will also withdraw similarly as soon as the work is completed.

As regards the lines of wire in front of the LALA BABA defences instructions will be sent to the Staff Officer 13th Division stationed near the well on the direct CHOCOLATE HILL road to close the gaps as soon as Div.HQ are informed that all the 2nd Mounted Division and Indian troops are within the defence. As soon as the Staff Officer in question is satisfied that the whole of the troops of the 13th Division are within the defences he will instruct the R.E. Officer (who will be with him) to close all the gaps, and the R.E. will then withdraw at once to the following forming up place.

The order to withdraw the troops holding LALA BABA defences to the forming up place will be sent direct to the officers concerned from Divisional headquarters.

Signed.

18th December, 1915.

The strength of the Battalion on 31 December 1915 was: 15 officers, 386 other ranks, 401 total.

<u>Casualties for December</u>

4 officers were hospitalised, wounded nil; other ranks: rejoined from hospital 151, killed 2, wounded 3, missing nil, hospital sick 278.

Evacuation of Helles

The War Diary states that the Battalion arrived at Mudros Harbour at 2 p.m. on 21 December and they remained on board until the next day, when they proceeded to camp and were joined by the Machine Gunners and advance party.

On 23–25 December they 'rested and celebrated Xmas'.

On 30 December they left camp at 8 a.m., arriving at North Pier to embark on board the *Princess Alberta* at 9.30 a.m. and disembarked about 11 p.m. at *River Clyde* landing. They arrived at Gully Beach at 4.15 a.m. and moved to bluff in Gully Ravine at 2 p.m. The Battalion was in Brigade Reserve.

At Helles on New Year's Day at 9 a.m., the Battalion marched from Gully Beach to dugouts about 200 yards below Eski Lines where they started making a new road from Zigzag to Gully Beach. During this time, the Machine Gun Section moved into the fire trenches, parties were on ammunition dumps loading up carts and employed the usual fatigues removing and destroying surplus stores, et cetera.

Command of the Battalion was taken by Lieutenant Colonel Geleman, who attended a conference at 39th Infantry Brigade HQ to discuss orders for the evacuation of 13th Division. After attending a conference of company commanders on 6 January, the CO reconnoitred Eski Line, this was also undertaken by all available officers on 7 January.

At 11.30 a.m., Turks began bombing the first line trenches. This bombardment gradually increased in intensity, reaching its maximum about 14.30. Such at the Battalion as could be collected were 'standing to', ready to move. At 14.45, the Battalion was ordered to move to Brigade HQ. A fatigue party of 100 men with officers there to meet them. The Battalion was then moved up to Frith Walk in support of 4th South Wales Borderers (SWB). A quantity of bombs and boxes had been brought up and sent forward to SWB.

The bombardment had now ceased and the rifle fire which had been heavy also slackened. The Turks had evidently contemplated an attack but were unable to get their men out of the trenches. The 7th North Staffs Regiment was attacked but the Turks were shot down as soon as they left their trenches. Men were sent forward to help the SWB in rebuilding their trenches. The Battalion was ordered to leave 5 officers and 130 men in Frith Walk in support of 4/SWB. The remainder withdrew to bivouac.

At 5.50 a.m., half of the 8th the Battalion moved up to occupy Eski Line in accordance with 40th Brigade 00.No. 1. (Order), 'B' Company held from Artillery Road to Great North Road; with 'C' Company to White house communication trench; 'D' Company to Gully Ravine in accordance with the same order and 70 men moved to Gully Beach. Later in the morning, three machine guns arrived which were posted in prepared emplacements, one with each company.

At noon on 8 January, orders were received (42nd (East Lancashire) Division), to destroy everything that could be of use to the enemy, and an orgy of destruction began. Huge dumps were made, or added to, the largest of these at 'W' and 'V' Beaches. Hundreds of cases of bully beef, condensed milk, biscuits and other rations, ammunition that could not be taken away, limbers, wheels and anything else that would burn, were piled up, and the mass soaked in paraffin.

Many horses and mules had to be shot, to the bitter grief of their drivers.

Preparations were made for the firing of the dumps at daybreak on 9 January, hours after the time fixed for the embarkation of the last batch of troops. As in the case of so many 'innovations' of the Great War – steel helmets, breastplates, catapults, darts and hand-grenades, for instance – a time-honoured device was resorted to. Candles were left burning in tins, their rate of burning having been carefully timed, so that when the flame reached a certain point it would ignite a train of oil and waste, which led to a mass of combustible material placed around and among the wooden cases. By means of a similar artifice, fixed rifles in the firing line continued to pop off at regular intervals in order to delude the Turk into the belief that the trenches were still occupied.

At 13.30 it was recorded that the day had passed quietly and there was little shelling. The weather was fine with a light breeze. Battalion orders for evacuation were issued.

At 16.45, 70 men from Eski Line and 70 men at Gully Beach joined en route, with the whole proceeding to West Beach for embarkation. At 17.25, the rest of the Battalion from Eski Line, one officer and 11 men, moved off via the same route and began embarking on HMT *Ermine* which sailed about 21.00 p.m. with 15 officers and 288 other ranks.

The diary of 9 January reports that the *Ermine* arrived in harbour at Mudros and the men disembarked in two tugs regardless of units, so the Battalion came back rather scattered. It had blown hard in the night and some of the troops had to be taken to Imbros, Battalion HQ and moved up to Portianos camp. The day was spent cleaning up and looking over equipment: small parties were coming in at intervals.

By midday, 15 officers and 320 other ranks were concentrated, 1 officer and 32 men had been with 8th Royal Welch Fusiliers and now rejoined camp. Companies were now at the disposal of Company Commanders for complete kit inspections of clothing, accoutrements, arms, ammunition and rations.

A draft of 372 other ranks and 6 officers should have joined, but due to very heavy rain tents were unable to be pitched, and the draft was postponed until 17 January. On 16 January, the Zion Mule corps was struck and rations had to be manhandled as the roads were in a very bad condition. With the draft complete on 17 December, Battalion for deployment to Egypt on SS *Ancona*.

List of Gallipoli Casualties, M.E.F. (Land Forces, Not Including French)
Killed, 28,200; Wounded and missing, 89,349–117,549

Sick (of whom a large number died) admitted to Hospital – 96, 683.
Total 214,232.

Material Points from the Conclusions of the Dardanelles Commission 1917

The report published in 1917, by the parliamentary commission investigating the Dardanelles campaign, concluded that sufficient consideration was not given to the measures necessary to carry out the operation with success. It was critical of the fact that as early as February 1915, serious operations might have been neces-sary. The report found that under these circumstances the conditions of attack on the Peninsula should have been studied with a general plan prepared by the Chief of the Imperial General Staff, Sir James Wolfe Murray, with special attention being paid to the possible effect of naval gun fire in support of the troops, and that it was the duty of the Secretary of State for War to ensure that this was done.

It found that the short naval bombardment in November 1914 gave the Turks warning of a possible attack, and the naval operations of February and March 1915 led to them strengthening their defences. The report highlighted the fact that as the Turks were known to be led by German officers, there would be no reason to think that they would not fight well and so assumptions that the resist-ance would be slight and the advance rapid were unfounded. These facts had been reported by Admiral de Robeck and Sir Ian Hamilton.

The report states that after the first attacks in April and early May, due exami-nation of the demands of extended operations when obligations in other theatres of war existed, were not considered.

This was the case for May, June and July, which made it impossible to supply the forces with necessary drafts, guns, ammunition, high explosives and other 'modern appliances of war'. The report found the Government at fault for 'not concentrating their efforts upon the enterprise', and for limiting the expenditure of men and material in the Western theatre of war.

After the failure of the attacks which followed the first landing, the report found that there was undue delay in deciding upon the future course of action. Also, Sir Ian Hamilton had requested reinforcements but this was not considered by the War Council or the Cabinet until 7 June, some six weeks later, due to Government reorganisation.

The plan of attack from Anzac and Suvla at the beginning of August was also open to criticism. Although the plan was agreed after consideration of other plans by the commander of the Anzac Corps, it was felt in hindsight that the terrain was difficult and the main advance of the Anzac force up the north-western spurs of Sari Bahr, which was undertaken at night, in order to obtain the element of surprise, incurred an increased high risk of misdirection and failure.

Added to this, the operations at Suvla were 'a severe trial' for a force consisting of troops who had never been under fire and consequently, after due considera-tion and making allowances for the difficulty of attack and the inexperience of the troops, the attack was not pressed as it should have been. The report attrib-uted this 'in a great measure' to a want of determination and competence in the

Divisional Commander and one of his Brigadiers. The leadership of the 11th Division and the attached 10th Division, which constituted the main body of the attack, was not satisfactory. The report blamed a failure in command and communication between senior officers and the condemnation of orders, which was partly responsible for the failure to supply the troops with water on 7 and 8 August.

The report came down heavily on Sir Ian Hamilton, in particular for regarding Lord Kitchener as a Commander-in-Chief rather than as a Secretary of State. Specifically, it was found that his judgement of the situation in general lacked a critical spirit, and a submission to the Secretary of State for War of a comprehensive statement of the arguments for and against a continuance of the operations should have been made. Consequently, Sir Ian Hamilton was relieved of his command on 15 October.

The report found that the failure at Anzac was due mainly to the difficulties of the country and the strength of the enemy. The failure at Suvla also prevented any pressure being put upon the Turkish force in that direction, and success at Suvla might have lessened the resistance at Anzac. It also found that the operations carried out on 9 December could not have been successfully carried out without large reinforcements. Although the failure to supply sufficient artillery and munitions was a critical factor, the commission pointed out that a considerable amount of artillery was available in Egypt and Mudros for the Suvla operations but it was not utilised.

The report concluded that the decision to evacuate when taken was right.

General Hamilton's consternation with the Dardanelles Commission's findings and of their not availing themselves of his formal offer to submit what he had written for their scrutiny, resulted in him privately publishing his diary, in which he had also methodically recorded his correspondence to Earl Kitchener, the War Office and others. His reasons for doing so were that in his lifetime he wanted to 'have the verdict of my comrades of all ranks at the Dardanelles, and until they know the truth, as it appeared to me at the time, how can they give that verdict?'

In the diary he rebuts, for instance, the readily available supply of ammunition:

The whole story of the artillery at Helles may be summed up in the following sentences: insufficiency of guns of every nature; insufficiency of ammunition of every nature, especially of H.E.; insufficient provision made by the Home Authorities for spare guns, spare carriages, spare parts, adequate repairing workshops, or for a regular daily, weekly or monthly supply of ammunition; guns provided often of an obsolete pattern and so badly worn by previous use as to be most inaccurate; lack of aeroplanes, trained observers and all the requisites for air observation; total failure to produce the trench mortars and bombs to which the closeness of the opposing lines at Helles would have lent themselves well – in short, total lack of organisation at home to provide even the most rudimentary and indispensable artillery requisites for daily consumption; not to speak of downright carelessness which resulted in the wrong shells being sent to the wrong guns, and new types of fuses being sent without fuse keys and new types of howitzer shells without range tables. These serious faults provoked their own penalties in the shape of the heavy losses suffered by our Infantry and artillery, which may have been in a great measure averted if sufficient fore-thought and attention had been devoted to the 'side-show' at the Dardanelles.

Sir Ian Hamilton's *Gallipoli Diary* (two volumes), published in 1920, can be read in full online.

Photographs of 6th Manchester's at 3rd Battle of Krithia, and Lord Kitchener's inspection of trenches at Gallipoli can viewed, along with many other photographs on the Gallipoli Association website.

Salonika: 28th Division 84th Brigade

James Riley M. M. Cheshire Regiment 2nd Battalion, service number 11222

James Riley volunteered for his country on the first day of the outbreak of war, catching the train from Altrincham to Chester. He joined the 8th Battalion, the first of the 'New Army', raised at the Castle. It was mustered entirely of men who joined up at once in their only clothes, many just off the street. The racecourse Grand Stand was the battalion Headquarters and the men slept outside on the racecourse itself, thankful that the weather was warm and dry.

On 20 August 1914 the men were entrained for Tidworth on Salisbury Plain. On arrival, and after drawing on equipment of a sort, they were marched 4 miles at dusk to Shipton Bellinger, where camp was pitched and a meal of bread and tea purchased from a grocer's car was issued. At this point the entire battalion consisted of 150 men. The ensuing days saw the attestation of drafts of men from Chester, the 'first hundred thousand'. Except for the first Company, the men had no uniforms, equipment or arms. This also applied to the 'New Army' officers who joined in their civilian clothes. Training continued until summer of 1915, when the battalion set sail from Avonmouth for Gallipoli.

Private Riley was wounded at Gallipoli and after recovery in Gibraltar, he was seconded to the 2nd Cheshire Battalion. In 1916, the battalion was transferred from the Western Front to the Southern Front at Salonika. The following accounts are his battle experiences in the Balkans, on the Southern Front of the war.

The Macedonian Front, known as the Salonika Front, was formed as a result of an attempt by the Allied Powers to aid Serbia which had come under attack from the Central Powers.

Six British Divisions were deployed to Salonika for the campaign: 10th (Irish) Division; 22nd Division; 26th Division; 27th Division; 28th Division; 60th (2/2nd London) Division under the command of George Milne overall Commander-in-Chief of British Troops (XVI Corps), in Macedonia from 9 May 1916.

As part of the 28th Division, the 2nd Battalion Cheshire Regiment arrived in Salonika (Thessaloniki) northern Greece, in 1915; and moved to the line of the River Struma. Greece was a neutral country during the war and Salonika served as an entrenchment camp for the Allies.

Macedonia in the Balkan Peninsula became a stronghold of the Bulgarians. It was here that the British fought alongside a multinational Allied force of 500,000 French, Greek, Italian, Russian and Serbian contingents against the Bulgarian Army, German, Austro-Hungarian and Turkish of 300,000 men. At full strength, the BSF totalled 220,000 men holding some 90 miles of front.

The Struma Valley

The Struma valley must be one of the most unhealthy places in the world. To sleep on the low swampy ground without elaborate precautions means, to the European, at the best, a sharp attack of malaria of a malignant form. The 2nd Battalion at Lozista was probably the worst place in the valley. They had no mosquito nets and no gloves, or other protection and practically no quinine. In three weeks, at this plague-spot, the Battalion lost 700 men, 400 of whom never rejoined. Men attacked by this disease dropped unconscious as if they had been shot. These casualties were as honourably earned as any in action. It was no fault of the regimental officers or men that they incurred. The hardships of the 1916–17 winter were increased by the submarine campaign which caused a shortage of rations and canteen stores. The troops felt this all the more from having been weakened by malaria during the summer. This loss from malaria was the outstanding feature of the Salonika campaign.

The men had much to do to preserve their health under the varied climatic conditions. The winters in Macedonia were bitterly cold, with heavy snow and rain, while the summers were excessively hot (43 degrees Celsius), and liable to heavy thunder storms which put rivers in spate and washed away camps and horse lines.

From the autumn of 1915 until November 1918, the 2nd (and 12th Battalions), in between raids were constantly employed on making outpost positions, reserve works, roads and bridges. During the winter months of 1916–1917 the Allies worked hard at offensive and defensive preparation. To give an example of the amount of engineering work that needed to be done: a journey by road from Salonika to the headquarters of 12 Corps at Janesh was, early January 1917, so uncertain of duration that, although the rectilineal map distance was 28 miles, it was necessary to start at 8.30 in the morning to arrive by 3.30 in the afternoon. The only throughfare in places was interspersed by thigh-deep mire.

The Germans sarcastically called Salonika their Balkan internment camp.

(Crookenden)

In July 1916, a French force of a cavalry and infantry Brigade advanced some ten miles beyond the Struma, but was attacked by the Bulgars and driven back over the Struma with some considerable loss. The 84th Brigade, to which the 2nd Battalion belonged, was brought up to cover the French retreat. The Bulgars halted and entrenched themselves some two miles from the Struma, which was held by our troops in part on both sides of the river.

Struma, 30 September–4 October 1916

In September, the 7th Bulgar Division attacked the position on the Struma held by the 84th Brigade and two Battalions of the 27th Division. The strength of the 84th Brigade was only 2,000 owing to malaria, and the Battalions of the 27th Division were not much better off. The Bulgar Division was 20,000 strong. The attack failed with 5,000 casualties to the Bulgars.

A Yeomanry Brigade, with some horse artillery, was ordered to follow up the Bulgars, who were retiring in confusion, but the yeomanry were driven back by artillery fire and could not advance. On the same day, before the yeomanry advance, two companies of the 2nd Battalion (Captains Cuff and May) attacked and captured the entrenched village of Navoljen, taking eighteen prisoners.

On the failure of the yeomanry advance, the 2nd Battalion was ordered to follow up and locate the Bulgars. The other two companies crossed the Struma in the night, and the Battalion moved forward at daybreak covered by a battery of artillery fire, crossing the pain and coming into contact with the Bulgar rearguard some 6 miles from Navoljen. The scouts under Lieut. Beckett, and two companies under Capt. K.-S. and May, got in touch. One scout was killed. The Bulgars were retiring up the Belashitza, apparently in panic, and Colonel Smyth, commanding the battalion, wired to the Brigade that he thought it possible to capture the pass if the remainder of the Brigade would support him.

An answer was received that supply arrangements would not permit an advance of this nature, and directing the 2nd Battalion to retire with the information gained. It was a great opportunity which was missed. A few days later the Bulgars, finding they were not pursued, came back to the foot of the hills, but not so far forward as before.

Railway lines were of significant importance during the war. They could be used for strategic purposes and the advancement of an occupying army. These military supply lines or arterial routes had to be cut off to disrupt the enemy's flow of troops, horses, munitions, food and other supplies.

Doiran
Extracted from various sources and Secret Reports, Raids by 2nd Battalion Cheshire Regiment at Butkova-Dzuma

The village of Butkova-Dzuma was about 3 miles away from British lines on the northern side of the Struma Valley and just in front of a railway line. The Bulgars had posts out in front of the village and on its right and left.

At dawn on 20 December 1917, two Companies 'A' and 'C' of the Second Battalion, commanded by 2nd Lieutenant (A/C) K.-S. with a detachment of the 506th Field Company R.E., raided Butkova-Dzuma.

The Bulgars occupied a line on the north side of the valley and the battalion a line on the south side. The two lines were about 3 miles apart with the Butkova river flowing between. It was discovered by observation that the village was occupied by one Company of Bulgars.

The raiding party assembled in Butkova in our lines. After tea and rum, the raiders moved off in a column of route, and crossed the river at 04.20. After moving through high grass, and marching by compass they reached the various landmarks without difficulty.

At 06.35, the party passed between two posts previously located, and could hear the garrisons talking. A certain amount of difficulty was experienced in crossing the ditch and hedge. As the rear company were getting through the gap in the hedge, the enemy opened fire on them, but there were no casualties. After crossing the railway, the raiders turned west and deployed along the embankment. Fire was opened on them without effect. Enemy encountered were killed or captured, unless they ran away.

Three green Verey lights were the signal to move towards our lines. As our men passed through the village many more Bulgars were met, all of whom were captured, almost without resistance, including the Company Commander. In spite of a barrage put down by the enemy on the west and south sides of the village, our men were all clear of it soon after 08.00. It was estimated that thirty Bulgars were killed. One officer and fifty-two men were captured. Our losses were two officers and eleven men, all slightly wounded. Our casualties were chiefly caused by a trip bomb, during withdrawal.

The raid resulted in the awarding of the Military Cross to the Commanding Officer and two Military Medals to members of the raiding party.

On the morning of 16 January, enemy aeroplanes bombed the vicinity of Butkova Lake and Tile Spur, with one bomb falling 150 yards from dugouts. Preparations were now made for another raid on Butkova-Dzuma and Companies were moved from their billets to Staros and the Monastery. Assaulting Companies and half of 'C' company left the front line to take up outpost positions and machine guns were put in place along the river. The second raid would come from the west instead of the east.

This raid took place on 20 January 1918. Captain K.S. led the raiding party on a long march by compass bearing over very difficult country. By 06.15, the Assaulting Companies had been deployed and began the advance toward Road Post and Rail Post which were found to be empty and not used for some time. In front of the wire a long tripwire was encountered with tins on it which rattled. Within half an hour the supporting troops were over the river and proceeded to towards Dry Ford.

Assaulting Companies first came in contact with the enemy 60 yards beyond White River, where a small party of the enemy fired at the left company and were charged. The right company dispersed six men (killing one) about 100 yards from Iron Bridge. At 07.01, three enemy Verey lights were seen to go up and a few minutes later the enemy's guns opened fire. Rifle fire and bombing were heard increasing in sound.

Our guns opened fire to the east of the Level Crossing and the advance of the right was not hindered as all the posts had been evacuated. Two of the enemy were killed on the way, not including the first party encountered. The advance of the left company towards Copper Tree was checked by some twenty of the enemy 200 yards before reaching Copper Tree; these were, however, dispersed by rifle and rifle grenade fire. They tried to reform once but were dispersed. It is estimated that about thirteen of this party were killed.

On Copper Tree being reached, he encountered a redoubt which was built three sides of a square, facing east, south and west. He found that about sixty of the enemy were holding the redoubt, and a short pause was made while rifle fire and rifle grenade fire was opened on the redoubt, before the Company charged. The Commanding Officer led the charge which captured the position, inflicting heavy casualties upon the enemy. It was during the charge that the Commanding Officer was wounded.

As soon as the enemy saw that this Company was charging, he made off in two parties, one about fifteen strong in an easterly direction. Both these parties were fired on, in the larger party a large number were seen to fall. The smaller party after going east returned, probably with the intention of re-joining the remainder; these were mostly killed at point blank range.

In a shelter at Copper Tree an empty leather telephone case and plugs were found. Eight men were found dead at the redoubt. After this no further opposition was encountered, although firing continued from the left. Machine-gun fire was also opened from a point 500–600 yards north of Copper Tree. At 07.27 the enemy barraged Butkova-Dzuma.

By 07.40 the Companies started returning. No bugle call was heard as the mouthpiece of the bugle was lost during the advance. Two platoons of the right company were delayed near Level Crossing and thinking that the Left Company had not withdrawn they remained there until 08.15 hours. Enemy artillery shelled Guide Tree as our troops were seen retiring. At 07.50 our Companies were still crossing Dry Ford and over Dry River Bed. During the return, the enemy put down a very heavy barrage on the Dry River and Guide Tree.

At 08.00 the enemy barrage ceased temporarily, and by 08.20 our men were still retiring south-west of Egg Tree. The enemy then barraged Dry Ford and the track from Dry Ford to Butkova-Dzuma Ford. Signals were then closed down at Copper Tree and our guns started shelling Copper Tree. The enemy continued shelling the area. At 09.20, the raiding party returned to Butkova. The half Company who went as far as Road Post returned to the 'X' line (decussate).

It is estimated that about forty-five Bulgars were killed in all. Thirty were actually seen dead and the remaining fifteen are estimated from the numbers seen to fall when the enemy were making off to the north. We had only one man killed and this was after two platoons of the Right Company (who were delayed) left Level Crossing.

The Commanding Officer who was severely wounded was Captain Ronald King-Smith M.C., who was awarded the DSO (Distinguished Service Order), for his part in the raid. He was rescued by Private Riley 'C' Company, who left the trench and, going out into no man's land, carried the officer on his back through the wire and to safety, whilst under heavy sniper fire from the Bulgarians. For this action, Private Riley was awarded the Military Medal for gallantry and devotion to duty in the field. After the war, Captain King-Smith married and had a son – the children's author Dick King-Smith.

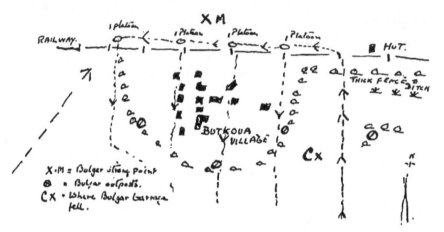

Sketch map of raid on Butkova village area. (Chester Military Museum)

Military Medal and service medals. (Christian Brady)

Operations, April 1918

As Bulgaria had aligned itself with Germany, the French High Command feared that Germany would call upon Bulgarian troops to take part in the German Spring Offensive on the Western Front. To countermand this, Britain and France agreed that their forces in Macedonia should make a series of limited artillery and infantry offensives. Instructions were received from the Commander-in-Chief of the Allied Armies.

The next few months saw the 2nd Battalion (28th Division) characterised by long marches (Arakli, Snevce, Rajaovo, Hodja, Mahale, Hamzai). The weather conditions were very poor and during this march they encountered heavy snow-storms and suffered severely from cold (frostbite). They reached Turica in late March and then marched on to Kumli to take part in operations in the Struma Valley on 14 April 1918.

The Corps Commander was notified of the instructions and decided on the following action:

Operation Order No. 32 of 11 April for 14–15 April 1918 saw the 28th Division take part in shared operations with the 1st Greek Division and 27th Division. It was part of a series of active local operations to be maintained along the Allied front in order to harass the enemy and obtain information regarding his intentions.

The object was to capture prisoners and occupy a series of some thirteen villages (See Appendix 1), by means of ambush and to push further forward. Another of the objectives was to make the enemy think that the appearance of guns on the left bank of the Struma was part of an advance; this would induce them to send forward reconnaissance forward patrols. By showing activity on the front of the 1st Greek Division, it would cause the enemy to move his forward trenches, et cetera, and present himself as targets for artillery and aeroplanes. The 28th Division were to link up with the left of 27th Division and occupy Kumli and Ormanli with the possibility of an extension further forward afterwards.

Operation Order No. 33 on 18 April 1918

The 1st Greek Division were to remain in occupation of the villages until 21 April and then withdraw and resume normal dispositions; and the 27th Division would withdraw from the forward line but would be responsible for the protection of the left to the forward troops of the 1st Greek Division until withdrawal took place.

The 28th Division were to withdraw from their forward line and resume normal dispositions for the night of 18 April. The village of Kumli was to continue to be held until the night of 20/21 April. (See Appendix 2.)

Report on Operations 14–16 April 1918; Elisan, Dragos, Prosenik

Head of Force crossed Struma at 2015 and halted S. of Elisan where force was divided into complete parties for allotted tasks. Main Body reached Elisan at 2130 hours and waited report from Advance Company that Kumli was clear. This not being received by 2300 hours force advanced on Kumli which was entered at 0030 hours. Strong patrols pushed on to Kujpri and Barakli.

After Kujpri was captured with little loss the first patrol was heavily counter attacked at about 0820 and the enemy appeared in a large force numbering about 500 men from E.N. & W. of the village at close range. In spite of rapid fire from our patrol the enemy advanced and rushed the three forward posts. Owing to the large number of the enemy, our patrol was outnumbered, and eventually after all the officers had been killed or wounded and having suffered losses of over 70 O.R. [Other Ranks] they were compelled to withdraw.

The Barakli Patrol which up to 0820 had a very similar experience, but had succeeded in holding its ground was withdrawn by Brigade orders about noon. The patrol suffered the loss of one officer and 50 other ranks wounded. The Support Platoon was ordered to withdraw last.

Amongst the battalion's total casualties, sixty other ranks were missing. These sixty 'missing' soldiers – the entire Support Platoon – had in fact been taken as prisoners of war by the Bulgarian Army. Private Riley was one of them. (See Appendix 3.)

The 4th Rifle Brigade from 80th Brigade (27th Division) also came to grief at Prosenik. The offensive was one of chaos and resulted in a high casualty rate: 3 officers killed and 118 killed, wounded or captured from a patrol of 134.

As a result, an enquiry was ordered under the direction of Lieutenant-General Briggs (16th Corps), in connection with the operations of the 4th Rifle Brigade at Prosenik and of the 2nd Cheshire Regiment at Kjupri and Barakli.

Court Findings
2nd Cheshire Regiment Operations at Kjupri and Barakli

1. The importance of making quite certain that troops can at least find the starting point even on the darkest night. Much delay was caused through neglect to take even the most elementary precautions to ensure this.
2. Neglect to take adequate measures for local security. Observation was by periscope alone, which, when the grass is high and the ground unknown, is no security at all. Good observation is a necessity for ambush operations so that when the enemy does arrive, he will successfully fall into the ambush, and his approach will not come as a surprise to our own troops.
3. In both cases (Kjupri and Barakli) the troops arrived at daylight, and the enemy was aware of their presence. The chances of an ambush had consequently increased, yet neither Coy Commander took steps to see that the troops were well placed to meet an attack.

4. The retirement from Barakli seems to have been conducted without any system. The 12 platoon was ordered to cover the withdrawal of the remainder of the Company and was then left to its fate, (which was apparently captured by the enemy). No attempt appears to have been made to assist by mutual support the withdrawal of No. 12 Platoon itself.

The 4th Rifle Brigade were criticised for failing to make proper local precautions to guard against surprise, which required personal reconnaissance on the part of Commanders at the time dispositions were being taken up. The lack of reconnaissance of the ground, even in the dark after arrival, was also cited as the reason for the flanks of 'C' Coy being insecure against enemy timed movements. Trenches were dug too deep to make it possible to see out of them, and high vegetation limited the range of vision even in the dark. Witness statements revealed how the troops kept digging the trenches ever deeper, so that they were of no use even as fire trenches, as orders were not given to stop. The enquiry criticised 'the lack of common sense' with regard to the absence of orders. It also cited the use of concealment at the expense of security and proper inter-communication. The enquiry was scathing in its findings that no attempt was made to clear up the situation with regard to 'C' Coy, and the fact that it was not until the following morning that reconnaissance was made, and then by a party of stretcher-bearers. Finally, it stated that the importance of the dangerous lines of approach afforded by the West Belica to the enemy should have been realised.

Lessons applicable to both the above operations (4th Rifle Bde, and 2nd Cheshire Regt).
1. No ambush can be expected to succeed if the enemy can approach to within a few yards of the ambush party without being seen. The only result can be the ambush party itself surprised.
2. The perimeters of these villages are far too large to be held by small platoon posts widely separated and out of touch with each other; each platoon is at once liable to be out flanked. The possibility of success will be much greater if more mutually supporting dispositions are resorted to, in which platoons or posts are distributed in depth, and no great distance from each other.
25th June, 1918.
H.L. Knight
Brigadier General,
General Staff, XVI Corps.

(Court of Enquiry papers)

The lessons were important as the Field Service Regulations (1914) stated: 'The correct application of principles to circumstances is the outcome of sound military knowledge, built up by study and practice until it has become instinct'. The Field Service Regulations deals with the 'General Principles', which govern the leading in war, of the Army. All the training manuals of the various arms are based on these regulations. (See Appendix 4 for regulations pertaining to the 'Findings of the Court of Enquiry').

Bulgarian Prisoners of War were released from captivity in September 1918 and the following report gives some further insight into the April operations that the 2nd Cheshire regiment took part in.

Report on Operations: 2nd Battalion Cheshire Regiment

Just after the Bulgarian Armistice (30th September, 1918), when our prisoners were returned, they were interrogated both by Lt-Col. E.C. Maxwell and Capt. M.S. Adshead. The NCOs said that the German Intelligence Officers with the Bulgarian Army knew of all our preparations for this operation and even asked such questions as the reason for postponing it as we had done.

In December 1916, the Bulgarian Ministry of War created Special Intelligence Units in prison camps to gather information which could support Bulgarian military operations. This was a direct contravention of the Hague Convention.

There were approximately twenty-one prison camps in Bulgaria during the First Word War, interning both soldiers and civilians. The administrators of the Bureau for Prisoners of War could not produce accurate figures for the numbers held. There was no official count of escaped or repatriated prisoners and the estimated figure given to the British government in 1917 stood at some 1,546 British prisoners.

After the War

Private Riley took part in the Victory celebrations and the unveiling ceremony of the Chapel Street Roll of Honour. He was demobbed from the army on 21 April 1919.

When James Riley returned home he found that his fiancé had not waited for him. When told that he was 'Missing in Action', she presumed that he had died, and she married someone else.

James Riley didn't return to Chapel Street to live, but instead went to sea for a few years serving as crew on HM *Mauritania* (sister ship of the *Lusitania*), voyaging between Liverpool and New York.

His wartime experiences never left him. Like many other returning soldiers and ex-POWs, he found it hard to settle indoors and the confines of four walls. He and his brother-in-law, who also served during the war, would sit out on the kerbside in greatcoats on cold nights, when the weather was below freezing, with a drink from the outdoor (off licence) and a pipe, and talk about the war.

Some years later, his nephew, as a child, found a photograph of him with soldiers in uniform, when he asked who they were, he replied that he wished he hadn't pulled it from the drawer – he wept and said they were all his friends who had died in the war, and he was the only one left. He suffered relapses of malaria throughout his life and died from the disease in 1966.

Salonika: 22nd Division 66th Brigade

Men from Chapel Street

Corporal John Rowan, service number 6047, Manchester Regiment

The 13th (Service) Battalion was part of the Third New Army (K3). In October/November 1915, the battalion embarked for Salonika, Greece to support the Serbian forces against the Bulgaria Army. The Manchester Regiment was stationed in Salonika up to 28 June 1918, when it was transferred to France.

In 1916, the Division took part in the Battle of Horseshoe Hill (10–18 August), and the Battle of Machukovo (13–14 September).

The following account is taken from various sources including Mann and Crookenden (12th Cheshires were also in 66th Brigade).

First Battle of Doiran, 22 April–8 May 1917 (To coincide with Nivelle's offensive of the Aisne)

The Terrain

Grande Couronne:

This was the name given to a cone-shaped hill immediately to the west of Lake Doiran. Crookenden states that by tunnelling through the apex from the rear, 'the Bulgarians had made an observation post such as only occurs in the dreams of artillery observers'. It was guarded by the 9th (Pleven) Division, the best soldiers of the Bulgarian army.

From the narrow window, the whole of the Allied position could be seen, laid out like a map. Crookenden furthers that no movement could have escaped the observer's notice, and except for an attempt at blinding with smoke shell on suitable occasions, no action was possible against this 'prince' of observation posts. It was known as the 'Devil's Eye' by British troops.

He gives this perspective: the ships in Salonika harbour some 40 miles away could be counted, and the arrival of reinforcements known long before they reached their destination.

'Pip' Ridge:
The name Pip came from the word *piton*, a French word meaning knoll or knob. These rose steadily from P4½ to P1, the highest.

The British general offensive in the Doiran-Vardar sector began after two days' artillery preparation on the night of 24–25 April 1917. The British 22nd and 26th Divisions attacked the Doiran Hills from Pip 4½ on Pip Ridge (13th Manchesters), in the west to Lake Doiran in the east. Some 100,000 shells were fired by the British. Approximately 2,000 gas shells were brought in for the offensive but two-thirds were defective. With half an hour before the offensive was timed to start, the enemy began to pour down a very formidable barrage. In front of them lay the boulder-strewn slopes of Jumeaux Ravine. It was here that troops from the 26th Division were always killed, captured or driven back by counter-attacks, and reinforcements and ammunition supplies failed to come forward. The Bulgarians filled the ravine with artillery and machine-gun fire, which cut down advancing troops, ammunition resupply parties and stretcher-bearers. The blast effect of shells killed more British soldiers in these narrow ravines than shrapnel did. Added to this was the fact that though two balloons were on duty their observers could not see into the deep ravines where the enemy batteries were concealed. This meant that it was not possible to locate the exact positions of the enemy's flashes, or for the gunners to reply with sufficient accuracy to put an end to the barrage.

Twelve companies attacked the Bulgarian 2nd Brigade and managed to take the 'Nezezov', 'Knyaz Boris' and 'Pazardzhik' positions, after a bloody fight. After a Bulgarian counter-attack the British were repulsed and had to retreat. The British assaults on the right and central fronts were also repulsed. The British attacks in the next two days were defeated by constant Bulgarian fire and counter-attacks. The British withdrew their initial positions on 27 April, and the Bulgarians immediately reconstructed the destroyed fortifications.

The Bulgarians gunners were assisted by two very strong searchlights; this meant that in this full glare our men had to leave their trenches and brave the barrage, to run to the bottom of the ravine, wade through a stream, and charge up a steep slope on the opposite side. In many places they did get a foothold in the enemy's trenches that ran along the top of the slope, but they were unable to stay there, as the deadly barrage, while it kept their own support from arriving, also followed them into the trenches they had captured.

General Vladimir Vazov ordered fire day and night on Allied positions. The initial several-hour struggle between British and Bulgarian batteries was followed by a one-hour Bulgarian counter-barrage in which 10,000 shells were fired.

On 5 May, the Greeks, who now occupied the sector on the immediate left, just across the Vardar, won their first slight success, and on the following day artillery preparation was recommenced in front of Doiran and Pip Ridge. This was where the enemy meantime had been considerably reinforced by both artillery and infantry. The attack it preluded was again directed across Jumeaux Ravine, but again, had no lasting result.

The French, Italians, Serbs and Greeks were equally baffled in their endeavours to advance by the natural and strongly fortified resources of the ground occupied by the Bulgars. The reason for this was that German experts had constructed very deep reinforced emplacements and concrete dugouts or trenches cut from the solid rock and had developed to the utmost all the natural advantages. The two main positions had two rows of continuous trenches, passages for communication. In front of these positions there was a two-lined system of wire entanglements. Between the rows of trenches watch points, shelters and in the concrete emplacements machine guns were planted, platforms for ammunition; ready at a moment's notice to sweep deadly hails of bullets along the deep and heavily wired ravines through which all the Allied attacking parties had to make their way.

On 8 May, after a long artillery barrage, they began another attack with waves of British troops attacking Bulgarian positions. After four attacks during the night of 8/9 May, the British were defeated and suffered enormous casualties. Due to this the British had to abandon all attacks.

General Vazov's successful defence of Doiran made him a hero to the Bulgarians.

Casualty figures were: 12,000 killed, wounded and captured, of which more than 2,250 were buried by Bulgarian defenders. The losses of the 9th (Pleven) Infantry Division were 2,000 of whom 900 died from disease or wounds.

Doiran, Pip Ridge, 18–19th September 1918

The military situation on the Struma was one of stalemate for nearly two years. Neither side was strong enough to make any move. To have advanced across the plain without capturing the mountains which dominated it to the north and south would have served no useful purpose and would merely have placed the troops in an unfavourable tactical position, as well as exposing them to malaria.

On 8 August, the decision was made by the Higher Command to put into operation the plan of the Serbian strategist Voivode Mischitch. Put briefly, this operation was a surprise attack on the Serbian front to be delivered where initial success would place the Allies in dominating positions, within measurable striking distance of the enemy's chief communications. It was hoped, by adopting this plan, to separate the Bulgar forces in the Vardar Valley from the Bulgar forces round Monastir, and to cut the road and railway running down the Vardar Valley. One of the factors for success of this plan was that no reinforcement of the enemy could be permitted. Therefore, to pin the enemy to his ground it was necessary to make him use up his local reserves, and at all costs prevent any movement towards the Monastir front at the critical time. On the front held by the British troops, the 'P' Ridge, 'the strongest natural fortress in Europe', was of predominant importance, and it was well known to both sides that the fall of the 'Pip' Ridge would be immediately followed by the invasion of Bulgaria and the cutting off of the Bulgar troops operating west of the Vardar river.

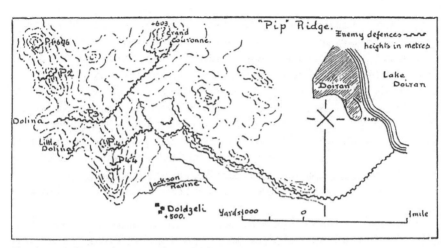

Sketch map of Pip Ridge area. (Chester Military Museum)

The attack began on 15 September, and by the night of 16 September six Serbian divisions and one cavalry division were pouring through the gap made the previous day, and the action was extended right and left with great rapidity. Pushing on with incredible speed, the Serbians reached the Vardar Valley on 21 September. The Bulgarian army was cut in two, one of their main lines of communication had gone and defeat stared them in the face. Before this point was reached, the British made their contribution to the finale debacle. No single enemy battalion must be allowed to move westward to the ever-widening gap in their front and one more attempt on the pitiless bullet and shell-swept slopes of the 'Pip' Ridge was ordered. After four days' preliminary bombardment and wire-cutting, the 66th Infantry Brigade, led by the 12th Battalion (22nd Division), attacked the Ridge.

The 12th Battalion left Pillar Hill at 12.45 a.m., on the night of 17/18 September, and moved along the mule track through Doldzeli village and on to Jackson's ravine, where the front line was. A few men were wounded by shrapnel from shell burst.

At 'zero', 5.08 a.m., the Battalion advanced to attack the formidable whale-backed ridge several hundred metres high with practically a knife-edge crest, and from which the original crest fell away on each side at a very steep gradient. On this account, the preliminary gas bombardment had very little effect. Furthermore, the artillery was unable to make any impression on the phenomenally strong dugouts and galleries, which the enemy had made on each successive rise of the ridge, and which in many cases were covered with as much as 20ft of concrete.

The 66th Brigade had to attack the end of this long spur named P. Ridge, and to capture the successive well-fortified and wired knolls with numerous trenches, forming a veritable fortress, which rose steadily from P4½ to P1, the highest. Owing to the confined space it was only possible to deploy one battalion at a time in the attack. It is difficult to imagine a more formidable task than that which faced the 12th Battalion, the enemy were stout fighters and well armed.

'A' Company carried P4½ by 8 a.m., after overcoming considerable resistance. The right platoon met some forty of the enemy coming out of a large dugout on the right of this work. Severe hand-to-hand fighting ensued in which, at length, all these men were killed, except for two prisoners. The dugout was bombed and set on fire. This opposition delayed the attack and Colonel Clegg-Hill led the remaining three companies forward to attack the next ridge, P4. This advance was checked by an explosion, either of a mine or a bomb dump, which caused many casualties and some confusion. At the same time, very heavy machine-gun fire, a barrage from trench mortars and from a *flammen-werfer* (flame-thrower) opened up the western end of P4. As a result, the companies began to lose the barrage and consequently, when they reached P4, they found the enemy manning the trench, ready for them. About this time, a bullet burst the tank of the *flammen-werfer* and blew it up.

In the face of very heavy fire, the companies pressed on, and 'A' Company penetrated the centre of P4. 'B' and 'C' Companies stormed the western portion of the work, but 'D' Company was held up on the eastern side.

Colonel Clegg-Hill was now wounded and assisted to a shell hole where he was bandaged (he later died).

Meanwhile, the enemy had mounted a number of machine guns at the western end of P4 and in the shell holes below it, and opened a close-range enfilade fire along P4, whilst trench mortars put a heavy barrage down on P4 as well.

However, portions of 'B' and 'C' Companies swept on to the attack of P3, but the enemy had by now occupied little Dolina and the men attacking P3 were annihilated. So severe a crossfire swept the column between P4½ and P4, that nothing could remain alive in the area.

The 12th Battalion had ceased to exist. The Battalion was brought out of action by 2nd Lieutenant L. Richmond, of whom the official history states he 'did well', to withdraw the fifty or sixty survivors to Jackson's Ravine, where the remnants of the Brigade were reorganised. The 66th Brigade, of which the 12th Cheshire formed a part, had 857 casualties. The casualties suffered by the Battalion which went into action on 18 September were: 8 officers killed; 10 wounded; NCOs and men killed: died of wounds and missing, 144; wounded, 130.

For their gallant action, the Battalion was awarded the Croix de Guerre by the French (Crooken: 1938).

The following account is from a paper entitled 'I Saw the Futile MASSACRE at DOIRAN, A Plan that was doomed to Failure'. It was authored by 'An Unprofessional Soldier' on the Staff of 28th Division and published in 1938/39, as part of the series 'I Was There'.

Introduction

The Battle of Doiran is now a forgotten episode of the Great War, overshadowed by the doings of Haig in France and Allenby in Palestine. There was no full contemporary account of the Battle in any British newspaper. Sir George

Milne's dispatch was not published and did not appear in *The Times* until January 23rd 1919, and then only in truncated form.

The very name of the Battle is unknown to most. Yet in singularity of horror and in tragedy of defeated heroism, it is unique among the records of British arms. The real work was entrusted to the men of the 22nd and 26th Divisions, who were able to attack the Doiran hills, co-operating with the Cretan Division of the Greek Army and a regiment of unreliable Zouaves.

Battle

In the early light of an almost unclouded morning the British and Greek forces advanced in order of battle. The noise of our guns had abruptly ceased before daybreak, and there came that awful pause in which defenders and attackers are braced to face the ordeal, with fear or desperation, with cool courage or with blazing ardour. Slowly the pale grey smoke lifted in layers of thin film above the ridges, blue shadows deep in every fold or hollow and a dim golden glow on scrub, rock and heather.

No one could tell what had been the effect of our gunfire upon those fortified hills. The infantry soldier relies upon the guns behind him, trusting in their power to smash a way for his advance by killing or demoralising the enemy and cutting up his defences. In this case, if he had any hopes or illusions, the infantry soldier was quickly undeceived.

Our attack on 'Pip Ridge' was led by the 12th Cheshires (22nd Division). The battle opened with a crash of machine-gun fire, and a cloud of dusty smoke began to blur the outline of the hills. Almost immediately the advancing battalion was overwhelmed in a deadly stream of bullets which came whipping and whistling down the open slopes. Those who survived were followed by a battalion of Lancashire men, and a remnant of this undaunted infantry, fought its way over the first and second line of trenches – if indeed the term 'line' can be applied to a highly complicated and irregular system of defence, taking full advantage of every fold on contortion of the ground. In its turn, a Shropshire battalion ascended the fatal ridge.

By this time the battle of the 'Pips' was a mere confusion of massacre, noise and futile bravery. Nearly all the men of the first two battalions were lying dead or wounded on the hillside. Colonel Clegg and Colonel Bishop were killed; the few surviving troops were toiling and fighting in what appeared to be inevitable and immediate death. The attack was ending in a bloody disaster. No orders could reach the isolated cluster of men who were still trying to advance on the ridge. Contact aeroplanes came roaring down through the yellow haze of dust and smoke, hardly able to see what was going on, and even flying below the levels of the Ridge and Grand Couronne. There was only one possible ending to the assault. Our troops in the military phrase of their commander; 'fell back to their original positions'. Of this falling back I will say nothing. There are times when even desperate heroism has to acknowledge defeat.

While the 60th Brigade was thus repulsed on the ridge, a Greek regiment was thrown into disorder by a counter attack on the right. At the same time a Welsh

Brigade was advancing towards Grand Couronne. No feat of arms can ever surpass the glorious bravery of those Welshmen.

There was lingering gas in the Jumeaux Ravine (probably ours!) and some of the men had to fight in respirators. Imagine, if you can, what it means to fight up a hillside under deadly fire, wearing a hot mask over your face, dimly staring through a pair of clouded goggles, and sucking the end of a rubber nozzle in your mouth. At the same time heat is pouring down on you from a brazen sky. In this plight you are called on to endure alone; you must vigorously fire back, and vigorously assail with your own bayonet. It is as much like hell as anything you can think of.

Welsh Fusiliers got up as far as the Hilt, only half a mile below the central fortress, before being driven back by a fierce Bulgarian charge. Every officer was killed or wounded. Following this came the 11th Welsh, who were also compelled to retire fighting. For a time, however, a few of the enemy's trenches, full of dead or dying men, remained in our possession. A third Welsh battalion was offered up, to perish, on that awful day. The 7th South Wales Borderers nobly stormed up through the haze of battle until they came near the hills of the Tassel and The Knot. Then, all at once, the haze lifted, and they were left open to a sweeping and overwhelming fire. Melting away as they charged, a party of Welshmen ran up the slopes of Grand Couronne itself and fell dead among the rocks. Of the whole battalion, only one officer and eighteen men were alive at the end of the day. All night, unheard in the tumult of a new bombardment, wounded men were crying on the hillsides or down in the long ravines.

Whatever Sir George Milne now thought of his own plans, he must have been gratified by the behaviour of his own troops. Those troops had been flung against positions no infantry in the world could ever have taken by a frontal attack, and they had proved themselves to be good soldiers. Two entire Brigades had been practically annihilated. Only on the right was there a temporary gain of ground by two Hellenic regiments in the neighbourhood of Doiran Town.

My own troops (if I may speak of 28th Division) were in support of the Cretans under the Krusha hill east of the Lake. These people intended to make a 'surprise' attack on the high positions to the north, though I do not see how anyone can be surprised by an attack which has to be launched over a three or four miles of perfectly open country – unless he is surprised at the futility of such a thing. The Cretans had lined up during the night along a railway embankment, which is immediately below the hills. At dawn they advanced over the plain of Akindzali, breaking through the enemy's outpost line. Our artillery, owing to a failure in co-ordination, did not properly support the advance, and our guns were eventually withdrawn under a heavy Bulgarian fire. There were casualties in the neighbourhood of Akindzali village (the scene of unmentionable Greek atrocities in the war of 1913). The attack rapidly collapsed, and by the evening the Cretans were back at the railway line from which they had started.

At nightfall the 28th Division took up a purely defensive attitude, overlooking the plain. It may well be asked why this Division was never given the chance of throwing its full weight into the battle. The enemy itself, as we afterwards learnt, was very much astonished by the absence or concealment of so large a body of troops. One of the first questions put to a captured British airman near Petrich was 'can you tell us what has become of your 28th division?'

A fresh and equally futile massacre on the Doiran hills was arranged for the following day, in spite of the total breakdown of the general scheme. It was now the turn of the Scotsmen-Fusiliers, Rifles and Highlanders of the 77th Brigade, undismayed by the dreadful evidence of havoc, ran forward among the Welsh and Bulgarian dead. Artillery demoralised the regiment of Zouaves on their left. A storm of machine-gun fire blew away the Greeks on their right, in uncontrolled disorder. Fighting on into a maze of enemy entanglements, the Scotsmen were being annihilated, their flanks withering under a terrible enfilade.

A fine battalion of East Lancashires attempted to move up in support. The 64th Brigade launched another forlorn attack on the Pip Ridge. The broken remains of two Brigades were presently in retreat, leaving behind more than half their number; killed, wounded or missing.

We had now sustained 3,871 casualties in the Doiran battle. Our troops were incapable of any further effort. A terrible high proportion had been lost or disabled. We gained only the unimportant ruins of Doiran town and a cluster of small hills immediately above it, never of any value to the enemy or strongly defended. The fortress of Grand Couronne was unshaken, with crumbled bodies of men and a litter of awful wreckage below it. No one can view the result of the operation as anything but a tactical defeat. Had it been an isolated engagement, there would have been every prospect of disaster. The whole plan of the battle and its conduct are open to devastating criticism; but so are the plans and the conduct of a great majority of battles. (The Cheshires, South Wales Borderers and the Argylls were awarded the French Croix de Guerre for their part – the Royal Scots Fusiliers lost 358, the Argylls 299 and the Scottish Rifles 228 men).

Luckily, the Franco–Serbian advance was continued with extraordinary vigour (elsewhere). Before long the Bulgarian Army was cut in two and a general withdrawal began to take place along the entire front. Our Doiran battle was now regarded as a contribution to victory for had we not been effective in pinning down the enemy reserves? British commanders are wonderfully philosophic after all. In other words a waste of lives.

The Franco–Serbian Armies were also attacking in better conditions further to the East and, In spite of desperate fighting by the Bulgarians and their Austrian allies, a gap was opened up in the Bulgarian line and the Serbian, French and British cavalry followed up the Bulgarian retreat and captured Kosturino and Strumitsa. Following the breakthrough the Bulgarains sued for peace. To add to the tragedy the battle honour 'Doiran 1918' was awarded to one yeomanry regiment and 22 infantry regiments. The campaign honour

'Macedonia 1915-1918' was awarded to 10 British yeomanry, 59 British infantry regiments and 4 Indian regiments.

Sir George Milne was never asked about these events but was hailed a victor.

The 2nd Cheshire (28th Division) were in the area of the battle, but saw practically no fighting.

Wakefield & Moody (p.211) state that the attack failed due to the lack of artillery support, problems with inter-unit communication and the reckless first attack by the Greeks.

The French and Serbian Allies did achieve an overwhelming success due to the breach of the defensive lines at Dobro Pole, which enabled the Allies to penetrate into Varda Macedonia and send reinforcements to Doiran. Falls (p. 246–53). The Bulgarians abandoned the position on 21 September and by 23 September the Bulgarian Army was in full retreat and was being actively pursued by other units of the British Salonika Force.

After the Armistice with Bulgaria came into effect on 30 September 1918, the 28th Division advanced across the country towards Turkey. The Ottoman Empire signed an Armistice on 30 October, after which the 28th Division was sent to occupy the Dardanelles Forts. It remained in Turkey on peacekeeping duties until October 1923.

In considering the utility of the Salonika force, it must be remembered that they brought the war to an end by defeating the Bulgars and the Turks, by advancing on Constantinople through Bulgaria and Western Thrace. The collapse of the allies of Germany, followed by that of Austria, put an end to Ludendorff's idea of prolonging the war into 1919 (Crookenden p. 42).

Asia: Mesopotamia (Modern Iraq), Asiatic and Egyptian Theatre

Men from Chapel Street

<u>8th Battalion Cheshire Regiment</u>
James Ratchford, service number 10455; William Ratchford, 11235.

The British Government had very large interests in oil in Persian territory at the head of the Persian Gulf. A large portion of the oil fuel for the British Navy came from the oilfields, making Britain dependent on the supply. Shortly after the outbreak of war, the authorities became anxious about the supply line and its protection became a serious consideration. Troop shortage led the First Lord of the Admiralty (Winston Churchill) to note in a Naval Staff Paper: 'We shall have to buy our oil elsewhere. The Turk can be better dealt with at the centre.' On the surface, the Government were reconciled to the loss of the supply.

On 26 September 1914, the Military Secretary to the Secretary of State for India produced a memorandum entitled, 'The Role of India in a Turkish War'. In this document he expressed the opinion that a Turco–Arab coalition would be a very serious danger to India. He recommended that a force should be dispatched from India at once, to the head of the Persian Gulf to protect the oilfields, and to send out a signal to the Turk and the Arab that 'we mean business'.

The memorandum was apparently seen by Lord Kitchener, the Secretary of State for War, but the opinion of the General Staff was not sought. However, it seems the document content so worried the Secretary of State for India (Lord Crewe) that he wired to the Viceroy that India might be called on to furnish a Division for service in the Gulf.

The warning telegram was followed up a few days later by another telegram, ordering India to send a Division and to dispatch the 1st Brigade immediately. The authorities in India had very little information to go on other than the destination of the troops. On receipt of the order, India telegraphed the Secretary of State: 'We assume you are sure the advanced Brigade is strong enough for its purpose. We cannot judge without knowing its instruction and objective.' And it asked the question: 'Do you intend that we should manage the Expedition or do you mean to run it direct from India Office?'

This elicited the information that the troops were to occupy Abadan (Abadan Island, near Mohammerah) to protect the oil tanks there and the pipelines to the wells. They were also to show the Arabs support against the Turks. Further, India was to manage the campaign, but the Secretary of State would define the objectives. The pipeline extended for 130 miles inland.

This was the beginning of the Mesopotamian Campaign.

The Siege of Kut

Encouraged by early successes, British and Indian forces advanced deep into Mesopotamia. At the Battle of Ctesiphon, British forces suffered heavily and the Allied units retreated to Kut (100 miles south of Baghdad), where they were surrounded and besieged by the Ottoman forces led by a German, General Goltz. General Townshend of the 6th (Poona) Division of the Indian Army was ordered to hold Kut, while Indian Army forces attempted to advance north up the Tigris to relieve the beleaguered garrison. However, the Indian Army was already strained due to the campaign's lack of planning, logistical support and communication problems, and was unable to maintain the force. It could not provide transport of sufficient scale either on land or water; it also had a supply shortage with commitments to two other forces, in East Africa and Egypt, and a frontier campaign. Added to this, the Division had been sent out without base organisations of any sort, and no expertise to organise one. The Indian Army were unable to break the siege and over 20,000 were killed in the ensuing battles.

Around 3,000 British and 8,500 Indian troops and 3,500 Indian non-combatants (attached ancillary support) were trapped at Kut. The siege lasted 147 days, from 7 December 1915–29 April 1916, and was also known as the First Battle of Kut. Conditions became increasingly desperate: food was rationed and supplies were dwindling, the weather was freezing with torrential rain, the garrison had poor drainage and sanitation and medical supplies were limited. Efforts were made to drop supplies from aircraft, with the Royal Flying Corps carrying out the first ever air supply operation, and by riverboat, but to no effect. By April, some 1,750 British and Indian troops had died from wounds or disease (CWGC).

The British Government offered £2 million (£122 million in 2017), and sent T. E. Lawrence (Lawrence of Arabia) as a negotiator, to broker a secret deal with the Ottomans in exchange for the release of the troops, but this offer was rejected by Enver Pasher, who had declared Jihad (Holy War) on Britain. The British Government also asked for help from the Russians who were in Persia (Iran) at the time, but the garrison was surrendered before they reached Baghdad (Falls: p.249).

The garrison was surrendered on 29 April, with some 12,000 servicemen taken prisoner. These men were exhausted and suffered malnutrition and illness. From here they were death-marched to Baghdad, and from there survivors marched a further 500 miles to prisoner of war camps in Anatolia, Turkey.

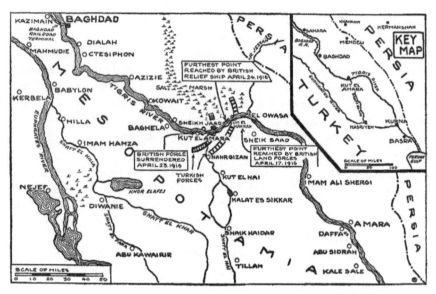

Key map of Kut El Amara. (Wikimedia Commons)

Casualties from the first attempt to capture Baghdad, the Siege of Kut and the battles to relieve the garrison resulted in 40,000 killed, missing, wounded or captured. The news of the surrender shocked the British public – it was another defeat at the hands of the despised Turks – and came on the back of the retreat from Gallipoli. Subsequently, a Parliamentary enquiry was held into the campaign.

Attempts to relieve Kut, 4 January–24 April 1916

In the middle of 1916, General Maude was appointed to take charge of the Army in Mesopotamia. Moving his Headquarters to Basra, he spent four months organising the Base and Base Services and despite pressure on him by the British Government to mount an offensive, he refused until his backward areas were in complete order. When these were working, he moved his headquarters forward, and was now able to make his fighting plans, secure in the knowledge that he could be supplied fully and regularly.

The 8th Battalion Cheshire Regiment reached Mesopotamia (or Mespot, as they called it) with the 13th Division on 28 February 1916. They had taken part in the evacuations at Suvla and Helles, they were now veterans and few of them were left in the ranks. The Battalion had been filled up with drafts but they had very little training and there was a shortage of young officers and of experienced non-commissioned officers – only three who had been with the Battalion since August, besides the quartermaster, arrived in Basra. They arrived when hope of relieving the garrison besieged at Kut was almost gone. The great attack on the Dujaila (Es Sinn) position had failed through too rigid adherence to the plan of attack, which itself was open to criticism on the grounds of rigidity and over-caution, when it

8th Battalion Cheshire Regiment marching in desert, 1917. (Wikimedia Commons)

would have been justifiable to take a risk. This failure was one of a series of failures, the like which the British Army had never before experienced. But as long as any small chance of relieving Kut remained, it had to be tried. The Battalion spent a month in training.

Action of Faliahiya

It was decided to make the next effort on the northern, or left, bank of the Tigris. The first Turkish position, and the only one on this side, was at El Hannah. Saps had been dug to within 50 yards of the enemy's wire, and with ample artillery available they were able to bring fire to bear on the Turks from both flanks. The 13th Division had rehearsed the attack during its month's training over full-scale dummy trenches. All the Battalions and companies knew their task thoroughly.

On 5 April, the 8th Battalion passed through the leading Brigade to the attack of the 3rd Turkish line. But the Turks had gone and the Battalion found itself the advance guard to the Division. Nothing could be seen of the enemy, but gradually fire was felt on the left flank. A change of direction was ordered with the Battalion covering a front of some 2,000 yards. After moving some 300 yards, the enemy fire became heavier, and advancement a further 300 yards was made by short rushes.

The Battalion halted and dug in, they were quite unsupported and remained there till dark when they were relieved by the 38th and 39th Brigades. The losses were heavy: 2 captains were killed, 7 officers wounded; 28 men killed, 170 wounded; and 7 missing.

After a bombardment, the 38th and 39th Brigades made a night attack, which was successful. The Turks were driven back to a position at Sannaiyat with one flank in the river and one on the Suwaikiya Marsh as before. An attack made in daylight by the 7th Division on this position was also defeated with terrible loss. And Kut was no nearer.

Second Attempt on Sannaitat

On 9 April, the 13th Division made an attack on Sannaiyat. The attack was a failure due to loss of control. Individuals reached and entered the Turkish position, but there were too few junior officers and experienced NCOs to push the attack home. The losses were again heavy, with 3 officers killed, 2 wounded and 5 missing; 7 men killed and 50 wounded, and 64 missing.

Operations from 6 April onward were much hampered by the marsh overflowing, flooding the trenches and that of the Turks. On 11 April, a violent thunderstorm preceded a waterspout and hurricane the following day. The left bank became impassably waterlogged and operations were moved to the right bank.

Action of Bait Isa, 17–18 April

This position might have been occupied when the troops withdrew from the unsuccessful attack on the Dujaila (Es Sinn) position, but was not.

The 8th Battalion relieved the forward Battalions of the 3rd Division early on 18 April and were continuously engaged in strenuous trench warfare till 19 May – with one day's rest for a wash and brush-up in a rest camp on 7 May.

After a third attack on Saaniyat by another Division on 22 April, Kut fell.

On 19 May, the Turks evacuated the Es Sinn position but held on to the trenches covering Kut in the Hai bridgehead on the south and the Khadairi Bend on the north. They also still held on to the Sannaiyat position.

Conditions were terrible: further military operations were prevented by the heat. The troops were worn out with diseases, dysentery, cholera and boils. There was a lack of vegetables. The temperature was 130° in the tents. The casualties from the heat in occupying the abandoned Es Sinn position were very heavy.

By the end of August, the 8th Battalion mustered only 8 officers and 279 men.

A long period of training at Amara followed and continued until December. During this time drafts arrived and by the end of November, the Battalion was 732 strong, and with the return of Colonel Glover from hospital, all ranks were ready for a renewed offensive.

Kut, 1917

The offensive began with a march on the Hai by the 3rd Corps – the 13th and 14th Divisions – while a bombardment kept the enemy in his Sannaiyat position. The 40th Brigade crossed the Hai at Atab around 8 a.m. of 14 December, dug a line of trenches on the east bank and were then withdrawn. On 20 December, the 40th Brigade made an unsuccessful attempt to force a passage at the Shumran Bend, in the daylight. Rain now stopped all operations for a fortnight. After much hard fighting, the Turkish position in the Khadairi Bend was captured on 19 January by the 9th Brigade. This meant that Kut and Hai defences could now be shelled.

Capture of the Hai Salient, 25 January–5 February

The 8th Battalion was now in reserve when the 40th Brigade successfully attacked the Hai salient on the east bank on the 25th January. The troops were strictly ordered not to go beyond the Turkish first line. On the west bank, the 39th Brigade was not so successful, in spite of very great gallantry.

On 1 February, the 40th Brigade made a further attack on the east bank of the Hai, the 37th on the west bank. The 8th Battalion led the way, capturing their objective, the Turks' second line, and then bombed outwards on both flanks until they had won the whole line between the Tigris and the Hai. A significant number of prisoners were captured, but a lot more Turks, who were coming to surrender, were mistaken for a counter-attack by another Battalion and were driven back by fire. After relief on 2 February, the Battalion was sent across to the west bank. They had no fighting, but had to endure a great deal of shelling, and 'overs' from rifle fire aimed at the front trenches.

On 15 February, the 8th Battalion took part in an attack on the west bank which proved to be the last effort in this period of trench scrapping and digging. The enemy surrendered en masse and the Hai salient was won. Casualty figures were: 3 officers wounded, including the Colonel, 4 men killed and 33 wounded. On 16 February, a terrific thunderstorm arrived with hail, flooded camps and trenches, just too late from the Turk's point of view.

Between 2–31 January, the 40th Brigade dug 7½ miles of fire and communication trenches, besides wiring and consolidating 4 miles of captured trenches.

It was all done in the open, but every man who fell whilst digging saved many lives which would have been lost by advancing across the open.

Two more desperate affairs were necessary before the Turks could be ousted from the area. The first was the forcing of the passage of the Tigris at Shumran by the 16th Division, the second the capture of Sanniyat, the prize of the 7th Indian Division.

The Turks' rear guard was well handled. On 25 February the 13th Division took up the pursuit. The passage of the Diyala by the Lancashire Brigade was one of epic of gallantry. In order to assist them, it was arranged for the 8th Battalion to be in the 'beetles', or armoured motor launches of the Gallipoli beaches, described by Hamilton (p.4) as barges which could carry 500 men under their own engines; (each 'beetle' had a 'brow' fixed on to her bows, like a drawbridge to be let down, over which men could pour ashore by fours; the same with mules, guns, supplies, they could all be rushed on land as fast as they could be handled on the beaches). They were to run ashore on to the Turkish trenches facing the river, and to rush the position. But one of the launches grounded on a sand bank and the engines of the other broke down, and the men were very fortunate to get out before the Turkish guns found them and consequently, the crossing was secured without the aid of the 8th Battalion.

Baghdad, 11 March

When the available troops entered Baghdad, the fighting continued.

The four objectives to achieve were:

- To pursue and complete the rout of the 18th Turkish Corps on the Tigris
- To seize the railhead at Samarra
- To fall on the flank of the 13th Turkish Corps which was falling back from Hamadan by Kermanshah in front of the Russians
- To take control of the inundations of the Tigris and Euphrates.

By pursuing these objectives, the paths of any possible Turkish offensives, down the valleys of the Tigris, Euphrates or Diyala, should be blocked. As Baghdad could be flooded out in the rainy season with all movement stopped, it was vital that the objective was to take control of the inundations.

The 8th Battalion, under Colonel Crocker, had some minor scrappings with the Turks in clearing the immediate neighbourhood of Baghdad. They captured a couple of barges with several hundred rifles, and assaults took the villages of Khan Jadida and Karsin (25 miles north of Baghdad).

The 13th Turkish Corps was moving west to join up with their 18th Corps on the Tigris. Owing to the revolution in Russia, the Russian pursuing army came to a standstill for want of food and ammunition. In consequence, two Cheshire brigades were sent to attack this Corps. But they were driven back and the 13th Turkish Corps crossed the Diyala and swung south-west towards its friends on the Tigris.

This junction was prevented by the action of Dogame (Duqma) on 29 March, when the 13th Division drove the 18th Corps back to the line of the Shatt El Adhaim, while the Cavalry Division held off the 13th Turkish Corps at Delli Abbas. In this battle, which took place on a marl plain, as hard and flat as a billiard table, the 8th Battalion was in reserve.

Ishan Bay, Commander of the 13th Turkish Corps, now made efforts to force his way into the plain from his base in the Jabal Hamrin Hills. News of this move came on 10 April, on the eve of an attempt to force the passage of the River Adhaim. The attack was postponed, and to support the Cavalry, facing the exits from the Jabal Hamrin, the 39th and 40th Brigades were at once sent across the desert, marching all night, to a point on the Sindiyeh light railway, some 6 miles from Chaliya – some 20 miles in all.

The 8th Battalion reached this spot about 5 a.m. and were at once sent forward in the front line on the right flank. A change of direction was ordered, but the left Battalion did not conform, and a gap of some 1,000 yards was caused. This was filled by reserve platoons. Owing to a threat to the right flank, other reserves were sent there, and the whole Battalion was deployed on the front line.

The Turks had been entrenched near Delli Abbas, but they had left their trenches and came in on long waves. The battle was an encounter battle, both sides racing for a small hillock which was the only local rising ground. 'Our men reached the crest first and lay down to shoot. Their steady fire, supported by the guns, soon checked the Turks, who gradually drew off as we gained fire superiority.' They fell back in the first instance a few hundred yards and later to a position some 6 miles away. The Turks were pursued for five days, by the end of which time they had disappeared into the hills. The Adhaim flank was now near, and the Shatt El Adhaim was forced on 18th April by the 38th Brigade, with a loss to the Turks of some 1,200 prisoners.

Casualties were: 6 officers wounded; 10 men killed and 54 wounded; Colonel Crocker was also wounded but remained at duty, and 1 officer died of wounds later.

The troops had suffered a good deal from the heat and lack of water, to say nothing from the maddening swarm of locusts which hopped incessantly over everything. Lying out in a 'cat stretch' all day in these conditions, in thick serge clothes was very difficult. Even after the battle, rest and sleep was almost impossible.

Affairs on the Shatt El Adhaim, 30 April

Despite its defeat on 11 April, the 13th Turkish Corps left a containing force at Deli Abbas and moved down the Shatt El Adhaim in an attempt to save Samarrah. After a great deal of marching they reached the defile where the Shatt emerges from the hills, but were too late to stop (our) crossing of the Adhaim or the capture of Samarrah on 24 April. They were attacked in position at Dahuba by the 38th Brigade on 24 April and driven back to another position close under the Jabel Hamrin range, where they awaited attack. The position was a strong one covering some 8 miles of front, with a 'splendid' field of fire over the open plain.

The main attack was made on the night of 29/30 April. The 38th Brigade was to threaten the enemy's left, while the 35th Brigade attacked the 'Boot' on the west of the river. The 40th Brigade attacked in the centre, the 8th Battalion on the left and the SWB (South Wales Borderers) on the right in front line. They advanced across the bare plain under the protection of an artillery barrage, and a screen of smoke and dust. They drove the Turks from their trenches, suffering few casualties. The enemy seemed surprised and retired behind Adhaim Village. The ground in front of the village was very much broken by deep nullahs running down to the river. This, combined with the rapid advance, caused some disorganisation in the companies, but the men pressed on into the village under a storm of rifle and machine-gun fire, and drove the Turks out with bomb and bayonet.

Both Battalions of the SWB and the 8th Cheshires swept on, missing the Turkish second line and strong points, where they had been ordered to halt and consolidate. Colonel Crocker was severely wounded and his Adjutant, 2nd Lieutenant Welsby, was killed, which may account for the failure of the Battalion to stick to the plan of attack. By now the battalions, much intermingled, had reached the enemy's gun line and captured some 800 prisoners.

Despite the Machine Gun Corps attempting to restore some order, a tremendous dust storm swept over the field. No one could see anything, nor could people at the back see anything, nor could people at the back realise what was happening to the two forward battalions, by now 2 miles ahead of their supports. Telephone communication was broken and the chain of command no longer existed.

The Turkish Commander was quick to seize his opportunity. Pouring in a heavy enfilade fire from the 'Boot', he sent in a smashing counter-attack of 2,000 men; hidden by the dust, right across the front of the 38th Brigade, which was advancing on the right. 'Our' guns could see nothing and so could not help. A bloody hand-to-hand struggle took place behind the screen of dust. The Turks regained seven of their guns and more than half of the prisoners.

However, thanks to a brilliantly handled Lewis gun, the Turks were held up long enough to enable (our) men to get back to the Turkish second line, where General Lewin had brought forward the machine guns of the rear Battalions when he saw the leading companies overshoot their objective. The Turks could not get forward from the village, out of which they were soon shelled when the dust storm subsided. By midnight the battle was won and the Turks were in full flight.

The strength of the Battalion going into action was only 247, their loss of 131 men made the engagement one of the bloodiest in this theatre of war. Casualties were: 1 officer killed, 24 men killed, 44 wounded and 58 missing.

The punishment the Turks received broke their morale and the bulk of the 13th Corps disappeared.

The following is a description of conditions giving an appreciation of the conditions endured by the soldiers: the heat was terrific. The thermometer stood at 110° in the shade and up to 130° in the tents. In the winter, when the snow was lying on the hills, water froze in the water bottles.

The constant dust storms parched the men's throats and filled the eyes and ears; locust, lice, dust flies, you could hardly get food in your mouth without swallowing a fly; rain, mud, mirage and dysentery, no fun, only the endless monotony of flatness and endless miles of trenches (Crookenden).

General Maude records in his dispatch that: 'Early on the 11th Lieut.-Gen. Marshall advanced rapidly on Baghdad, and entered the city amid manifestations of satisfaction from its inhabitants.' He notes that a state of anarchy had existed for some hours with Kurds and Arabs looting bazaars and setting fires indiscriminately. He points out that the Infantry guards soon restored order, and the British flag was hoisted over the city. He points out that a fortnight before Baghdad was liberated the enemy had been removing articles of military value and destroying property, he furthers that an immense quantity of booty, part damaged, part undamaged remained. Significantly, this included all the guns which fell into the enemy's hands at the capitulation of Kut in April 1916. His dispatch reports that on 19 March, British troops occupied Feluja, 35 miles west of Baghdad, driving out the Turkish garrison.

The 8th Battalion also fought at the second and third Actions of Jabal Hamrin (18–20 October 1917 and 3–6 December 1917). The Battalion was now some 800 strong, having been reinforced by many men who had served in France with the 5th and 6th Battalions.

General Maude's death on 18 November was a real sorrow to the troops. They held him in the high confidence which thoroughness in preparation and skill in leading always inspires.

The Batttalion, as part of the 13th Division, fought its last engagement as a whole at the Action of Tuz Khurmatli – part of the Kirkuk Operations (25 April–24 May 1918). In these operations, Colonel Crocker had his own column consisting of the 8th Battalion, half a squadron of the 12th Indian Cavalry, a section of mountain battery and a small R.E. Cable Section. This column bore a decisive part in the battle of Tuz Khurmatli (near Kifri) in which several small columns boldly rounded up outlying detachments of Turks.

In July 1918, the 40th Brigade was detached from the Division with the Division's artillery to support the drive to Mosul and north. The Division remained in the Mosul area on occupation duties until evacuated at the end of 1918. From here, the rest of the Division proceeded to Amara, where it was demobilised on 17 March 1919. Private William Ratchford was demobbed in April 1919.

James Ratchford was discharged from his military service on medical grounds in October 1917, and was awarded a Silver War Badge.

The following newspaper report cites the heroic action taken by him whilst on leave in November 1916, when he rescued two people from drowning in a dock at Liverpool.

SOLDIER'S HEROIC RESCUE: EXCITING DOCK INCIDENT: 21 NOVEMBER 1916

Private Jim Ratchford, of the Cheshire Regiment, whose home is 56, Chapel Street, Altrincham, has been rewarded by the Royal Shipwreck and Humane Society with £1 and a vote of thanks for his gallant rescue on the night of October 17th, of the Foreman of the Silloth Shed, who had fallen into Clarence Dock, Liverpool. A policeman had previously attempted a rescue, and was in the water some time in an endeavour to bring the man out of the dock. He finally became exhausted, and it was then that Ratchford jumped into the water and saved both the Foreman and the policeman. His gallantry in relation to the policeman has been brought to the attention of the authorities,

Private Ratchford in November 1892, was on the steamer off the Nova Scotia coast when the vessel ran on to a sandbank. He swam with a lifeline a good distance, and was the means of saving many lives. He is a well-known boxer and club swinger …

(Nantwich Guardian)

His bravery was officially recognised by the Liverpool Shipwreck & Humane Society, which bestows honorary awards, and brings to the attention of the authorities people who voluntarily put their own lives at risk by saving or attempting to save other people who are in danger.

With the reputation of the British Army now restored after its defeat at Kut Al Amara, the governance of the area was embroiled in a political and administrative dispute. The Mesopotamian Administration Committee, actioned to determine ultimate governance, was to rule for a British administration and not an Anglo–Indian administration for Basra; and an Arab authority for Baghdad.

(Adapted from *The Oak Tree: War and the Twenty-Second*.)

The 8th Battalion arrived in Mesopotamia from Gallipoli to take part in last attempts on the Tigres to relieve Kut-Al-Amara. Two battles were fought and casualties incurred. After Kut-Al-Amara fell, reorganisation of the rear was required to ensure supplies and reinforcements. After the fall of Baghdad, the 8th took part in other engagements necessary to clear the Turks from the area. It is noted that losses at Band-l-Adhaim were higher in proportion to the troops engaged than in any other Mesopotamian battle.

Middle East: Sinai and Palestine Campaign (Gaza and Jerusalem), November–December 1917

Egyptian Expeditionary Force (EEF)
27 October–7 November 1917 (Official Record)

After the failure to capture Gaza at the second battle on 19 April, there was no more serious fighting until the autumn. General Allenby was sent out from France to replace General Murray as G.O.C.-in-Command.

During August, the 53rd Division was withdrawn from the line to Belah, a mile or so south of the Wadi Ghuzze to undergo intensive training for the forthcoming operations. At this time of the year the country, which in the spring is green with crops and grass, is burnt up and there is no sign of vegetation other than a few fig trees. The soil itself is light and the passage of troops very soon cuts the surface up, resulting in clouds of choking dust. After the rains, this dust becomes thick mud, making transport movement almost impossible.

Training was carried out by day and night and much practice was given in the night marches. The water ration was cut down and no man was allowed to drink until after his return to the bivouac area. This was a real hardship in the heat of summer when marching in clouds of dust, but it proved its value later when the water supply failed north of Beerheba. During this period, the commanding officers and company commanders made numerous reconnaissances towards the Wadi El Sheria and Beersheba.

A third attempt on Gaza was planned on a more ambitious scale than the previous two, and was really an attack on Beersheba. This meant dealing with a front of some 30 miles. On the west lay Gaza, near the sea, which was now converted into a well-wired, well-dug, strong, modern fortress – offering no prospect of success to a frontal attack. Eastwards, the defences consisted of a series of field works, mutually supporting as regards gun fire, these positions ended at Tel Es Sharia. Then a gap of about 14,000 yards – 8 miles. The defences of Beersheba covered the last 4 miles.

The country beyond Wadi Ghuzze was an arid roadless desert, which required careful and thorough organisation to ensure a minimum provision of ammunition, food and, above all, water for the force, not only for the attack and assault, but also for maintaining a rate of pursuit that would ensure inflicting a very severe blow on the enemy.

The plan of attack was to feint in front of Gaza and the enemy right centre, and to make the main attack by XX Corps and mounted troops on Beersheba; to then turn west and to attack Tel Es Sharia, based on the water at Beersheba, without which further advance was impossible. If the water supply could not be captured in a single day, the alternative would be to return to the starting point. The question of water governed all the operations, tactical and strategical. The official history (p. 19) states that: 'Time after time in the days to come the Desert Mounted Corps was faced by the problem of whether to allow a beaten enemy to withdraw and re-coup or to founder invaluable horses by continuing the advance without water.'

Every ruse was employed to make the enemy think that the main attack would be on Gaza. One of the simplest, which had the greatest effect, was the preparation of a staff officer's portfolio, containing a mock agenda for a conference at GHQ indicating that the main attack would be made on Gaza, along with other items to make it appear genuine. This portfolio was taken out by the staff officer on patrol, who allowed himself to be chased by the Turks: he pretended to be wounded and dropped the papers. These were picked up and carried to the Turkish HQ and made a marked difference to their preparations.

On the night of 24 October, the 53rd division (XX Corps) which included the 4th and 7th Cheshire Battalions came up to the Wadi Ghuzze between Hisea and Shellal. The infantry had a very long and trying march, which needed careful reconnaissance and leading. Although 'done in', the Welshmen and Cheshire men had no thought but to make their point, and in the 159th Brigade only four men were admitted to the ambulance.

On the morning of 23 October, the Division was holding an outpost line running from El Baqqar to the Wadi Esh Shari and covering the left flank of the corps. The other Divisions, 60th and 74th on their right, and facing Beersheba: while the mounted troops were preparing to move further to the east. All movement was by night and done without a hitch, thanks to outstanding staff work and skilful leading by the young officers who acted as guides. During the day, the troops remained hidden at the bottom of the wadis, suffering severely from the heat.

The official history records:

> Hardly had dusk screened the land from view when the whole area swarmed into life like a stirring ant-hill. From Shellal the labourers hastened along the railway East of the Ghuzze, stripped of the brown camouflage which screened their uncompleted work, set about plate-laying and the screwing up of the pipeline. Regiment after regiment of Australians, New Zealanders and Yeomanry, rode South-eastward, till by 30th October there were 12,000 men and as many horses at Asluj and Khelasa. Closer to the enemy's front advanced the infantry's divisions. Huge columns of camels, having picked up the loads stacked ready for them in long rows, filed out across the Ghuzze almost in silence, to disappear in the dust raised up by their own feet. The supply tractors ground

their way forward, the lorry columns, railed up from Cairo, were at work; half a dozen wheeled divisional trains marched with their burdens. Each column had its allotted route, not necessarily on an existing track; for movement across country was not much more difficult in the light of a moon nearly full. The transport column of the Desert Mounted corps alone from Tell El Fara on the night of the 28th was six miles long. By midnight vast clouds of dust hung over the teeming plain. But by dawn all was still once more.

On the night of the 28/29 October, the Brigade was pushed forward to cover the construction of the branch railway to Karm, and on the following night an outpost position was taken up on the forward slopes of the Wadi Hanafish, opposite to the Turkish Rushdi system of trenches. By the morning of 30 October, the 53rd Division was dug in on this line. It held a line of hastily entrenched posts on a front of some 7 miles, to secure the left bank of the Corps. It was also to be prepared to attack the Turks if they retreated from Beersheba towards Gaza. The main infantry attack was on that part of the Turkish line South of the Wadi es Saba.

The 60th Division advanced with the 'utmost gallantry' and was supported by guns of all calibres, and actually carried the whole of the enemy's first line by half past eight in the morning, by two o'clock in the afternoon the two attacking divisions had swept over the enemy's second line. The 74th Division then swung to their left and took out the enemy's works to the north of the Wadi Saba. Meanwhile, the cavalry had worked their way round to the north-east of the town to cut off the escape of the enemy, and captured some 1,300 prisoners and eight guns. The town itself was entered by the cavalry just after sundown, and the water supply, which was essential to the later operations, was secured.

On 31 November, the 53rd (Welsh) Division moved across to the right flank of the force to the north of Beersheba and was soon in touch with the enemy in the mountains in front of Towal Abu Jerwal. On this day, the 4th Battalion (Cheshire) marched 20 miles and no men fell out. The advance of the 53rd was apparently a great surprise to the enemy who hurriedly collected portions of four divisions to oppose them. The task of this division from now until the final breaking of the Turkish centre on 6 November, was to hold off this large enemy force, an object which could only be attained by continuous fighting under very difficult conditions.

The hill country into which they now penetrated was very different to that which had previously been encountered in Palestine. Instead of soft sand or hard earth, which soon disintegrated into fine dust, they found barren stony country, intersected by deep wadis at the south end of the central ridge of the Judean Hills, which runs north and south with only one break from Dan to Beersheba.

Further to the north it may be likened to the backbone of a flatfish, the centre bone being the ridge up which the only main road in the hills runs from Beersheba through Jerusalem to Nablus and to the north, and its side bones are the ridges intersected by deep wadis running east and west, to the Jordan Valley and Dead Sea on the one hand, and to the fertile plain to the other.

This central ridge, which rises up to 3,000ft near Jerusalem, gradually decreases in height as it goes south, and the last few miles just north of Beersheba are very broken, with wasis running east, south and west in a 'bewildering manner'. It was in this country that the action of Khuweilfeh took place.

The second phase of the operations could not be undertaken until six days after the capture of Beersheba, due to the necessity of building up a sufficient forward reserve of ammunition and supplies, and a bad *khamseen* (a very hot wind) which blew continuously for three days.

Meanwhile, the XXI Corps had captured the whole of the enemy's first line at Gaza, and were inflicting heavy casualties on the garrison by continuous bombardment and by the repelling of many counter-attacks.

The main objective of the second phase was the water supply at Sharia, which involved the capture of the Rushdi system of trenches, by the 10th (London), 60th (Irish) and 74th Divisions. At the same time, the 53rd Division was to attack Tell El Khuweilfeh and protect the right flank of the XX Corps. In the main attack, everything depended on the progress of the 74th Division on the right, who had to capture all the enemy trenches on the east of the railway. These were strongly held by the enemy and bristled with machine guns, and in addition, the attack had of necessity to take place over very open ground. The 74th, however, though only after very heavy fighting, captured all their objectives, taking many prisoners. With their right flank secured, the 60th (London) and 10th (Irish) Divisions quickly stormed the main system.

The 60th (London) Division then captured the water supply at Sharia and the 10th (Irish) Division took the Hareira Tepe redoubt. The 53rd Division beat off enemy attempts on the right flank, and on the 7th, a gap was ready for the cavalry. The enemy evacuated Gaza and mounted troops set off in pursuit.

The operations of the 53rd (Welsh) Division began on 3 November, when the Division advanced in two main columns, the 159th Brigade on the left. It is almost impossible to ascertain exactly what took place in this battle, which lasted from 3–6 November. The ground in this district was extremely broken and no large-scale maps were available. The map in use, 1/250,000, had been prepared by Kitchener and Condor in 1882, and whilst very accurate, it was not contoured, and minor features, though of great tactical importance, were not shown; added to this, much of the fighting took place at night.

The weather was hot and the men suffered severely from thirst. The Brigade moving on Ain Kohle, had several skirmishes with the enemy.

The Division attacked Tell El Khuweilfe on 4 November. The 159th Brigade had the secondary task of capturing Ain Kohle, but with only one battery to support it, it was unable to get forward. The position was not captured in spite of the efforts of the other two Brigades and the Yeomanry. But this costly attack had prevented the enemy from withdrawing any troops, or guns, to deal with (our) main attack.

During this period, a *khamseen* was blowing and everyone suffered greatly from thirst. The advance had begun with all the troops carrying two bottles, but with transport difficulties it could be 48 hours before further supplies could be brought up. In addition, units were very scattered and in some instances were in such exposed conditions that supplies could only reach them by night.

As an example of the difficulty of keeping touch in this particular district: during the battle, a party of Turks got in between the left of the 160th Brigade and the right of the 4th Welsh and the 4th Cheshires, and sniped advanced Divisional Headquarters. It was impossible to get at them, and eventually they were dispersed by an 18-pounder which was (with great difficulty), manhandled into a position from which it could deal with them.

After this the 53rd Division was to have the task of protecting this flank preventing the enemy coming through the hills from Hebron, while the main force moved on by the coast roads. The prospect of success now depended on the valour of the 53rd Division.

Casualties, Cheshire Regiment: 4th Battalion: 6 men killed, 2 officers and 48 men wounded; 7th Battalion: 1 officer and 2 men killed, 1 officer and 21 men wounded.

Operations Leading to the Capture of Jerusalem, 8 November–9 December 1917

The following is an account of the part played by the 4th and 7th Battalion Cheshire Regiment in the liberation of Jerusalem, 1917.

From 8 November until the end of the month, the troops of the 53rd (Welsh) Division (known as Mott's Detachment) remained in the Khuweilfeh area to protect the right flank of the force. The pursuit was now transferred to the coastal plain on the line of the Huj to Ended. This required all available transport, so that the 53rd (Welsh) Division was, for the time being, immobilised.

The character of the hill country formed a great contrast to the fertile plain. In place of orange groves, vineyards and cultivation were barren and boulder-strewn ridges, separated by narrow valleys. There was the occasional cultivation on terraces, and in the bottom of the valleys. It was a hard, barren, stony country. One fairly good road ran from north to south through Nablus, Jerusalem and Hebron to Beersheba. Water was scarce, being mostly rainwater stored in rock cisterns. During this period reconnaissances towards Hebron were carried out, and the infantry spent much time improving the main road running north and clearing up the Khuweilfeh battlefield.

On 19 November, the weather broke and there was a heavy rain for two days, and the temperature dropped considerably. The troops were still dressed in khaki drill shorts and serge jackets and steel hats, but all spare clothing had been left behind at Belah, and the troops had a very uncomfortable time with no chance of a change of clothing. In addition, the boots began to give them trouble. They had been on sand or soft ground for about two years, and although they had marched the whole way from the Suez Canal, as soon as the rains came, coupled with stony ground in the hills, the boots gave way, the stitches which had been weakened by wear in the sand broke, and the soles came off the boots. On the march up to Dhaheriveh at the end of the month, many men had to use their puttees wrapped around their boots to keep the soles on. Before the final advance to Jerusalem, however, a small quantity of new boots was received, with the worst cases re-shod.

Some idea of the difficulty of maintaining this detached force in the hills will be gained from the supply arrangements. The supplies of the Division during their advance along the hills came by railway to Karm. They were carried by 'caterpillar' tractors to Bir Abu Irqaiyiq, and then by mules along the old Turkish railway to Beersheba, and then by lorry to Hebron, and finally delivered to the troops by camel.

El Mughar, 13 November 1917

Though this name appears on the Cheshires Colours, neither the 4th or 7th Battalions were engaged in the battle. They are included in the troops engaged because it was only the presence of the 53rd Division, moving alone up the hill country through Hebron on Jerusalem, that enabled the main advance to continue along the coastal plain, unmolested on its right flank. The account of what the Division did in its essential task has been overshadowed in the histories by accounts of the fighting in the plain. The City of Jaffa was occupied as a consequence of the Battle of Mughar Ridge.

Capture and Defence of Jerusalem, 7–30 December 1917

The attempt to capture Jerusalem without bringing it into the zone of operations by cutting it off from the north having failed, it was now decided to attack it directly from the west. In this plan, the 53rd Division moving up from Hebron was to cooperate by covering the right flank of the attack and threatening Jerusalem from the south. The 158th Brigade was left behind to guard the road back to Beersheba.

On 3 December, the 159th Brigade moved from Burj El Bemareh to Dilbeh by Ed Dhaheriye. On 4 December, the Brigade was 3 miles south of Hebron, and on 5/6 December, the 7th Battalion took up an outpost position 3 miles north of that town.

On the morning of 6 December, the 7th Battalion advanced, acting as advanced guard at the north of Beersheba, and in the evening the line through Beit Fejjar, a total of 23 miles.

At dawn on 7 December, the 7th Battalion moved against Sherifeh, a strong hill, held by the Turks and, assisted by the 4th Welsh, captured the hill by 7 a.m. Meanwhile, the 4th Battalion were advancing on the right of the main road, conforming with the movements of the 7th Battalion. During the day the weather broke again, and fog or mist descended on the hills and blotted everything out, though the Mount of Olives was to be seen in the distance through breaks in the clouds. Bethlehem lay about 2 miles away directly in front, and enemy artillery could be seen in action shelling the main road, but (our) guns could not reply as orders had been given that no fighting was to take place in the immediate vicinity of Bethlehem or Jerusalem.

The night of 7/8 December was not a night that would be forgotten by those who were unfortunate enough to be in the hills. The state of the road prevented all transport movement, and no rations could be delivered. Off the main road there was a sea of mud, and though mules and donkeys could move with difficulty, no other forms of transport could move at all. The main road had been much improved by the Germans, and had been very well engineered up the steep hillsides. However, the stone of the district is soft limestone and as the wheels of the German lorries were, in the absence of rubber, tyred with iron, the roads had been terribly cut up and by now were a soup of liquid grey mud, and still full of potholes. Teams of artillery horses came down wholesale on the slippery roads, and blocked the traffic, camels' legs splayed out and split the poor creatures at the quarters, and many of the drivers died of cold. There was no shelter, and the driving rain beat down unmercifully and everyone was wet through, cold and miserable.

Thinking that he had come up against the main Turkish defences of Bethlehem, and influenced by the failure of the transport, in face of instructions to respect at all costs the Church of the Nativity and Rachel's Tomb, General Mott decided to wait until the next morning before resuming the advance.

On the morning of 8 December, the 4th Battalion were withdrawn to the main road, and on arrival found the previous day's rations waiting for them. For the first time in weeks there was bread and fresh meat, but as the bread was soaked with water, and there was no dry fuel, the troops remained hungry. The line advanced a little, but the Turks were still holding Bethlehem, and were shelling the troops and main road with 5.9s and .77 guns, and a small number of casualties were sustained.

During the night of 8 December, the Turks withdrew from Bethlehem, and the 159th Brigade passed along the main road west of the town in the early morning of 9 December, some three hours after the Turks had left. The road had been blown up in places, and the advance was slow, but by midday the 4th and 7th Battalions arrived at Mar Elias, with the remainder of the Brigade on the main road as far as the outskirts of Jerusalem and joined hands with the main army which had moved eastwards from the coast. Here they swung round and took up an outpost line facing due east from Mar Elias to Jerusalem.

Jerusalem surrendered on 9 December.

Casualties between 3–9 December for the Cheshire Regiment were: 4th Battalion: 9 men killed, 2 officers and 61 men wounded; 7th Battalion: 1 officer and 3 men killed, and 2 officers and 35 men wounded.

On the morning of 9 December, the 159th Brigade were on the line of the Jerusalem–Bethlehem Road, facing about east from the walls of the city to Mar Elias, in the order 5th Welsh, 4th Welsh, 4th Battalion, 7th Battalion. During the day, the Brigade was ordered to cover Jerusalem from the north and north-east, and advance down the Jericho Road.

Jerusalem stands some 2,600ft above sea level, and is surrounded by hills a few hundred feet higher, except at the south-west, where the Valley of the Kedron falls away steeply to the Dead Sea. Jerusalem stands at the head of this valley, one branch of which separates the Mount of Olives from the east side of the city, and the other branch, the Valley of Hinnom, runs round the south of the city.

The ground south and south-west of the city is broken by steep-sided deep valleys, and there are no roads running east from the Jerusalem–Bethlehem main road. So, to get to the Jerusalem–Jericho road from the south one must go right round, or through the city and on to the Mount of Olives, which lies east of the city.

In order to carry out the plan, the 4th Welsh went round the west and the north of Jerusalem and attacked the Mount of Olives, where they were held up. The 5th Welsh were accordingly sent to assist via the south and east of the city, but were held up by the deep valleys, and only got forward after considerable delay. In the meantime, the 4th Battalion captured some high ground east of Mar Elias, from which fire could be brought to bear on the Jerusalem–Jericho Road. The 7th Battalion were held in reserve, and in the evening provided the guards on the gates of Jerusalem.

On 10 December, the 4th Welsh occupied the Mount of Olives, but the Turks still held the ground to the east of it.

On 11 December, the 4th Welsh occupied Aziriyeh (Bethany) and the 4th Battalion Abu Dis, taking some prisoners.

On 12–13 December, the line remained in approximately the same position. On 14 December, the 7th Battalion who had been finding guards in Jerusalem, advanced through the line held by the 5th Welsh, and seized a ridge, in the face of enemy fire. On the same day, a post held by the 4th Battalion (Bullocks Post) was raided by the Turks but was subsequently reoccupied by the Battalion.

On 16 December, the 4th Battalion was withdrawn to Bethlehem. On 17 December, 7th Battalion attempted to capture Ras Ez Zamby, but were unsuccessful. It was captured by the 16th Brigade on 21 December.

About 23 December, the weather broke and there were heavy falls of rain accompanied by high wind, and the weather became very cold.

On 24 December, the 4th Battalion were moved up to Sir John Grey Hill's house on the top of the Mount of Olives. This house, which now forms part of the Jewish University, stands right on top of the ridge where the view is magnificent. To the north can be seen ridge after ridge, culminating in the high ground around Tel Asur (captured on 9 March), to the west lies Jerusalem, and to the south-east the Dead Sea. A few hundred yards south-east along the ridge stands the German Hospice, later used as XX Corps HQ.

This house was in full view of the enemy, but strangely enough it was not shelled, even during the attacks which took place a few days later.

Christmas Day was a hopeless day of sleet and driving rain, and all the valleys became full of water, and the roads deep in mud. Owing chiefly to the weather conditions there was very little activity during the day.

On 26 December, in the evening, the 4th Battalion were relieved by the 7th RWF (Royal Welch Fusiliers) and went back to billets in the Convent of Notre Dame De France in Jerusalem.

On the night of 26/27 December, the Turks attacked to recapture Jerusalem but without success. On the divisional front, the chief attacks were on White Hill and Zamby, and though the Turks managed to capture the former they were shelled off, and it became for the moment no man's land.

During the day, the 4th Battalion were 'standing to', ready for action if neces-sary, and in the late morning two companies were sent up to the west slope of the Mount of Olives to make a new road for the artillery limbers. Owing to the heavy rain of the preceding few days, it was quite impossible for wheeled vehicles to travel across country, quite apart from the fact that the ground was intersected with wells. The guns, or rather howitzers, were in position just behind the German Hospice on the Mount of Olives, and the only road along which ammunition could be brought ran right along the top of the hill and was there-fore in full view of the Turks. The task was to break down walls, and make a new track lower down the hill.

Nearby was the Hospice, the tower of which was being used as an O.P. (Observation Post), and strangely enough the Turks did not shell it, probably because it was German property. From the top a most wonderful view of the battle could be obtained, and every movement of both sides could be clearly followed. Observers on the tower saw a Turkish force, which had massed in the bottom of a wadi preparatory to launching an attack on Zamby, caught in the fire of our how-itzers and almost completely wiped out.

On 28 December, it appeared that the Turkish attack was losing its power and the 159th Brigade was put in the left of the 158th Brigade to join up with the 60th Division, as the latter advanced. During the day, the 4th Welsh reoccupied Ras Eztawil, and the 7th Cheshire Battalion a ridge further north.

On 29 December, the Turkish opposition died away and they were in full retreat. The 4th Battalion left Jerusalem at 1 a.m. and during the day occupied in succes-sion Hizmeh and Jeba and the high ridges beyond without very much difficulty.

As a result of these operations, the Turks, instead of recapturing Jerusalem, found themselves 6 miles further away and Jerusalem was now out of range of artillery fire.

The *New York Herald* front page of 11 December carried the headline: 'Jerusalem is Rescued by British After 673 Years of Moslem Rule'

Prime Minister David Lloyd George described the capture as: 'A Christmas present for the British people'. (The British Museum).

Britain would hold Jerusalem until the end of Mandatory Palestine in 1948.

Tell Asur, 8–12 March 1918

At dusk on 6 March, the 7th Battalion moved out of Rummon Rise to occupy Nejmeh by dawn, followed by the 4th Battalion who were to remain in support at Kilia. The 7th Battalion accomplished a very fine performance. After a long and trying march over most difficult country, intersected by deep ravines and the precipitous Wadi Dar El Jerir, both objectives were reached, the enemy outpost being entirely taken by surprise and driven off both hills.

At 17.00 hours on 8 March, the 159th Brigade began an attack, the 4th Battalion supported by the 7th, having to capture Pear Hill, and then to move on to Kefr Malik.

British soldiers marching into Jerusalem. (National Library of Israel Collection)

The 159th Brigade operated in two columns owing to the impassable nature of the Wadi El Jerir. The right column composed of the 4th and 7th Battalions was directed on Munatir Ridge, Pear Hill and Kefr Malik, the left column, composed of the 4th and 5th Welsh, on Dar Jerir and Drage's Hill. The 4th Welsh was under the command of the Colonel Pemberton of the 4th Battalion.

At 4.30 a.m. on 9 March, the 4th Battalion cleared Munatir under considerable opposition, but was held up by very heavy fire from Pear Hill. However, artillery was turned on and at 7.45 the hill was gallantly stormed by the 4th Battalion in spite of the bare open approach. The 7th Battalion was now moved forward and both Battalions cleared the Wadi Dar El Jerir, on the line Taiyibah–Munatir.

At 5 p.m., the forward part of Rock Park was captured under heavy shell fire by the two Cheshire Battalions.

On 10 March, the 7th Battalion, after intense bombardment of the ridge which was very strongly held, drove the enemy off and entered Kefr Malik about 2 p.m.

In this battle, the 4th Battalion (Cheshire) lost 2 officers and 5 men killed, and 4 officers and 35 men wounded; and the 7th Battalion (Cheshire), 3 men killed and 1 officer and 27 men wounded.

Chapel Street Prisoners of War

It is known that at least three soldiers from Chapel Street were captured as German prisoners of war (POWs). Two of the men were brothers in different units. All the men had divergent experiences and endured disparate captivity. The effects of war and imprisonment stayed with the men for the rest of their lives: Reports state that effectively they served a *Durance Vile* (a very long prison sentence).

Sergeant Martin de Courcy, 22nd Cheshire Regiment 10421

Sergeant Martin de Courcy was taken prisoner at Ypres. His official documentation shows him held captive in January 1915, and in March 1915 he was moved to Wittenberg. The prison camp was situated on a sandy plain some 10½ acres in extent at a place called Klein Wittenberg, 2 miles from the city. It consisted of eight sections and compounds, with a capacity of 13,000. Wittenberg is 59 miles south-west of Berlin and was the cradle of the Reformation (Pope-Hennessy: 1919).

The *Chester Observer*, 22 January 1916, gave a detailed account of the experiences of a soldier from the 1st Cheshire Regiment who had been imprisoned at Wittenberg for fourteen months. It was reported that, 'He went out to the front with a smartness that did credit to his regiment but he returned from Germany a cripple on crutches, with both feet amputated from the instep, through the fearful neglect he suffered while in captivity at the camp in Wittenberg.'

The soldier described his experiences:

For over six months they never allowed me to write home or receive parcels, and I never had a change of shirt for over six months, and they had taken my cap and great coat when I was captured. The Germans took delight in keeping us short of clothing as well as food. Through marching about without boots in the wet and snow, my feet soon began to swell up and pain me so horribly that I could not walk. It was not until three captured British doctors came to the camp that my feet received attention, and one of them, Captain Vidal, told me that through my feet being neglected for so long, gangrene had set in and was spreading so rapidly, that to save my life, it was necessary to cut both of my feet at the instep.

An epidemic of typhus broke out at Wittenberg camp. Reports state that due to the weakened condition of the men the 'scourge' soon spread, with the result that the German doctors 'took fright and bolted'. The camp was left in charge of the Russians, who were the most numerous of the prisoners and the captured doctors, three of whom subsequently died. Further reports state that the cruelties worsened until the American Ambassador visited the camp. This was in direct conflict of the Hague Convention (Chapter: 11 Prisoners of War Hague Convention. 1907).

Patrick de Courcy, 4th Hussars (The Queen's Own) 4163

Patrick de Courcy entered the theatre of war on 16 August 1914, embarking on the SS *Atlantian* with the Household Cavalry and Cavalry of the Line, 3rd Cavalry Brigade, 4th Hussars (The Queen's Own). He was an experienced cavalryman having previously served with the 8th Hussars (The King's Royal Irish) during the Boer War. The regiment took part in the Battle of Mons and the Great Retreat.

Battle of Mons

The Gazette (Official Public Record) states that by 22 August, the BEF (British Expeditionary Force), had arrived in Mons and taken up positions along 20 miles of the canal that ran east to west through the town. The BEF were to hold the canal for 24 hours and dig trenches to the south side of the canal. If the line couldn't be maintained, the fall-back plan was to withdraw south to the pit villages and slag heaps and form another defensive line.

The battle began on the morning of 23 August, when the Germans opened up an artillery barrage on the British positions. For a time, the battle was in favour of the British riflemen, who were trained to fire fifteen times per minute and hit targets at 300 yards, and who were so accurate the Germans thought they were facing batteries of machine guns. The combined rifle fire, machine-gun and artillery fire devastated the German columns. They changed tactics from marching in columns towards the BEF, to adopting more open, looser formations. They also had superior manpower (160,000) and 600 artillery.

By the afternoon, the British position was untenable. Casualties were mounting and the Germans had begun crossing the canal in force. By 6 p.m., in a coordinated withdrawal, new positions were taken a few miles south of Mons as the British prepared their second line of defence. The French 5th Army also retreated and this left the British right flank exposed. At 2.00 a.m. on 24 August, Sir John French ordered a general withdrawal of troops. A total of 1,638 British servicemen lay dead on the battlefield.

Cavalryman de Courcy was captured by the Germans as a prisoner of war at Mons. Records reveal he had been held a prisoner at Minden, some 40 miles from Hanover. Minden camp was described as 3 miles from the town and surrounded by farms. It consisted of a big square with six blocks of huts. Its capacity was 18,000 (Pope-Hennessy: 1919).

Research into ICRC documents reveal he qualified for release as a repatriated prisoner, and he arrived in London on 20 January 1918, via Boston, Lincolnshire. Boston was used as a repatriation port from 1916–19. Bilateral agreements and exchanges of prisoners under certain circumstances existed before the Armistice of November 1918. The countries involved in the repatriation schemes were principally Switzerland, Holland and Denmark (Treaties, States Parties and Commentaries Geneva, 6 July 1906).

His condition was described as 'Mental?' and he was referred for treatment at the 1st London Hospital. It is possible he was suffering from the condition that was then described as 'barbed-wire disease', or a Psychasthenia psychosis; a psychological condition recognised by the German War Ministry in 1917. Jones & Wessely (2010) state that though this condition was recognised in captivity, the post-release effects were not recognised. The authors point out, however, that the consensus of psychiatric orthodoxy of the First World War in Britain and Germany, concluded that POWs were protected against 'war neurosis'.

Michael Groark(e), 1st Battalion Cheshire Regiment 9278

Documentation held by the International Swiss Red Cross shows Michael Groark(e), of the Cheshire Regiment, as a POW *'desparu en nov'*; but there are no further details about his capture date or captivity. He was awarded the 1914 Star (known as the Mons Star).

Repatriation of Prisoners of War from Germany 1918

At the end of 1918, there were some 140,000 British POWs in Germany. By December 1918, some 264,000 prisoners had been repatriated. A very large number of these prisoners were set free en masse and sent across Allied lines without any shelter or food. This created difficulties for the receiving Allies and many of the prisoners died from exhaustion. In spite of protests from the English and French governments, this 'inhuman' procedure was continued. (*Statistics of the military effort of the British Empire during 1914–1918*, p.730).

The released POWs were met by cavalry troops and sent back in through the lines in lorries to reception areas, where they were fitted with boots and clothing and dispatched to the ports in trains. Large camps were set up in Dover and Hull and all combatant prisoners were directed there upon arrival. Arrangements were made for prisoners returning from Germany or the Baltic via Switzerland, Holland, Copenhagen or directly across the lines in France and Belgium.

Extracted from Hansard, 14 November 1918, and related sources

Extra medical supply and transport staffs are being sent out, and besides a very large stock of emergency parcels from the central Prisoners of War Committee, 30,000 full kits and 30,000 rations for a month will be sent immediately as a first instalment. Red Cross workers, V.A.D.'s (Voluntary Aid Detachment), and medical personnel now in Holland will be retained for the present to cope with the emergency if required. Besides such Dutch ships as may be available, seven ships carrying 9,000 persons have been ordered to Holland to bring back the prisoners; and three of them sailed yesterday.

All the combatant prisoners, on their arrival in England, will go to large reception camps, where it is hoped they will receive the heartiest of welcomes, their medical wants will be attended to, and arrangements will be made for giving them leave as soon as possible.

Official recognition

All returned British prisoners of war received a framed letter of appreciation dated '1918', from King George V and Queen Mary, on their release and return to Great Britain at the end of the First World War. This was written in the King's own hand and was reproduced and distributed in the form of a lithograph. It was written in blue pen on embossed paper; the King requested that each man's name was written on the letter. The letter's distribution was arranged by the Mobilisation Department of the Central Prisoners of War Committee. There is no record in the Royal Archives of the names or numbers of those to whom the message was given (*Daily Telegraph*). It was the first ever mass communication from a reigning British monarch.

It read:

Buckingham Palace 1918

The Queen joins me in welcoming you on your release from the miseries and Hardships, which you have endured with so much patience and courage. During these many months of trial, the early rescue of our gallant Officers and Men from the cruelties of their captivity has been uppermost in our thoughts. We are thankful that this longed for day has arrived, and that back in the old Country you will be able to once more enjoy the happiness of a home and to see good days among those who anxiously look for your return.

George RI. (Rex Imperator – King and Emperor).

[It is difficult to find information on POWs, as in many cases it does not exist. Prisoner of war camps were inspected during the war by the International Red Cross. Details for the above prisoners were obtained using the ICRC (International Committee of the Red Cross) archives.]

PART TWO

Those Who Also Served

The Royal Army Service Corps (RASC)

Men from Chapel Street
James Barrett; James Gormley T/30671 Driver; David Norton T1/879.

On 1 August 1914, the Army Service Corps comprised 498 officers and 5,933 other ranks. The figures for other ranks rose exponentially to 156,190 for 1915 and by 1 August 1918 the figures were: 10,477 officers and 314,693 other ranks.

The Royal Army Service Corps was divided into three main sections:

1. *Horse Transport Section*. In 1918, some 40,000 servicemen served in the Horse Transport Section including Saddlers and Farriers in France; 6,439 in Egypt; 8,450 in Salonika. The chief depots were at Aldershot and Woolwich.
2. *Mechanical Transport Section*. The maximum number of vehicles was in the region of 125,149 mechanically-propelled vehicles, including 53,107 motor lorries; 31,098 pneumatic-tyred vehicles and ambulances; and 36,953 motorcycles. The Corps provided drivers for all the field ambulances. It conveyed the ammunition for all branches of the Royal Artillery and for the tractors of the heavy Siege Artillery. It also provided a large number of clerks at Headquarters and in the various Commands. The chief depots were at Winchester and Bulford.
3. *Supply Section*. At the outbreak of war, the Corps was providing rations for 186,400 men and forage for 28,742 animals. By the time of the Armistice, 11 November 1918, it was feeding 5,500,000 men and 895,000 animals. The chief home depots were at Deptford, Avonmouth, Northampton, Newhaven, Reading, Southampton, Leeds, Glasgow, Liverpool and Manchester.

The casualty figures for the Corps were: 16,000 officers and other ranks either: Killed in action, dying of wounds, disease (5,872), wounded, prisoners of war or missing presumed dead.

In recognition of 'Splendid work' during the war, the distinction of 'Royal' was conferred by the King under Army Order 362 of November 1918.

The following record gives an interesting insight into one man's recognition of service and pension rights:

William Taylor T/20230 (50 Chapel Street)

William Taylor served with the ASC (Army Service Corps) as it was originally called. He enlisted in the Horse Transport section in 1903, extending his service for a further eight years with the Colours in July 1905. He was qualified in the management of horses, and was a head groom and driver. His records reveal he had tattoos on both arms; on his right arm of a Japanese lady, and the left arm of a lady and feathers. In 1908, he was treated for gonorrhoea.

He completed eight years' service with the Colours, and he rejoined his unit for mobilisation at the outbreak of war on 5 August 1914 in Dublin. In the same month, he went to France and served with the BEF (British Expeditionary Force) until December 1915, when he was then sent to Aldershot for discharge after completing thirteen years' time expired. Private Taylor maintained he received a letter about this time stating if he again enlisted for a further period of eight years, he would complete twenty-one years for a service pension. On the basis of this he attested in July 1916, and embarked for Salonika.

His early record reveals that his overall conduct was good, though in 1916 he was reprimanded for having a light in his tent after 'lights out'. In May 1918, he was tried in Malta, for neglecting to obey orders and for conduct to the prejudice of good order and military discipline; he served a period of fourteen days' detention.

In July 1917, his health suffered from a shell burst and he suffered breathing problems whilst serving with 237th Company, and in early May 1918 he was invalided from Salonika in 1919, with Bronchopneumonia. He was awarded a Silver Badge (B287596), 'on account of disabilities contracted following service overseas in a theatre of operations', under King's Regulation 392. xvia. This regulation applies to qualifying persons who are 'no longer physically fit for war service and are *surplus to military requirements* (having suffered impairment since entry into the service)'.

Up until 1921, Private Taylor's right to a pension was in dispute. In a statement citing his service details in December 1920, and written in a strong hand, he requested his case be looked into and with a favourable circumstance. However, the authorities, who had misplaced his records, stated that as they were not registered with the Ministry of Pensions in Chelsea there was no pension entitlement; they also discounted his military service during the war as 'normal' attestation.

In February 1921, Taylor's previous service was acknowledged. In a Statement of Service he was classed as a 'Regular', having enlisted for three years and nine years Reserve Service; he was consequently awarded a thirteen years pension.

Royal Flying Corps

MOTTO: *Per ardua ad astra* (Through adversity to the stars).

Men from Chapel Street

Walter Oxley; Thomas O'Connor; James Murray.

In 1912, King George V signed a royal warrant establishing the Royal Flying Corps (RFC). It consisted of a Military wing and a Navy wing, with training provided by the Central Flying School.

Mechanisation

By August 1914, the Royal Flying Corps personnel consisted of 103 officers and 1,097 other ranks and was very much a fledgling unit. There was a shortage of serviceable aeroplanes and a severe shortage of experienced pilots available at home and to act as instructors. At the outbreak of war, the country was practically without an aeroplane engine industry. Out of a total of sixty-six aeroplanes, only twenty at the Central Flying School were operational, and the rest were worn out or unserviceable through accident. From 1912–14 the RFC were still in a process of aircraft testing for artillery spotting, aerial photography and night flying. Three of the standard Government designs of aeroplanes were in a state of transition with production a mixture of Government design, private design and using different contractors. The military wing of the RFC was equipped almost entirely with machines of Royal Aircraft Factory design, with the Navy preferring to develop British private enterprise by buying machines from private firms.

Consequently, for the first six months of the war, engine supply was met entirely by France. In May 1915, orders were placed for 2,260 aeroplanes with 123 delivered, some 191 contractors were working directly for the Military Aeronautics Directorate in the manufacture of aviation equipment, with 721 sub-contractors employed on aviation work. The mechanical transport required for the Royal Flying Corps also increased considerably with 351 vehicles with the Expeditionary Force, 370 at home and 640 on order.

Official statistics reveal that due to the impossibility of obtaining the required number of skilled men for the technical work of the corps, recruits, unskilled and partly-skilled men were trained as armourers, acetylene welders, blacksmiths, coppersmiths, magneto repairers, fitters, wireless mechanics and operators, clerks, storemen, sailmakers, drivers and cooks. And in photography, camera repairing and rigging. A whole industry was evolving around aviation with hundreds of different firms building aeroplanes and parts; motor-car firms, coach-builders, upholstering and furniture firms. To meet the demand for labour, women and apprentices were employed. By 1917, the number increased to over 1,000, and it was not uncommon for a firm to have capital of £1 million. In 1916, the Air Board was formed to co-ordinate effort and to ensure adequate supplies of material reached both the RNAS and RFC.

Flying

Training was carried out at the Central Flying School and by May 1915, 109 finished pilots were turned out. Training in flying was being also carried out at eleven different stations, with 215 pilots and 19 observers under instruction; during this same time, 153 officers gained the Aero Club certificate, the first step in the training of a pilot. By March 1917, there were 78 Service Squadrons and 59 Reserve Squadrons formed. More stations were needed for supply to meet the demand and 3 Service and 9 squadrons were under formation. Squadrons were stationed in huts, billets or under canvas. Between September 1916 and March

1917, 1,193 pilots graduated with 300 on the waiting list. By March 1918, the numbers of personnel increased to 18,286 officers and 144,078 other ranks.

Vivian (1921), in discussing the great inventions of the war, recognises the synchronisation of engine-timing and machine gun, which rendered it possible to fire through the blades of the propeller without damaging them. He notes how the early days of crude bombing developed from bombs thrown by hand and bombs strung like apples on wings and undercarriage, to bomb racks with releasing gear. As reconnaissance work and aerial photography became integrant to the work of the RFC, he denotes how photographs gave information the human eye had missed and could, for example, reveal the impression of ground marched on by troops which the aerial observer was unable to detect. Ariel photographs were exclusively used in compiling the British Army's highly detailed 1:10,000 scale maps introduced in mid-1915. Wireless became available and this further expanded the role of the RFC. By 1915, each corps in the BEF was assigned an RFC squadron solely for artillery observation and reconnaissance duties.

The RFC took part in nearly all the major battles of the First World War. The role of the RFC very quickly extended to aerial battles, strafing – attacking repeatedly with bombs or machine-gun fire from low-flying aircraft – to the bombing of military airfields and strategic bombing of industrial and transportation facilities. Casualty figures killed and missing on the Western Front from July 1916 to July 1918 show 3,610 men with an average of 200 hours flown. To meet the increased demand for Flying Officers, recruitment extended from the existing arrangements in England to Scotland, Canada and South Africa, but the official statistics note that the project in Ireland was discontinued.

On 1 April 1918, the Royal Flying Corps and the Royal Naval Air Service were merged into the Royal Air Force.

Footnote: Under the Infractions of the Armistice Clauses, it is noted that though Germany did surrender some 2,000 aeroplanes, 600 were absolutely unfit for use; 1,000 were in bad condition; and about 200 were observation aeroplanes.

Canadian Expeditionary Force (CEF)

Men from Chapel Street
Hugh Arnold, Sapper 11 (4th Field Company) 2nd Division Canadian Engineers

The Canadian Expeditionary Force was created by the Canadian Government for overseas action in the First World War. It relied on volunteers as Canada did not see conscription until 1918.

Throughout most of the war, each division had three field companies of engineers and one pioneer battalion. After training in England, the 4th Field Company disembarked in France as part of the 2nd Division and was immediately sent to the front where it experienced trench warfare first hand. The company saw its first major action at the St Eloi craters. It supported operations during the Somme offensive and was later involved in the fall at Courcelette.

Winter 1916–17

The Official History of the Canadian Army records that a pattern of limited hostilities continued throughout the winter of 1916–17, established against the enemy formations of the 6th Bavarian Reserve and 12th Reserve Divisions:

> The largest number of raids mounted in January 1917 was one by the 20th and 21st Battalions (4th Brigade) on the 17th. These units were represented by some 860 specially trained all ranks, assisted by sappers of the 4th Field Company. The object was to inflict casualties, take prisoners and booty, and destroy enemy dug-outs three miles east of Lens in the area of the Lens-Bethune railway. Parties of the 18th and 19th Battalions carried out demonstrations on the flank as the assault went in at 7.45 a.m., a time when the enemy usually relaxed his alertness following morning 'stand down'. Corps and divisional artillery provided adequate fire support in which Canadian machine-gun units joined, while special Royal Engineer units laid down smoke. In one hour the attacking force, operating on a 850-yard front, blew up more than 40 dug-outs, exploded three ammunition dumps, captured two machine-guns and two trench mortars and destroyed several others taking 100 prisoners of the 11th Reserve Division. Canadian casualties numbered about 40 killed and 135 wounded. The enemy, recording the repulse of 'an extraordinarily forceful undertaking' by the Canadians, reported losses of 18 dead, 51 wounded and 61 missing.
>
> (Nicholson, 1962)

The Fourth Canadian Infantry Brigade History of Operations details the raid under the heading:

A Famous Raid

January 1917. To signalise the New Year, the Brigade resolved to put on a more extensive raid than had yet been attempted. This was carefully planned with a smoke barrage. The attack was to be made by two Battalions, the 20th and 21st in two waves, with two complete Companies from each Battalion. The first wave to capture the German front line trench and clean it up; the second to pass over in the open and go on to the final objective. One half of the first wave was to follow the second to help in the final work.

After waiting several days for a favourable wind, on the 17th a force of 930 men entered the enemy's trenches in daylight and made a new record for the British Front. The results were highly satisfactory. The number of enemy dead is unknown, but the prisoners included 1 officer and 99 O.R.s. Our casualties were 36 killed, 73 wounded, and none missing.

For the purpose of the raid, the Brigade was reinforced by the M.G. Company of the Household Cavalry and an M.G. Company and the Artillery of the 1st Canadian Division.

A message was later received, which read: 'The Army Commander congratulates the 2nd Canadian Division on the great success of their enterprise, and is pleased that their careful and through preparations have been rewarded with such substantial results.'

The War Diary states there was a heavy snowstorm on the night of 17 January. The raid was carried out by 4th Infantry Brigade accompanied by fifteen sappers. The purpose of the raids was to inflict damage on the enemy, plunder resources, take prisoners and wear down morale of the enemy, to gain information, i.e. maps which would give details of the front line, machine-gun posts, bunkers, communication trenches, defensive positions behind the front line.

The raid resulted in the following Military Medal commendation:

Sapper 11 Hugh Arnold.
   Northeast of Calonne, January 17th, 1917.
   For conspicuous gallantry and devotion to duty.
   This sapper went forward with the assaulting party troops and personally blew a number of enemy dugouts, emplacements, and large bomb store. In one case he cut the chains of a machine gun with explosives and assisted in bringing it back.
   Awarded the M.M. on 7/2/17 (Byng).
   LG date for award 12/3/17.

The next planned major operation would be the assault on Vimy Ridge. From March onwards, the Canadians raided the enemy lines every night. The purpose was to destroy fortifications, supply lines and barbed wire defences. Intense training and the development of new tactics were essential to the preparation. A replica of the ridge was built behind the Canadian lines and platoon-level tactics employed. Each platoon member was trained to carry out all platoon responsibilities, including those of the men above them and beside them, detailed maps were issued to soldiers not just officers and NCOs, front-line troops were briefed, and each platoon was given a designated task by the commanding officers rather than orders received by remote chain of command. Added to this was constant patrolling of the enemy defensives and training in the use of counter-battery fire and German weapons, which could be turned once trenches were taken.

The War Diary entry reads: 'New Establishment is based on the New French System. Each platoon is trained and organised as an independent fighting unit. Each platoon is composed of four sections, 2 of which are called "Rifleman", one a Lewis Gun Section, and the fourth a grenade section.'

Further entries reveal that extensive training took place in musketry, grenade practice, bombing and bayonet fighting. Lectures were given with regard to German weaponry including *flammen-werfer* (flame thrower) and the application of lessons learned at Verdun. Added to this, the 4th Field Company were also engaged in the underground fortifications of Zivy Cave.

Vimy Ridge was a military engagement fought as part of the Battle of Arras, situated in the Nord-Pas-de-Calais region of northern France. The objective was to take the German-held ridge, which stretched from Vimy to Givenchy-en-Gohelle; 7km long on a north-west to south-east alignment and across the top of a further escarpment – the Lorette Spur, lying on a more east–west alignment and which gave control of the surrounding Artois plain. An unsuccessful attempt had been made by the French in 1915, which resulted in 150,000 casualties. For the first time, four divisions of the Canadian Corps were to be brought together, joined by the British 5th Infantry set against three divisions of the German 6th Army. The 2nd Division were tasked with the capture of Thelus and Farbus Wood.

Vimy Ridge is Canada's most celebrated military victory and marked its coming of age as a nation. Despite many casualties, the triumphal assault was a turning point in the war in terms of precision planning and execution, raising both the national pride of Canada and the morale of the Allies. The Germans acknowledged the Canadians as worthy opponents, granting them the accolade of 'Stormtroopers', a term used in connection to its own elite infantry. Some 97,000 Canadians saw engagement in the initial attack.

The 4th Field Company took part in further successful battles including Passchendaele, the third battle of Ypres, which is synonymous with the imagery of WWI soldiers fighting trench warfare in quagmires of mud (due to the collapse of an ancient drainage system and torrential rain). The battle was fought on a terrain which Currie considered unsuitable; his objections were overruled and he predicted the ensuing casualty rate with great astuteness. They fought at the Battle of Amiens, and the victory secured there is now considered to be decisive in terms of determining the outcome of the war. On 11 November 1918, the 4th Field Company also fought in the last battle of the war, on the last day of the war when they took part in the liberation of the town of Mons from German occupation, showing a supremacy of Allied victory that was intended to live in the German psyche, and mark the end of the Great War.

During the war, some 40,000 Canadians served as engineers.

Hugh Arnold's Attestation Papers can be viewed on the website of the Canadian Expeditionary Force (CEF): www.bac-lac.gc.ca/eng/discover/military-heritage/first-world-war/personnel-records/Pages/personel-records.aspa

Thomas Arnold and John Bagnall
(Service unidentified at this time)

Royal Irish Rifles

Men from Chapel Street
Patrick Burke (47 Chapel Street)
John Hanley (10 Chapel Street)
James Hughes, 6th Battalion Service number 2579, died of wounds 7/6/17
John McNicholas
Michael Quinn (42 Chapel Street); originally from Co. Mayo, religion C of E
Patrick Quinn (42 Chapel Street); originally from Co. Mayo, religion C of E
Thomas Riley, 16th Battalion Service Number 45813
James Scarfe Jnr

Thomas Scarfe
James Sheehan

The Royal Irish Rifles Regiment was officially formed in 1881. During the First World War, the Regiment raised twenty-one battalions, serving alongside the regular battalions and seeing action on the Western Front, Egypt, Palestine, Salonika, India and Dardanelles.

In 1921, the Royal Irish Rifles Regiment was renamed as the Royal Ulster Rifles. After undergoing various merges and amalgamations, in 1992 it was joined with the Ulster Defence Regiment to form The Royal Irish Regiment.

1st Battalion Royal Irish Rifles

The 1st Battalion of the Irish Rifles Regiment came under the command of 25th Brigade in 8th Division, until 3 February 1918 when it transferred to 107th Brigade in 36th (Ulster) Division. It suffered very heavy casualties, losing two Colonels during offensives. In one attack in 1916, the battalion was down to one surviving officer and sixty men.

The 36th (Ulster) Division was made up of members of the Ulster Volunteers Force, previously called the Ulster Volunteers who were a Unionist militia founded in 1912 to block Home Rule for Ireland. In 1913, they organised themselves into the Ulster Volunteer Force to give armed resistance to the prospective Third Home Rule Act (enacted in 1914). The 36th (Ulster) Division formed thirteen additional battalions for three existing regiments: the Royal Irish Rifles, the Royal Irish Fusiliers and the Royal Inniskilling Fusiliers. The Royal Irish Rifles had traditionally recruited in Dublin and the surrounding areas.

German Spring Offensive, 1918

Battle Honour St Quentin, 21–23 March 1918
Edward Lowe, 1st Battalion Service number 10990, died 21/3/18

21 March: Operation Michael

The 1918 Spring Offensive (Kaiserschlacht) was a major German military offensive. In an attempt to break the deadlock on the Western Front, a series of four attacks was planned with the code names: Michael, Georgette, Gneisenau and Blucher-Yorck. Operation Michael was launched from the Hindenburg Line in the area of Saint-Quentin, France with the objective to breaking through the Allied lines and outflank the British forces, which held the front from the Somme River to the English Channel. The other offensives were divisionary tactics designed to divert the Allied forces from the main offensive on the Somme. British suffered heavy losses with some 20,000 dead and 35,000 wounded. The British were forced to retire.

The 1st Battalion War Diary for 20 March reveals that a German offensive was expected the following morning, with the information coming from prisoners. The German artillery bombardment began at 4.40 a.m. on 21 March.

The bombardment hit targets over an area of 150 square miles in the biggest barrage of the war. Over a million shells were fired in five hours. Trench mortars, mustard gas, chlorine gas, tear gas and smoke canisters were concentrated on the forward trenches, while heavy artillery bombarded rear areas to destroy Allied artillery and supply lines.

In detail the diary reveals:

> 4.30 a.m. Heavy bombardment of Battle Zone, Front line, Redoubts & gun positions by artillery of all calibres. Gas shell extensively used. 'Man Battle Positions' being received at 4.40 a.m. 'A' Coy (Capt. Reed, M.C.) occupied Battle Zone Trenches RIGHT; 'B' Coy (Capt. Brown, M.C.) Battle position LEFT; 'C' Coy Counter Attack Trenches. 'D' Coy Redoubts right of Bn.HQ Fog was thick until 12.30p.m. Intense shelling of Battle Zone developed about 9.a.m. particularly 'B' & 'C' Coy trenches, the Battalion being on all day until ordered to retire on HAMEL about 11.00p.m.

There follows a list of known officer casualties, including Captain Brown recorded as wounded and missing.

On 22 March large bodies of men and transport were seen along St Quentin–St Simon Road. The Battalion engaged until ordered to fall back to position near Happencourt, until dusk, when the right flank was seriously threatened. Orders were received on the line Sommette Eaucourt–Cugny behind the Canal. At 11.00 p.m., the Battalion then moved across country crossing the canal at Pithon by the light railway bridge and proceeded to billets at Eaucourt, arriving 3 a.m.

The diary for 23 March reveals that the village was shelled with 5.9 guns and the battalion moved out north-west and west and dug in. Heavy fighting was heard in the direction of Ham and Esmert Hallon. Orders were received at 1 a.m. to move to higher ground south of Cugny. They dug in with the enemy occupying woods on the opposite height, which lasted until 11 p.m. The 14th Division then fell back and the Gloucester Entrenching Battalion on the right were retiring, when they were rushed by the enemy and the Commanding Officer ordered a retirement on Beaumont, where the battalion reassembled at 1 a.m. and dug in. There were some casualties and the Battalion HQ in the sunken road was rushed, without casualties.

By the end of the Spring Offensive, the 36th (Ulster) Division had suffered 7,310 casualties.

Engagements of Royal Irish Rifles World War One

Battle of the Somme
Battle of Cambrai (1917)
Battle of Messines (1917)
Battle of Passchendaele
Battle of the Lys (1918)
Battle of Courtrai (1918)

Battle Honours Awarded for Service in the Great War

Mons, Le Cateau, Retreat from Mons, Marne 1914, Aisne 1914, La Bassee 1914 '17 '18, Armentieres 1914, Ypres 1914 '15 '17 '18, Nonne Bosschen, Neuve Chapelle, Frezenberg, Aubers, Somme 1916 '18, Albert 1916, Bazentin, Pozieres, Guillemont, Ginchy, Ancre Heights, Pilckem, Langemarck 1917, Cambri 1917, St Quentin, Rosieres, Lys, Bailleul, Kemmel, Courtrai, France and Flanders 1914–18, Kosturino, Struma, Macedonia 1915–17, Sulva, Sari Bair, Gallipoli 1915, Gaza, Jerusalem, Tell Asur, Palestine 1917–18.

Tribute to the Royal Irish Rifles by King George V

> I recall the deeds of the 36th (Ulster) Division, which have more than fulfilled the high opinion formed by me on inspecting that force on the eve of its departure to the front. Throughout the long years of struggle, which now so gloriously ended, the men of Ulster have proved how nobly they fight and die …
>   George V

The Ulster Tower Memorial

On the first day of the Battle of the Somme, 1 July 1916, the 36th Ulster Division went into battle in their sector of operations, which stretched from the edge of Thiepval Wood to the village of Hamel. The Division took a German strongpoint called the 'Schwaben Redoubt', and made the furthest advance of any Division north of the Bapaume Road. However, they were forced to withdraw due to German counter-attacks. The 36th Division suffered over 5,000 casualties on that one day alone (killed, injured, missing or prisoner of war).

A symbolic memorial tower stands at the place where the men fought and died. The 'Ulster Tower' is a replica of Helen's Tower from the Clandeboyne Estate in Ireland, where the Ulster Division trained. The memorial was built in 1921, from public subscriptions and is a memorial to the soldiers of the Ulster Battalions, and the Regiments of the Royal Irish Fusiliers, Inniskilling Fusiliers and the Royal Irish Rifles who fought in this area of the Battle of the Somme.

In the park, a plaque has been placed by the Royal Irish Rangers to the memory of the 36th Irish Division and to the nine Victoria Cross recipients. There is also another memorial beyond the park which commemorates the Irish men from the Orange Order who fought here.

Further information from www.irishsoldier.org

Email: sommeassociation@btinternet.com

Notable War Memorials

Thiepval, France; Menin Gate Memorial Ypres, Belgium; Island of Ireland Peace Park Messines, Belgium; Irish National War Memorial Gardens, Dublin; Guildhall Derry, stained-glass window commemorating the 10th, 16th and 36th Irish Divisions; 8th Infantry Division Memorial, Aldershot.

More information:
Royal Ulster Rifles Regimental Museum
5 Waring Street
Belfast
BT1 2EW
rurmuseum@yahoo.co.uk

Royal Dublin Fusiliers

The Royal Dublin Fusiliers Regiment raised six battalions for service in the First World War.

Regimental Battle Honours

Le Cateau, Retreat from Mons, Marne 1914, Aisne 1914, Armentieres 1914, Ypres 1915 '17 '18, St Julien, Frezenbuerg, Bellewaarde, Somme 1916 '18, Albert 1916, Guillemont, Ginchy, Le Transloy, Ancre 1916, Arras 1917, Scarpe 1917, Arleux, Messines 1917, Lanemarck 1917, Polygon Wood, Cambrai 1917 and 1918, St Quentin, Bapaume 1918, Rosieres, Avre, Hindenberg Line, St Quentin Canal, Beaurevoir, Courtrau, Selle, Sambre, France and Flanders 1914–18, Helles, Landing at Helles, Krithia, Sulva, Sari Bair, Landing at Suvla, Scimitar Hill, Gallipoli 1915–16, Egypt 1916, Gaza, Jerusalem, Tell Asur, Palestine 1917–18, Kosturino, Struma, Macedonia 1915–17.

Easter Week, 24–29 April 1916

Two events during the Great War in 1916 were to have a profound effect on Ireland. Both centred on Dublin City and its people. They involved the Royal Dublin Fusiliers (largely Catholic soldiers of Dublin) and other Irish regiments who had gone to war in defence of their country, Ireland, against the Germans, and who were supporters of Home Rule; and a dissident group of Irishmen, who wanted Ireland to be a self-determining republic, and who seized the advantage of war and the absence of a large majority of able men to mount an armed insurrection, known as the 'Easter Rising', in pursuit of that ideal with arms smuggled into the country from Germany.

The report of 'The Royal Commission on the Rebellion In Ireland of 1916' states that the policing of Dublin fell to the Dublin Metropolitan Police Force, who were undermanned, as many of its officers had enlisted in the army; the military authorities keen to recruit from a body of men with 'splendid physique and a fine record of honourable service'. Also, as the force was unarmed officers were forced to withdraw. The rest of Ireland was policed by the Royal Irish Constabulary (RIC) who were a quasi-military force and whose officers were trained in the use of carbines (long-arm firearms). It was stated that if Dublin, like Cork and Belfast, had been policed by the Royal Irish Constabulary – 1,000 armed and disciplined policemen, knowing the city, and with 1,000 soldiers available to them – the anarchists would have been quelled. Another factor was that the Special Crimes Branch (which each of the forces had) was not especially qualified to deal with political crime.

Due to these circumstances the 4th, 5th and 10th Battalion Royal Dublin Fusiliers, amongst other Irish and English regiments, were called on to quell the insurgency. Parts of the City of Dublin were so badly shelled by the army that Dublin resembled the ruins of Europe. Many of the civilian population were killed, including children. The Dublins took the formal surrender of rebels.

16th (Irish) Division, 48th Brigade (9th Battalion)

Men from Chapel Street
Edward Birmingham, service number 6127: Enlisted 4/11/14 (Aged 39 years old). Discharged on 1/5/18 awarded the Silver War Badge (407232).

Gassing of the Irish

War Diary Extracts for 26 & 27 April
Battle of Hulluch, France

> Wind changeable to calm wiring principally in front of CHALKPIT SALIENT. Bombing Officer, Intelligence Officer and several bombers went out and bombed the crater opposite POSEN ALLEY, where work was carried on nightly, between 12 m/n & 2.a.m. Gas attack was signalled back from A coy at 4.45 a.m. there was an almost imperceptible breeze from the EAST, a dense cloud of black gas and smoke was between us and the sun and gradually spreading over our lines, at 5.20 a.m. a heavy bombardment of our front line trenches began during which time heavy rolls of whitish gas was seen to come from all the sap heads in front of Hulluch sub section and the POSEN CRATER and pass over the lines of the 49 Inf. Bde on our left; the bombardment lifted to our reserve and communication trenches and under the gas the enemy entered a section of our front trench where nearly all the men were killed or wounded: they were put out again and the line held for the rest of the day by the remnants of the two coy reinforced by B coy from the reserve trench and later (at dark) by A coy of 9 Dublins from GUN TRENCH.

The diary goes on to state that the night passed in evacuating wounded, burying the dead and identifying where possible. A strong barrage was put up with some shelling and repairing trenches. The dead were evacuated at night.

War Diary for 29 April

> At 3.20 a.m. the gas attack signal was given again and the gas issuing from saps, one cloud from about Puits 14 bis and one from Hulluch Front met over our front and shelter down on our trench, without wind to move it, no

bombardment or attack took place and scarcely a man could survive this attack the battalion moved out tonight relieved by the 47th Bde. The casualties from gas poisoning were more severe than on the 27th owing presumably to gas clouds meeting and remaining stationary and concentrated over the trenches. Our casualties during the two days were (officers names) and casualties Other Ranks killed 81; 53 wounded; 122 gassed; 102 missing; total casualties OR's 368 leaving Battalion strength 578. The 47 Brigade relieved the 48th tonight … Identification of dead carried on today and burials at night.

An appendix remarks and references state that those 'missing' are believed killed.

Armistice Day

On 11 November 1924, an extraordinary Armistice Day parade and ceremony took place in the City of Dublin. Two contingents of marching the First World War veterans set off from different routes, namely Dame Street and the rebuilt General Post Office (GPO) – the birthplace of the Republic of Ireland (Proclamation of 1916: Easter Rising). They converged at College Green for a wreath-laying service and the unveiling of the Guillemont Cross (bound for France). Present at the service was Lord French Lord Lieutenant of Ireland (1919–22). A wreath was laid by Mary Kettle on behalf of her husband Tom Kettle MP (9th Battalion, died 9/9/16 at Ginchy), leading Irish Nationalist protagonist for Home Rule and founding member of the Irish Land League, who has no known grave.

The Celtic Cross was 13ft 6in high made of solid granite weighing 3 tonnes. It was enclosed by a metal railing measuring 15sq. ft. It was inscribed in Irish and English: 'Do chum Gloire De agus Onora na hEireann' (To the Glory of God and Honour of Ireland); 'In commemoration of the victories of Guillemont and Ginchy Sept 3rd and 9th 1916 in memory of those who fell therein and of all the Irishmen who gave their lives in the Great War RIP.'

As two enormous wreaths were carried over the heads of men to the base of the cross, the Union flag was hoisted over Trinity College and a sea of thousands and thousands of men sang 'God Save the King'. (www.britishpathe.com)

What made the Armistice Remembrance service remarkable was that it took place some eight years after the Easter Rising, after the Irish War of Independence and the Irish Civil War. It puts to rest the myth that Irish soldiers were to be forgotten on their return to Ireland. Clearly these were vociferous Irishmen, proud of their victories and proud to have done their duty in defence of Ireland at a time of international crisis.

On 27 April 2001, the Irish government officially acknowledged the role of the soldiers of the Royal Dublin Fusiliers who fought in the First World War by hosting a state reception at Dublin Castle for the Royal Dublin Fusiliers Association.

The Regiment lost over 4,777 men during the Great War.

Connaught Rangers

Men from Chapel Street
John Kelly (Service unidentified at this time)
Patrick Mahone (Service unidentified at this time)

The Connaught Rangers made famous the song, 'It's a Long Way to Tipperary'. It saw service during war on the Western Front, Gallipoli, Mesopotamia (Iraq), Salonika and Palestine. During the first two months of the First World War, the regiment raised four Service and Reserve battalions.

The New Armies

5th (Service) Battalion (29th Brigade in 10th (Irish) Division)
Saw service at Gallipoli in 1915; Salonika in 1915; Palestine 1917 and the Western Front in 1918. The National Museum of Ireland (Curator: Military History) states some 15,000 Irishmen were at Gallipoli. It is said: 'The Sea at Gallipoli ran red with Irish blood.'

6th Service Battalion (47th Brigade in 16th (Irish) Division)
Saw service on the Western Front at the Battle of the Somme, losing 23 officers and 407 other ranks. The Battalion was decimated during the German Spring Offensive, when in one week it lost 22 officers and 618 other ranks. Those surviving were transferred to the 2nd Battalion the Leinster Regiment.

Battle Honours for the Great War
Mons, Retreat from Mons, Marne, 1914; Aisne, 1914; Messines, 1914, '17; Armentieres, 1914; Ypres, 1914, '15, '17; Langemarck, 1914, '17; Gheluvelt, Nonne Bosschen, Festubert, 1914; Givency, 1914; Neuve Chapelle, St Julien, Aubers, Somme, 1916; '18; Guillemont, Ginchy, St Quentin, Bapaume, 1918; Rosieres, Hindenburg Line, Cambri, 1918; Selle, France and Flanders, 1914–18; Kosturino, Struma, Macedonia, 1915–17; Sulva, Sari Bair, Scimitar Hill, Gallipoli, 1915; Gaza, Jerusalem, Tell Asur, Megid-18.do, Sharon, Palestine, 1917–18; Tigris, 1916; Kut al Amara, 1917; Bagdad, Mesoptamia, 1916.

During the Easter Rising, some of the Connaught Rangers in Dublin on leave volunteered for attachment to other units of the British Army, namely, Royal Irish Fusiliers and Royal Dublin Fusiliers. The 3rd Battalion was involved in patrols, capturing volunteers and weapons in the outlying provinces.

The Connaught Rangers Association holds papers, diaries, publications, letters, photographs and memorabilia associated with the Connaught Rangers. It also organises lectures and trips to battle sites and can be contacted by the following:

The New Connaught Rangers Association,
King's House,

Boyle,
Co. Roscommon,
Ireland
Website:conaughtrangersassoc.com/about/

Royal Horse and Field Artillery

The Royal Field Artillery was the largest branch of the Royal Artillery, providing howitzers and medium artillery near the front line.

Men from Chapel Street

John Brennan; George Jones; John Leonard; Frank O' Shea; Acting Corporal John Naughton, service number 31313, disembarked France 8/5/15; John Scanlon, Driver Service number 78279; John Taylor, service number 1002380; Peter Taylor; Thomas Taylor; Corporal Felix Tyrell, Driver Service number 67210, disembarked France 22/9/14; William Tyrell, Gunner Service number 24682; James Tyrell, Driver Service number 15445; Simon Tyrell, Gunner Service number 243924; Thomas Wyatt Driver Service number 35246.

William Curley, Gunner 81st Brigade 'C' Battery, service number 78269; died of gas wounds 28/12/18.

Vincent Maguire (McGuire on the Roll of Honour), No. 8 Chapel Street

Vincent Maguire, service number 77441, served as a signalman in the 9th Brigade, 28th Battery, which was part of the 7th (Meerut) Division of the Indian Army. The Brigade saw action in France in 1914, Mesopotamia in 1915 and Palestine in 1917.

He experienced many dangerous exploits, family reports state that Vincent Maguire had served in India and France, where he was gassed with mustard gas and suffered trench foot.

In April 1918, he was aboard the ship HT *Kingstonian*, a steam ocean liner used for transport, and en route back to France with the 52nd Division, when it was torpedoed by German submarine U-boat (UB-68).

The War Diaries record the dramatic events as follows:

> 1 April. Orders received to move to Alexandria. All horses handed into remounts, all harness to Ordanance.
> 3rd April. Alexandria Docks. Arrived about 5 a.m. and embarked on H.T. Kingstonian.
> 4th April.
> At sea. Sailed at 4.30 p.m. in a convoy of 26 ships including escort.
> 10th April.
> H.T. Warwickshire torpedoed about 6.30 a.m. 82 miles from Bizerta.
> 11th April.

H.T. Kingstonian torpedoed West of Sardinia at 5.33 a.m. Troops transhipped to H.M.S. Lychnis, who came alongside. Some of the men who were sent away in the ship's boats were picked up by H.M.S. Berberis. Two men were named as killed by the explosion. 6 B.O.R.s [Brigade Other Ranks] missing, wounded by explosion 2 B.O.R.s. H.T. Kingstonian taken in tow by H.M.S. Berberis, & eventually beached on coast of Sardinia. A Lieut. and 35 B.O.R.s were left to guard kit.

12 April. Marseilles.

Arrived early morning, disembarked, & after being fitted with missing clothing, marched to no. 8 Camp.

17 April. Grand Laviers.

Arrived Abbeville Station 8.a.m. & marched to billets, no guns, wagons, horses or baggage.

The diaries note that from 23–26 April the Brigade was still trying to draw supplies of horses and ammunition. Already exhausted by 27 April, the Brigade marched 26 miles to billets, only to find watering facilities poor. The next day they marched a further 13 miles to Linzeux, leaving at 10 a.m. and arriving at 2.00 p.m., and here the watering facilities were bad. This entailed another march on 29 April of 15 miles to Crequy, here the watering facilities were good but the billets were scattered.

The ship was destroyed by the Germans on 29 April 1918. The Navy tug HMS *Dalkeith* was repairing the *Kingstonian* when the submarine UB-48 torpedoed and sunk both the ship and tug, resulting in one death on the stranded ship and nine on the salvaging tug.

This was not the end of the signalman's heroic adventures.

In 1919, Vincent Maguire was awarded the Distinguished Conduct Medal (DCM) for his bravery and gazetted with the following citation:

77441 Sig.V. Maguire, 28th Bty., 9th Bde., R.F.A. (Altrincham)
(LG 3 Sept. 1919).

Has shown greatest coolness and contempt of danger in maintaining communications under heavy fire as Battery Signaller, and especially during the recent open fighting when he has spared no effort to maintain the line, frequently under heavy shell fire.

The Norton Family

The Norton family of Chapel Street were a large family who were very well known in the Altrincham area. Mrs Charlotte Norton, a widow, was heralded for her exceptional patriotism; she was the proud mother of eight sons (some of whom had seen service during the Boer War and in India), all of whom volunteered to fight for the country in the spirit of heroism that was prevalent to the era.

She was also grandmother to twelve of her married sons' children, including five of her widowed son Thomas.

Their service was as follows:

Sergeant-Major Joseph Norton, Grenadier Guards; Sergeant-Major John Norton, an Instructor with the King's Own Royal Lancashire Regiment; Sergeant Michael Norton, a Bomb Instructor who served in the Cheshire Regiment before transferring to the Prince of Wales's Volunteers (South Lancashire) Regiment; James Norton Royal Rifle Corps (who died in the service of country at Modder Spruit); David Norton, 2nd Cavalry Regiment and Robert Norton, Driver with the Army Service Corps (who enlisted at the same time); Thomas Norton, who volunteered for the Royal Garrison Artillery.

Mrs Norton's eighth son, Peter (twin of David), was a gymnastics instructor and reputable boxer who also volunteered his services, attempting to enlist with the Black Watch Royal Highlanders. However, Mrs Norton appealed against this on her own behalf and that of her two invalid daughters, and was successful in gaining his absolute exemption from military service.

Company Sergeant-Major Joseph Norton, 3rd Battalion Service number 10330

Company Sergeant-Major Joe Norton was a Musketry Instructor with the Grenadier Guards. At the outbreak of war, he acted as instructor to the New Army, before giving this up to volunteer for service in France, disembarking in November 1914. As part of the 2nd Battalion (1st Guards Brigade) he took part in the Battle of Loos (28 September–8 October). In 1916, he was transferred to the 3rd Battalion (2nd Guards Brigade) which engaged in the later stages of the Battle of the Somme at the Battle of Flers-Courcelette (15–16 and 20–22 September), the capture of Lesboeufs (25 September), and the Battle of Morval (25–28 September). He sustained injuries during the Battle of the Somme, and on recovery returned to the regiment and was seconded to the 4th Battalion. He retired from the Grenadier Guards in 1923 after twenty-one years of service.

In September 1916, during the battle of Flers-Courcelette, part of the Somme Offensive, Sergeant-Major Norton showed his gallantry when, under the cover of night, he led a search party to find and rescue the future Prime Minister Harold Macmillan, whom he had witnessed falling, injured.

Macmillan had been leading an advanced platoon in no man's land. They were caught by machine-gunners from the left flank. Macmillan, severely wounded in the left thigh and with a bullet in his pelvis, rolled down into a slit trench and lay for ten hours, waiting for nightfall and rescue. After spending the time in a morphia-induced sleep, drifting in and out of consciousness; feigning death as Germans skirted round the shell hole and reading the classical playwright Aeschylus's *Prometheus* in the original Greek (afterwards stating: 'It was a play I knew very well, and seemed not inappropriate to my position …'), he further recollected: 'Company Sergeant-Major Norton, a splendid man, I can see him now … bottom of shell hole, sloped rifle:"Thank you, sir, for leave to carry you away," as if he'd been on a parade ground!' Macmillan's legs being unable to take his weight necessitating stretcher-bearers to be brought in, with the noise of their movements bringing shelling from Ginchy village.

Thorpe (p.57) states that in May, Macmillan's father had, at his request, sent him a batch of books, including *Prometheus Vinctus*. It would seem that the following last verse in the play was Macmillan's point of reference:

> Now his threats walk forth in action
> And the firm Earth quakes indeed.
> Deep and loud the ambient Thunder
> Bellows, and the flaring lightening
> Wreathes his curls around me.

Sergeant-Major Norton was also mentioned in dispatches three times, with one citation reading:

> He showed conspicuous gallantry in March in the fighting round Ervillers (a village between Arras and Bapaume). He was commanding the men of battalion headquarters, which came under very heavy shell fire for some hours, and severe casualties incurred. He superintended the removal of wounded men under this heavy fire, and greatly helped on their removal. By his gallantry and devotion to duty he set an inspiring example to all ranks, and his conduct throughout nine days heavy fighting was magnificent.

His actions entitled him to wear the emblem of the oak leaf cluster with his medals. He was also the recipient of the Italian Bronze Medal for Military Valour.

Joe Norton first saw service as a volunteer with the King's Own Royal Lancaster Regiment at the age of 16, spending his birthday in the trenches during the Boer War. Acting as a dispatch rider he had many narrow escapes, including on one occasion having his horse shot from under him. He was awarded the South Africa Medal and clasps; the Queen's Medal with bars (Cape Colony and Orange Free State); and the King's Medal. When the South African campaign ended, he joined the First Battalion Grenadier Guards.

After the war, Joseph Norton went on to a further distinguished career of daily service. He served as Doorman of 10 Downing Street, overseeing the visits of eminent statesmen and influential people from the world of national and international politics, and served under and had personal contact with five prime ministers: Ramsey McDonald, Stanley Baldwin, Neville Chamberlain, Winston Churchill and Clement Atlee.

He was a bearer and one of the bodyguards at the funeral of King Edward VII. He also used to go on royal shoots, and had the distinction of instructing King George V in the art of shooting.

PART THREE

Compassion

Commemorating Those Who Died in Battle
<u>Memorial to the Missing: Belgium</u>
Ypres (Menin Gate) Memorial

Designed by Sir Reginald Blomfield with sculpture by Sir William Reid-Dick, unveiled by Lord Plumer on 24 July 1927.

Ypres (now Ieper), is a town in the Province of West Flanders. The Ypres (Menin Gate) Memorial bears the names of more than 54,000 officers and men whose graves are not known.

The site of the Menin Gate was chosen because of the hundreds of thousands of men who passed through it on their way to the battlefields. It commemorates the forces of Australia, Canada, India, South Africa and the United Kingdom who died in the Salient. The memorial enshrines the names of United Kingdom casualties prior to 16 August 1917 (with some exceptions). Those after that date are named on the memorial at Tyne Cot.

Each night at 8 p.m., the traffic is stopped at the Menin Gate while members of the local Fire Brigade sound the last post in the roadway under the memorial's arches.

<u>Men from Chapel Street</u>
<u>Cheshire Regiment, Panel 19–22</u>

Joseph Booth Jnr, 2nd Battalion Service number 8851, died 8/5/1915 age 29 years. Disembarked France: 16/1/15.

Charles Henry Croft, 2nd Battalion Service Number 24973, died 8/5/1915 age 31 years. Disembarked France: 7/3/15. Lived at 20 Chapel Street.

Frank Collins, Service 1st Battalion Service number 10816, died 27/5/1915. Disembarked France 23/3/15. Lived at 9 Chapel Street.

Martin Donnelly, 10th Battalion Service number 49484, died 4/8/1917 age 33 years.

William Haughton, 2nd Battalion Service Number 16626, died 25/5/15. Lived at 39 Chapel Street.

King's Own Royal (Lancashire) Regiment

Alfred Oxley, 2nd Battalion Service number 17298: died 8/5/1915 age 35 years. Disembarked France 23/2/15. Lived at 20 Chapel Street. Married with seven children.

War Diary Extract

Between 4–9 May, the Battalion marched out and took over trenches in front of Frazenburg. The trenches were new and had not been completed. The enemy shelled the trenches throwing them in, rendering them untenable. The enemy then advance and captured them, and advanced against the support dugouts. There were nearly 1,000 casualties with 721 men reported 'Missing'.

Ralph Ryan, 1st Battalion Service number 3508, Killed in Action 14/5/1915 age 44 years. Disembarked France 4/12/14. Lived at 48 Chapel Street. Married with five children. He served in the terror of the Boxer Rebellion in China in 1900. He wrote to his wife: 'They will be very lucky fellows that get home from here.' She was a widow by the time she received his letter three days later.
Panel 12.

Ypres Town Cemetery Extension

Designed by Sir Reginald Blomfield.

   The Ypres Town Cemetery Extension (on east side of Ypres Town Cemetery) is located 1 kilometre east of the town centre. The extension was begun in October 1914 and was used until April 1915, and on two further occasions in 1918. The cemetery contains 145 Commonwealth burials of the First World War.

Cheshire Regiment 11.C.2

William Bagnall, 2nd Battalion Service number 8382, Died of Wounds 5/2/1915 32 years old. Disembarked France 16/1/15. Married with five children (Medals returned K.R. 1743).

Memorial to the Missing: France
Thiepval Memorial

Designed by Sir Edwin Lutyens, built between 1928 and 1932 and unveiled by the Prince of Wales, in the presence of the President of France, on August 1932.

   The Thiepval Memorial to the Missing of the Somme bears the names of more than 72,000 officers and men of the United Kingdom and South African forces who died in the Somme sector before 20 March 1918 and have no known grave. The memorial is sited next to the village of Thiepval, of the main Bapaume to Albert road. The village had been an original objective of the 1 July offensive, by the end of September it was captured.

Cheshire Regiment 9th Battalion

Dennis Hanley, service number 12477, died 4/7/1916 age 24 years. Addena Panel.
John Green, service number 11820, died of wounds 4/9/1918. Disembarked
France 19/7/15. Lived at 10 Chapel Street. Pier and Face 3C and 4A.

2nd Welsh Regiment

Peter Morley, service number 53568, died 22/9/1916. Lived at 41 Chapel Street.
Pier and Face 7A and 10A 1.J.28.

Guards Cemetery, Windy Corner, Cuinchy, France

Designed by Charles Holden.

Cuinchy is a village near the town of Bethune in the locality of Pas de Calais.
A little west of the crossroads known to the army as 'Windy Corner' was a house
used as a battalion headquarters and dressing station. The cemetery grew up
besides this house.

The original cemetery is now Plots 1 and 11 and Rows A to S of Plot 111.
It was begun by the 2nd Division in January 1915, and used extensively by the
4th Guards Brigade. It was closed in May 1916, when it contained 681 graves.
After the Armistice, it was increased when more than 2,700 graves were brought
in from the neighbouring battlefields – in particular, the battlefields of Neuve-
Chapelle, the Aubers Ridge and Festubert and certain smaller cemeteries (some
79 soldiers from the United Kingdom of various regiments). There are 1,247
identified casualties.

The King's (Liverpool) Regiment

Sergeant Thomas O'Connor, 4th Battalion Service number 6146, died 4/7/1915.
Married with six children.

Loos Memorial, Belgium

*Designed by Sir Herbert Baker with sculpture by Charles Wheeler. It was unveiled by Sir
Nevil Macready on 4 August 1930.*

The Loos Memorial forms the sides and back of Dud Corner Cemetery,
approximately 6km from Lens.

The Loos Memorial commemorates over 20,000 officers and men who have
no known grave, who fell in the area from the River Lys to the old southern
boundary of the First Army, east and west of Grenay. On either side of the cemetery is a wall 15ft high, to which are fixed tablets on which are carved the names
of those commemorated. At the back are four small circular courts, open to the
sky, in which the lines of tablets are continued, and between these courts are three
semi-circular walls or apses, two of which carry tablets, while on the centre apse
is erected the Cross of Sacrifice.

Cheshire Regiment 2nd Battalion Machine Gun Corps
Arthur Garner, service number 10419, died 3/10/1915. Panel 49 and 50.

Barlin Communal Cemetery Extension, France

Designed by Sir Edward Lutyens.
Barlin is a village about 11km south-west of Bethune. The Barlin Communal Cemetery Extension lies to the north of the village. The extension was begun by French troops in October 1914 and when they moved south in March 1916 to be replaced by Commonwealth forces, it was used for burials by the 6th Casualty Clearing Station. In November 1917, Barlin began to be shelled and the hospital was moved back to Ruitz, but the extension was used again in March and April 1918 during the German advance on this front.

The Barlin Communal Cemetery Extension contains 1,095 First World War Commonwealth burials, two being unidentified. There are French and German burials interred.

South Wales Borderers 1st Battalion
Joseph Lowe

Tancrez Farm Cemetery, Belgium

Designed by Charles Holden.
Tancrez Farm Cemetery stands behind a rebuilt farmhouse, which during the war housed an aid post. It is located 17km south of Ypres town centre on a road which connects Ypres to Wijtschate and on to Armentieres. Work on the cemetery was constituted in December 1914 and was carried on by field ambulances and fighting units until March 1918. The cemetery contains 333 Commonwealth burials and commemorations of the First World War. Six of the burials are unidentified but there is a special memorial to one casualty known to be buried among them. There are also two German war graves.

Cheshire Regiment 10th Battalion
John Inions, service number 12653, Killed in Action died 3/1/1917. Disembarked France 9/7/15. Married with three children. Memorial reference 11.C.12.

Lijssenthoek Military Cemetery, Belgium

Designed by Sir Reginald Blomfield.
Lijssenthoek Military Cemetery is located 12km west of Ypres town centre, it is the second-largest Commonwealth cemetery in Belgium. During the First World War, the village of Lijssenthoek was situated on the main communication

line between the Allied military bases in the rear and the Ypres battlefields. Close to the front it became the obvious place to establish casualty clearing stations. The cemetery was first used by the French and in June 1915 by the casualty clearing stations of the Commonwealth forces. The clearing stations fell back before German advance and field ambulances took their places. The cemetery contains 9,901 Commonwealth burials, of which 24 are unidentified, and graves of other nationalities including French and German.

Cheshire Regiment 20th Battalion transf. (36264) 61st Coy.

Thomas Peers, service number 41763, died of wounds 15/8/1917 age 26 years. XVI1.AA.6.

Pozieres Memorial, France

Designed by W. H. Cowlishaw, with sculpture by Laurence A. Turner. The memorial was unveiled by Sir Henry Smith-Dorrien on 4 August 1930.

Pozieres is a village 6km north-east of the town of Albert.

The memorial encloses Pozieres British Cemetery, Plot 11 of which contains original burials of 1916, 1917 and 1918, carried out by fighting units and field ambulances. The remaining plots were made after the Armistice when graves were brought in from the battlefields immediately surrounding the cemetery, the majority of them soldiers who died in the autumn of 1916 during the later stages of the Somme, but a few represented the fighting in August 1918.

The Pozieres Memorial commemorates over 14,000 casualties of the United Kingdom. The Corps and the Regiments most largely represented are the Rifle Brigade with over 600 names; the Durham Light Infantry with approximately 600 names; the Machine Gun Corps with over 500; the Manchester Regiment with approximately 500 names and the Royal Horse and Royal Field Artillery with over 400 names.

Royal Irish Rifles 1st Battalion

Edward Lowe. Panel 74-76.

Soissons Memorial, France

Designed by G. H. Holt and V. O. Rees, with sculpture by Eric Kennington. It was unveiled by Sir Alexander Hamilton-Gordon on 22 July 1928.

The town of Soissons stands on the left bank of the river Aisne, approximately 100km north-east of Paris.

The Soissons Memorial is a massive white Portland stone construction which commemorates almost 4,000 officers and men of the United Kingdom forces who died during the Battle of the Aisne and the Marne in 1918 and who have no known grave. Names are listed on the memorial by Regiments in order of precedence, under the title of each Regiment by rank, and under each rank alphabetically.

Cheshire Regiment 9th Battalion
William Johnson, service number: 32623, died 30/5/1918.

Lapugnoy Military Cemetery, France

Designed by Sir Edward Lutyens.
   Lapugnoy is a village 12km west of Bethune in the Pas de Calais.
   The first burials were made in Plot 1 of the cemetery in September 1915, but it was most heavily used in the Battle of Arras. The dead were brought to the cemetery from casualty clearing stations, primarily the 18th and the 23rd at Lapugnoy and Lozinghem, however between May and August 1918 the cemetery was used by fighting units. The cemetery contains 1,324 Commonwealth burials of the First World War, with 3 being unidentified.

Somerset Light Infantry 1st Battalion
Michael Hines, service number 44416, died 26/5/1918.VI11.F.26.

Rocquigny–Equancourt Road British Cemetery, Manancourt, France

Designed by Sir Reginald Blomfield.
   The cemetery lies between the two villages Rocquigny and Equancourt in the Department of the Somme, some 13km north of Peronne and 12km south-east of Bapaume.
   The cemetery was begun in 1917 and, until March 1918, mainly used by the 21st and 48th Casualty Clearing Stations posted at Ytres and to a small extent by the Germans, who knew it as 'Etricourt Old English Cemetery'. Burials were resumed by Commonwealth troops in September 1918 and the 3rd Canadian and 18th Casualty Clearing Stations buried in it in October and November 1918.
   The cemetery contains 1,838 Commonwealth burial and commemorations of the First World War. Twenty-one of the burials are unidentified and nine Commonwealth graves made by the Germans which cannot be found are represented by special memorials. The cemetery also contains 198 Germans war burials and the graves of ten French civilians.

Manchester Regiment 12th Battalion
Albert Oxley, service number 54772, died 20/2/1918.

Lancashire Fusiliers 1/7 Battalion
William Hughes, service number 52884, died of wounds 25/10/18 age 19 years.
XIII.A.20

Asiatic and Egyptian Theatre (Southern Front)

Turkey
Helles Memorial

Designed by John James Burnett. Unveiled in 1924.
The Helles Memorial stands on the tip of the Gallipoli Peninsula. It takes the
form of an obelisk over 30m high and can be seen by ships passing through the
Dardenelles.
The Helles Memorial is the Commonwealth battle memorial for the Gallipoli
Campaign and commemorates many of those Commonwealth servicemen who
died there and who have no known grave. There are panels for those who died or
were buried at sea in Gallipoli waters. Total commemorated: 20,885.

Cheshire Regiment 8th Battalion
William Groark(e), service number 11267, died 18/8/1915. Panel 76 to 78.

India
Jubbulpore Cantonment Cemetery

The cemetery has ninety identified casualties and is on the Bilhari–Mandla Road.

Cheshire Regiment 2nd Battalion
Joseph Hollingsworth, service number 9939, died 14/8/1914.

Egypt
Alexandria (Chatby) Military and War Memorial Cemetery

Chatby is a district on the eastern side of the city of Alexandria. The cemetery is
located centrally within the main Alexandria Cemetery complex and was used
for burials until April 1916.
The Chatby Memorial stands at the eastern end of the cemetery and commemorates 1,000 Commonwealth servicemen who died during the First World
War and who have no grave but the sea. Many of them were lost when hospital ships or transports were sunk in the Mediterranean, sailing to or from
Alexandria. Others died of wounds or sickness while aboard such vessels and
were buried at sea.

<u>Cheshire Regiment 4th Battalion</u>
Lance Corporal William Hennerley, service number 19832, died of disease 5/10/1915. F.56.

Those Buried in the United Kingdom

William Curley, Gunner Royal Field Artillery 81st Brigade 'C' Battery Service number 78269, died 28/12/1918. Lived at 28 Chapel Street. Married with two children. Gassed while on active duty. He was taken to a military hospital in Manchester but died just after Christmas 1918. Hale Cemetery N.362.

James Ford, King's Own Royal Lancashire Regiment, 1st Battalion Service number 6523, died 30/6/15 of wounds (perforated duodenal ulcer and general peritonitis) in hospital at Lancaster, suffered a shell wound to leg in September 1914. Originally enlisted in 1900 serving two years in Malta. Married. Lancaster Cemetery R.C.7.

War Graves and Memorial Photographs

British War Graves: Memorials to the Missing is a website which can supply a photograph of a particular grave or memorial panel free of charge.

A photo request form is available and if the cemetery details are unknown, assistance can be given in tracing the information.

If you are interested in taking some photographs for the site, your contribution is welcome and an email form for messages is provided.

Website: www.britishwargraves.co.uk

The Commonwealth War Commission

The Commonwealth War Graves Commission (CWGC) is an inter-governmental organisation of six independent member states of the Commonwealth of Nations. Its principle function is the administration of records, maintenance of graves, cemeteries, memorials and places of commemoration of war dead and civilians killed in enemy action, during both the World Wars. Since its inception, the Commission has constructed approximately 2,500 war cemeteries, it is responsible for the care of war dead at over 23,000 burial sites and the maintenance of 200 memorials worldwide.

The Commission's founder, Fabian Ware, arrived in France in September 1914 to command a British Red Cross Unit. He noted there was no organisation in place to record the final resting place of casualties and became concerned that graves would be lost forever, so his unit took it upon themselves to register and care for all the graves they could find. By 1915, Ware's unit was given official recognition by the War Office, becoming the Graves Registration Commission. As reports of the grave registration work became public, the Commission and the Red Cross began to dispatch photographic prints and cemetery location information, in response to requests from relatives for information. As a consequence of this expanding role, the Graves Registration Commission in 1916 became the Directorate of Graves Registration and Enquires.

As the war progressed, Ware, concerned about the fate of the graves once the war was over, became convinced of the need for an official organisation representing the Imperial nature of the war effort, the equality of treatment due to the dead and the permanence of graves or memorials. With the support of the Prince of Wales, Ware submitted a memorandum to the Imperial War Conference in 1917. It was unanimously approved and the Imperial War Graves Commission was established by Royal Charter on 21 May 1917.

The Commission's work began in earnest after Armistice. Once land for cemeteries and memorials had been guaranteed, the enormous task of recording the details of the dead began. By 1918, some 587,000 graves had been identified and a further 559,000 casualties were registered as having no known grave.

Post-war saw the clearing of battlefields, individual graves and battlefield plots. The location and sites of many graves were no longer known, and individuals still lay unburied in areas where fighting had been fiercest. It is in this context that the majority of the CWGC Archive casualty records came into existence. To assist with the collation of information, details were provided by Labour Companies and Graves Concentration Units which were set up under the control of the military authorities. They were tasked with searching for unburied bodies, the remains of the war dead, isolated graves and small cemeteries (usually less than forty graves), and conducting the battlefield exhumation and reburials which resulted.

Despite the difficulty and unpleasantness of the work, the exhumation squads were methodical and meticulous in their searches and, as most of these had seen active service themselves, were painstaking in their search for anything that would help identify a fallen comrade. Nevertheless, battlefield conditions meant that many of these vital identification indicators were lost and a high proportion of the bodies found remained unknown.

It was the job of the officer in charge of these search parties to record details about each body recovered, including the location where the remains were found, whether a cross was found on the grave and any regimental particulars or other means of identification found at the time. These details were written on a ticket which was attached to the remains prior to their removal and reburial. The cemetery officer would be present at each reburial, and it would be his duty to record, on a Burial Return form, all the information that had been written on the original ticket, as well as the plot, row and grave number of the reburial.

These forms were collected daily and passed to the Army Burial Officer, who would then arrange for a copy to be sent to the Department of Graves Registrations and Enquiries. The Registration Officer was then responsible for registering the new graves, and for preparing comprehensive reports of the new cemeteries. The grave registration, concentration and exhumation records produced as a result of this work were passed to the Imperial War Graves Commission. From these core records the Commission was able to produce various other documents, including the register entries and headstone schedules (which were used to record what should be engraved on their headstones).

Many of the grave registration and concentration records would have been typed up by an army of administrative staff based in offices and base camps at various locations, from handwritten reports produced in the field, in all types of weather and conditions. For accuracy and verification purposes hundreds of thousands of verification forms were sent to next of kin, seeking corroboration of the details it held, and additional information where needed. Where the details recorded on the original documentation were shown to be inaccurate, corrections were made and the documentation annotated.

Cemeteries and Memorials

The Commission set the highest standards for all its work. In 1921, it built three experimental cemeteries. Of these, Forceville in France was considered the most successful and was the template for the Commission's building programme. Three of the most eminent architects of the day were chosen to design and construct the cemeteries and memorials: Sir Edwin Lutyens, Sir Herbert Baker and Sir Reginald Blomfield; Rudyard Kipling was to advise on inscriptions. Garden designer Gertrude Jekyll advised on planting, with the Commission raising its own garden nurseries.

The Commission set out the following principles: each of the dead should be commemorated by name on the headstone or memorial; headstones and memorials should be permanent; headstones should be in uniform; and, significantly, that there should be no distinction made on account of military or civil rank, race or creed.

The graves that were found were gathered into 'concentration' cemeteries, either newly created or built up around already existing burials grounds. Men were also buried in churchyards and civilian cemeteries. Where burials had occurred in established burial grounds with clearly marked graves, the graves were simply recorded and registered. Cemeteries were created on or close to the battlefield, or within the vicinity of the military medical facility where they died (known as a casualty clearing station). A very few men still lie where they died or were originally buried.

Memorials were often built as part of the cemetery, known as 'expansion' cemeteries, they were characterised by their high proportion of unknown soldiers. The Commission was provided with a list which enabled the registration of the details of those soldiers classed as 'Missing in Action'. This facilitated the decision as to the most appropriate place of commemoration for each individual, and to set out the design and layout of the memorial panels on which their names would be recorded; sometimes this would be in the form of a wall around the perimeter of the cemetery.

One of the great challenges the Commission faced was the provision of over 500,000 headstones, which involved sourcing high quality stone. In addition, the engraving of regimental badges and inscriptions was a labour intensive process, with each headstone taking a week to be chiselled by hand. Innovatively, the Commission contracted a Lancashire firm to design a machine which traced details on to the headstones which quickened the process. At one point, some 4,000 headstones a week were shipped to France.

The official commemoration of men that died on the Western Front constitutes some 1,620 cemeteries and memorials in France, and 372 in Belgium; while work progressed in Italy, Egypt, Palestine, Macedonia, Mesopotamia and on the Gallipoli Peninsula.

Albert Oxley's war grave, France 1917.

Illness

The Silver War Badge

This was a sterling silver badge originally issued to officers and men who were discharged or retired from military forces, as a result of sickness or injury caused by their war service. The serviceman's record would show that they had been released under Paragraph 392 (XVI) section 2b of the King's Regulations, as being permanently physically unfit. The recipient would receive a certificate with the war badge which would be worn on the right breast of a recipient's civilian clothes, and could not be worn on a military uniform. Roughly 1,150,000 Silver Badges were issued.

Sometimes the nature of the qualifying reason of discharge would be given, i.e. wounds, sickness or gassed. Chapel Street recipients of the medal included: Sergeant James Arnold, 38 years old, 1st Battalion Cheshire Regiment, service number 6463; Edward Birmingham, 39 years old, 9th Battalion Royal Dublin Fusiliers, service number 6127, discharged 1/5/18/ wounds; John Booth; Edward Caine, 22 years old, 6th Battalion Cheshire Regiment (Territorial Force), service number 267909, discharged 5/2/16; Patrick de Courcy, Queen's Household Cavalry and Cavalry of the Line, service number 45429, discharged 23/10/18, permanently physically unfit; James Ratchford, The Royal Welsh (Welsh) Fusiliers, service number 71258, discharged 1/10/17; Thomas Ratchford, 19 years old, Royal Shropshire Light, service number 31618, discharged 8/10/18; Richard Ryan, 4th Battalion Manchester Regiment, service number 2643, discharged 6/6/15; Alfred Shaw; Thomas Norton, Royal Garrison Artillery, service number 155890, examined 24/4/17, gunshot wound to the head.

They Also Served

Private Peter Gormley was a holder of the Distinguished Conduct Medal (DCM) the highest recognised award for bravery next to the Victoria Cross. In September 1918, a red line was drawn under his record, and all his medals forfeited under Paragraph 392 (XI) of the King's Regulation. He had 'deserted' – two months before the end of the war. Private Gormley had served in the 1st,

11th, 15th and 9th Battalion of the Cheshire Regiment and will have fought at Mons, Ypres, Loos and on the Somme. Latterly he was attached to the Infantry Base Depot.

Desertion was associated with cowardice, and this was the generally accepted reason as to why the offence was committed. Desertion was a serious offence and those found guilty after a court martial could be executed (some 240,000 courts martial were held and 3,080 death sentences handed down, with 346 sentences carried out). Clearly Private Gormley was not a coward; he was an experienced soldier, so his posting to the Infantry Base Depot may hold a clue to the real reason of his desertion. It is possible he was suffering from 'trauma' or battle fatigue, and was unfit for active military service so was redeployed to auxiliary military duty.

The First World War gave rise to new medical phenomena, which became known as 'shell shock'. It was thought by some that shell-shock was damage to the nerves in the brain caused by proximity to repeated shelling, that shock waves produced cerebral lesion. It is estimated that up to 40 per cent of Somme casualties were affected by shell-shock. It is also important to note that during 1917, 'shell-shock' was banned as a diagnosis in the British Army, and mentions of it were censored in medical journals. In 1922, the British government produced a *Report of the War Office Committee of Enquiry into 'Shell-Shock'*, which contained recommendations for Forward Areas, Neurological Centres and Base Hospitals. 'Neurasthenia' became a cover-all term for new types of injuries: physical, emotional, psychological. Until then, diagnosis and treatments varied, as did the range of symptoms experienced by the casualties. An example of emerging therapy is in the writing of Colonel Rogers, RMO 4/ Black Watch, who stated:

> You must send your commotional cases down the line. But when you get these emotional cases, unless they are very bad, if you have a hold of the men and they know you and you know them (and there is a good deal more in the man knowing you than in you knowing the man) … you are able to explain to him that there is really nothing wrong with him, give him a rest at the aid post if necessary and a day or two's sleep, go up with him to the front line, and, when there, see him often, sit down beside him and talk to him about the war and look through his periscope and let the man see you are taking an interest in him.

During the war years the Red Cross established some 3,000 auxiliary hospitals under the supervision of medically qualified staff and volunteers. Large houses, Assembly Rooms and Congregational Schools and other appropriate buildings were utilised and returning injured soldiers not in need of general hospitals could be treated and convalesce locally to their homes. Altrincham had several such facilities within a 5 mile radius.

The following newspaper accounts give an insight into dependency and ignorance, coping strategies and breakdown.

Drink to Wounded Soldiers

At Altrincham, today, Margaret Johnson, of Chapel Street. Altrincham, was committed for a month for supplying intoxicants to two wounded soldiers, and Gertrude Poole, who lodged with her, was fined 40s. Many beer bottles were found on the premises, and there was evidence of excessive drinking.

Superintendent Sutherland said that the Red Cross Hospitals in the district had terrible difficulty through wounded soldiers getting drink, and the Chairman (Mr T. W. Killick) said this was a very cruel and wicked case.

(M.E.N. 15 January 1917)

Broadheath Tragedy

This is the newspaper account of Mr Healey, an ex-serviceman of the Royal Engineers, who had lived at the Rose and Shamrock (when his father had been the landlord), and who was a resident of Chapel Street at the start of the war:

BRICKLAYER'S SUICIDE IN PRESENCE OF WIFE

A remarkable story was told at an inquest on John Healey (42), a bricklayer of Bridgewater-road, Broadheath, who was found with his throat cut in the early hours of Tuesday morning of last week. It was stated by his wife that he cut his throat with a razor in her presence.

The Coroner (Mr H. C. Yates) conducted the inquiry at the Rigby Memorial Schools on Friday.

The medical evidence, as given by Dr Harry G. Cooper, was to the effect that Healey had suffered from nervous debility. An examination of the body after death revealed the fact that the wound in the throat was such that it could have been self-inflicted. Death would ensue within a couple of seconds.

The Coroner:- It was done so quickly that one can only come to the conclusion that it was impulsive.

Dr Cooper:- It must have been.

Mrs Healey said her husband had been in indifferent health. On Monday he did not get out of bed until the afternoon, and after tea went back to his bedroom again. She sat up with him that night, and at one time he seemed to imagine that he heard somebody knocking at the door. She went downstairs, and answered the door just to satisfy him, but there was no one there.

Afterwards he seemed to fall into a sound sleep and she left him, continued the witness. At about a quarter to one o'clock she heard a noise which sounded like bare feet moving about on the floor. She saw him come out of the spare bedroom, where he kept his razor, but did not notice whether he had anything in his hands. He went to her bedroom, and she followed him in, and when asking him what he was doing she heard a gushing noise. Her husband then fell face downwards, and she ran out of the room, and went to a neighbour's house for help.

Answering the Coroner, Mrs Healey said her husband had never threatened to take his life. Although unwell he refused to stop working and 'would not give up'. He was an Army Reservist and served with the Royal Engineers at Mons. He was a spirit drinker.

An engine fitter, living in a neighbouring house, said that he was called by Mrs Healey, and on going upstairs found Healey lying dead on the bedroom floor.

Sergeant Lowry, of the Cheshire Constabulary, said Healey had a deep wound in the throat. A bloodstained razor was lying near the body, and there was an enormous quantity of blood on the floor.

Summing up, the Coroner said that it was perfectly fair to assume that Healey took his life. Where there were 'nerves' there was generally some trouble with the heart or brain afterwards. There was no doubt, he added, that the man was not asleep, but only shamming, and that he afterwards deliberately cut his throat in the presence of his wife. He would record a verdict that, while suffering from impulsive insanity, Healey, took his life.

Mr Healey's character and reputation were publicly vilified by the coroner in open court. At that time, suicide was a criminal offence which meant that if Mr Healey had lived, he could have been jailed for up to seven years. As he unfortunately died, the law stated he must be buried in an unmarked grave, in unconsecrated ground away from other graves. Mrs Healey and her children were to suffer the public stigmatisation and ignominy of being related to someone who fell short of the image of heroism.

It should be noted that during the war, cut-throat razors were army issue to serving soldiers.

Roll of Honour

The King's Telegram, Unveiling of the Plaque and the Roll of Honour

After the war, Chapel Street was a very different community. Some twenty-nine men had died during the conflict with between twenty and thirty more succumbing to injuries within a short time afterwards. The street was filled with widows and fatherless children, and without breadwinners in families, there was much poverty. A memorial plaque resembling a penny coin was issued after the war to the next-of-kin of those who died, they were made of bronze and became known as the 'Dead Man's Penny'. But unfortunately, they could not be spent and families had to rely on parish relief from the local churches to help with food parcels, children's clothing and days out.

On 5 April 1919, Lord Stamford unveiled a commemorative Roll of Honour, and read out a telegram from King George V acknowledging the brave actions of the men of Chapel Street, in their duty to king and country.

The Roll of Honour had been willingly subscribed to by the inhabitants of Chapel Street, who were 'properly proud of the record and fame it had won'. However, there was a remaining outstanding sum of £15 (approximately £5,116 in 2017) needed, and an approach was made on behalf of the appeal fund to the council. The council, for its part; felt it could not officially recognise the appeal, and it was suggested that personal donations from members could be made to the clerk of the council. One councillor, Mr Barber, was disgusted with this response, especially in light of the great personal sacrifice that had been made and he duly made a handsome personal donation.

The Roll of Honour was designed and executed under the direction of Mr Butler of George Street, who 'took a great personal interest, and with enthusiasm carried it through with success'. In recognition of the 161 men who volunteered their services for the Great War, the District Council gave permission for the erection of the Roll of Honour on the narrow kerb adjoining the church of All Saints, which stood at the entrance to Chapel Street. This was accorded as a privilege which is reported at the time as 'adding a pleasure and satisfaction to the many subscribers to the fund'.

Before the unveiling of the Roll of Honour by Lord Stamford, there was a procession through the town made up of the men belonging to Chapel Street, and at least 100 others, who had fought in the war and who put on their khaki and all were wearing their ribbons. (Not all the volunteers of Chapel Street attended the ceremony as many were still serving with the armies in France, Russia, Egypt and India.)

They gathered in the new marketplace, and were paraded by Sergeant-Major Norton, of the Grenadier Guards. Sergeant-Major Norton wore all his medals and decorations, Private Hennerley displayed the Mons Star of 1914, and Private Riley the Military Medal. There were others with South African and Mons ribbons, and there was one, whose name was Corfield, who on completion of his service after eighteen month in the trenches – re-enlisted and went back into the firing line and only received his discharge after the armistice. There were few without a decoration of some kind or other. And Altrincham looked on at the parade with a genuine feeling of pride. The procession was led by the Altrincham Borough Band over a route that must have measured a couple of miles, and on every side its course was watched with interest and delight.

The gallant boys of Chapel-street, 70 strong followed the band with a sprightly tread; and behind them, bearing them honourable company, were a hundred demobilised men and a Landen with three or four disabled. Two Colleens lent a merry and picturesque air of colour as they danced to the music of the band.

The local paper stated that:

> On reaching the Town Hall there was there was a short halt to allow the public representatives taking part in the ceremony to join the procession. When the procession got to Chapel Street it was with difficulty that a way could be forced for it through the dense and cheering crowd. It was managed somehow, mainly through the good offices of the police and the assistance of the sons of Chapel Street, whose sense of order was adequate to the occasion.

The street was decorated end to end with flags and bunting. A raised platform had been built in front of the Roll of Honour for the speakers and a big cheer greeted the opening words of the chairman of the District Council when he announced that he had received a message from His Majesty, which he asked the Earl of Stamford to read.

The King's Message read by the Earl of Stamford:

Buckingham Palace
Three o'clock

To George F. Turner, Esq.,
Chairman of the District Council,
Town Hall,
Altrincham.

Your telegram of yesterday was duly submitted to the King, and I am commanded to convey the thanks of his Majesty for the inhabitants of Altrincham for their loyal assurances to which the message gives expression. The King congratulates them, and especially those living in Chapel Street, that out of its 60 houses 161 men served in the war, 30 of whom have made the supreme sacrifice. His Majesty is proud to think that a roll of honour has been subscribed for and will be unveiled to-day as a record of the patriotism and fighting spirit so prominently displayed by the people of Altrincham. – Stamfordham.

After the National Anthem had been sung, the chairman of the council introduced the Earl of Stamford, who was dressed in uniform, who stated that he was taking a warm and keen interest in Altrincham. His Lordship assured that any help he could give in the important work that was to be undertaken by the council in the future, he would be only too pleased to offer it (Cheers).

The speech of the Earl of Stamford:

'A Proud And Triumphant Moment'

Fellow citizens we have met here to-day to pay a tribute to a number of brave men from our town who gave their services in defence of our country during the Great War through which we have passed. And the fact that strikes us all to-day and fills us with admiration is that from this small street of about sixty houses no fewer than 161 men went forth and joined our country's forces. Their names are inscribed on the roll which I am to have the honour of unveiling in a few moments. It is a glorious and wonderful record (A chorus: 'We can do it again'). No tribute that we can pay and no appreciation that we can express can, I feel, adequately reflect our feelings of pride and enthusiasm at the honour and distinction which these men have conferred on our town no less than on themselves. It is a proud and triumphant moment for us in Altrincham, and, so, it is a solemn moment. For we know that thirty of these men we shall not have the joy of welcoming back again. They have laid down their lives for their country. They have given, as a great man once expressed it, that last full measure of devotion, they have sacrificed themselves confident in the hope that a new and happier world should emerge from the wreckage of the war. (Cheers.) Let us keep that thought in our minds on this day of sadness and rejoicing.

This little ceremony will soon be over; we shall disperse, and go our separate ways, but from now on that roll of honour will deliver its message to you and me and to those who come after us. I conceive it as a clarion call to us to make ourselves the task of seeing that such courage and such devotion to a great cause shall not have been in vain. Each of us according to our individual powers and abilities can take a share in this collective work. Let us then, for unity of heart and mind, for unity of effort and of purpose, for a banishment of unworthy differences that hamper and delay the attainment of an ideal standard of living, a bright and more uplifting social life for the whole of the community. This new and better England that is coming; fashioned and built up by the energy of our

The Roll of Honour. (Designed by Mr Butler)

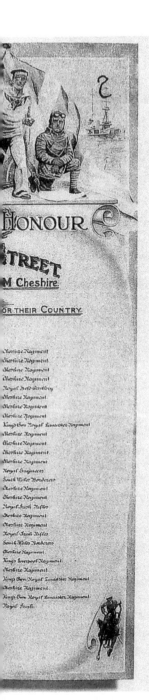

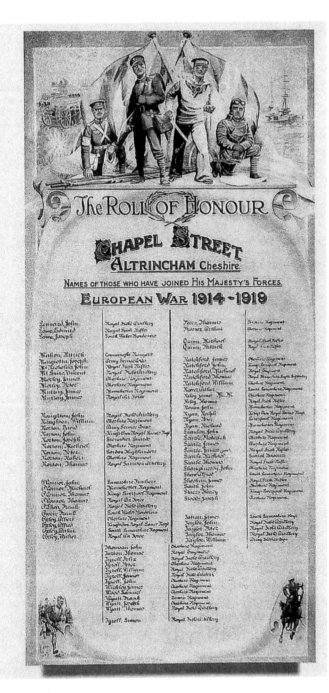

The Blue Plaque ceremony, 2009. (Hennerley family)

minds and hands, shall constitute our testimony of gratitude to the gallant men whom the war has spared to us, shall constitute England's last memorial to her death-less dead. (Cheers.) I now have the honour to unveil this roll of service.

On finishing his speech, Lord Stamford, amid great cheering, unveiled the memorial and the band played 'In Memoriam'. Lord Stamford was widely hailed for his mastery of public speaking, delivering this, his first public address, at the age of 23.

It is worth noting that in January 1919, the Irish Republican Party had formed a breakaway government (Dail Eireann) and declared independence from Britain. Lord Stamford's citing of the 'expressions of a great man', was in reference to the speech of Abraham Lincoln, and the quotation was from the Gettysburg Address. His Lordship would seem to be drawing a parallel between civil war and unity and the relationships of politics and difference; drawing on the suggestion of the 'banishment of unworthy differences'. His Lordship would have been aware that he was addressing a mostly Irish crowd, and sought to instil a new positive purpose and direction for the future, in a collective spirit of shared co-operation for a better England; founded on the common shared experience of the tragedy of the Great War.

If a country was worth living in, it was worth fighting for; conversely, if the country was worth fighting for, it should be worth living in. Many of the Chapel Street men attending the ceremony were Class Z Reserve, which meant that though they were now civilians, they had an obligation to return to service if called upon. It was in force should Germany ignore the conditions of the peace treaty and return to hostilities. It was abolished in March 1920.

Sir Arthur Haworth was called upon to give a speech in which he stated that the record of Chapel Street 'not only bore favourable comparison with that of any street in the country, but that during the period of voluntary enlistment, which was the most honourable period of all, it led the way above all streets in the country'. This brought great cheers from the assembly.

Chapel Street was thus accorded the accolade of 'The Bravest Little Street in England'.

Sir Arthur further implored that the great sacrifices, made for no selfish purpose and for the benefit of humanity, should not be frittered away, stating: 'One we were, one we are, and one we will be ever in our pursuit of the betterment of mankind.' (Cheers.)

The mayor also gave a speech of hearty congratulation in which he gave testament to Altrincham, which had stood as one of the first towns in the country; for its allegiance, its honour and self-sacrifice and its wonderful spirit. He stressed the importance of duty to see that it was manifested in the new world which was being entered into, so that the great blessings of peace might result in a purer and a better life. (Cheers.)

In a letter of acknowledgement to the local paper, Mr Clarke of Chapel Street wished to express his thanks to the people who made the proceedings so successful. He duly mentioned Thomas Corfield and Mr J. Ratchford for the decorations of the street, and Mr Tom Furness for his services. He went on to thank the members of the committee to whom the residents of Chapel Street were indebted to for the arrangements: Mr J. Butler, Mr Dennis Hennerley, Mr James Ratchford, Mr J. W. Davies, Mr P. de Courcey and John Rowan.

Description of the Roll of Honour after the dedication

The Roll of Honour was supported on stands which were screened by box shrubs in pots and protective railing; a wrought-iron canopy was attached to the wall of the church to give protection to the area from the elements. The king's telegram (which was five telegrams, forming the message) along with a photograph of the king was mounted and framed and given a place of prominence adjacent to the roll. The Roll of Honour was encased in glass with a decorative scrolled finial above the frame, its centre inscribed in gold lettering. All the names of the volunteers and their service were recorded in fine calligraphy, on parchment type paper, alongside artistic representations of servicemen in the different units, in a colourful and dramatic fashion. In between these a large crucifix of Jesus Christ was placed. Above the king's telegram a plaque had been erected which bore the date of the dedication. Surrounding all of this were wreaths of flowers, eternal candles, vases and rosary beads; so that it effectively became a shrine and place of pilgrimage. And so, the Roll of Honour came to symbolise the principle aesthetics of an Arts and Crafts installation; it was designed to transform the perception of a space.

The king's telegram and the Roll of Honour are on permanent display at Altrincham Town Hall. A copy of the Roll of Honour now stands in Dunham Memorial Gardens opposite St Margaret's church.

Walking With The Wounded

The charity was launched in 2010 by ex-servicemen Ed Parker and Simon Daglish.

Walking With The Wounded's mission is to support all veterans with physical, mental or social injury to gain the skills and qualifications necessary to develop new careers outside the military, reintegrate into society and provide long-term security for themselves and their families. The aims of the mission statement are met by focusing on housing, employment, retraining and education.

In 2015, in a first-of-its-kind partnership, the BBC's *DIY SOS* television programme brought together Walking With The Wounded, Manchester City Council and Haig Housing in a project aimed at transforming sixty-two homes and creating a veterans' housing community, within the existing community. Added to this was an advice centre with private space for therapy and counselling. Time, expertise, materials and supplies were donated to the project by volunteer contractors, along with many suppliers, utilities and smaller specialist companies.

Princes William and Harry with Nick Knowles. (Walking With The Wounded)

The project was supported by Princes William and Harry who personally donned white helmets and got stuck into the build. The television programme was screened in two parts and the BBC *DIY SOS* team has since revisited the site.

The charity runs a number of programmes designed to assist and support veterans in different ways. Home Straight Employment Advisors help unemployed veterans on the 'Home Straight', to find employment and rebuild their lives. Advisors work with people to build confidence, organise work placements, source funding for any required training and assist in gaining suitable employment and are located in major cities in the UK.

Many ex-servicemen who have served with the Forces for a long time may struggle with the transition to civilian life; from leading an institutionalised life to suddenly being forced to become independent can present problems for individuals, as well as families. Walking With The Wounded work closely with Head Start, a programme which complements NHS and other third sector organisations in the provision of mental health support to ex-service personnel.

Stigma within the military population is known to have a negative impact on accessing help with mental illness, as they tend to associate seeking care as a weakness. Fear, guilt, anger and shame are often encountered in relation to their military experiences. Avoidance or denial is also common in order to avoid feeling vulnerable. Ex-servicemen often present under duress following an ultimatum from a concerned partner or other family member.

Alcohol misuse is much higher than in the general population, and there is a correlation between alcohol misuse, mental health issues and violence. In order to cope with their symptoms and distress, ex-servicemen can self-medicate with alcohol or drugs. Brushes with the law, housing, employment, indebtedness and relationship difficulties can be associated factors.

Canada Street, Manchester. (Walking With The Wounded)

TO COMMEMORATE THE VISIT
OF

HRH THE DUKE OF CAMBRIDGE
AND

HRH PRINCE HENRY OF WALES

TO CANADA STREET
IN CELEBRATION OF THE RENOVATED
VETERANS HOMES AND SUPPORT CENTRE
23RD SEPTEMBER 2015

Commemorative plaque, 2015. (Christian Brady)

HRH Prince Harry, patron of Walking With The Wounded, has stated that he is personally determined to rid the stigma around mental health and has pledged that he will dedicate his life to helping mentally ill ex-servicemen and women.

Through a national network of accredited therapists, funding is provided for private face to face therapy for those with mild to moderate mental health difficulties such as depression, anxiety or PTSD (Post Traumatic Stress Disorder), and adjustment disorder including those who simultaneously misuse substances.

The NHS is central to ex-service personnel receiving support with their mental health. However, where the local NHS and its veteran specific services have limited geographical coverage and long waiting lists, Head Start offers an alternative and provides ex-service personnel with choice.

The charity is dependent on donations in order to fund its work and it relies on public support, volunteers and publicity.

Fundraising has recently included expeditions to the North Pole in 2011, Mount Everest in 2012, the South Pole in 2013, the Walk of Britain in 2015, Kilimanjaro climb 2016. Events around the UK have involved walks, marathons, dog events, car boot sales, holding swish parties, cycling and the Cumbrian Challenge.

All of these activities require sponsorship and participation!

References and Educational Resources

Bibliography

Bayliss, D. (2006) *A Town in crisis: Altrincham in the Mid-Nineteenth Century.* Manchester: Manchester Print Finishes.

Becke, Major A. F. (1938) *Order of Battle of Divisions Part 3A. New Army Divisions (9–26).* London: His Majesty's Stationery Office.

Becke, Major A. F. (1945) *Order of Battle of Divisions Part 3B. New Army Divisions (30–41) & 63rd (RN) Division.* London: His Majesty's Stationery Office.

Birchall, S. (2010) *Dissent in Altrincham: Religion, Politics and a touch of Scandal 1870–1905.* Manchester: Author House.

Edmonds, J. E. (1993) [1947] *Military Operations France and Belgium 1918: 8th August–26th September, The Franco British Offensive.* History of the Great War Based on Official Documents by Direction of the Historical Section of the Committee of Imperial Defence. IV. London: Imperial War Museum and Battery Press.

Laurie, G. B. (1914) *Great Britain, Army Infantry Regiments: Royal Irish Rifles.* Aldershot: Gale & Poulden.

MacPherson, W. G.; et al. (1923). *Medical Services: Diseases of the War: Including the Medical Aspects of Aviation and Gas Warfare and Gas Poisoning in Tanks and Mines* (PDF) History of the Great War Based on Official Documents by Direction of the Historical Section of the Committee of Imperial Defence. II. (online ed.). London: HMSO.

Miles, W. (1992) [1938] *Military Operations in France and Belgium: 2 July to the End of the Battles of the Somme.* History of the Great War Based on Official Documents by Direction of the Historical Section of the Committee of Imperial Defence. II. (Imperial War Museum and Battery Press ed.). London: Macmillan.

Murphy, David (2007) *Irish Regiments in the World Wars.* Osprey Publishing.

Richards, Frank (1933) *Old Soldiers Never Die.* (Library of Wales) (Kindle Locations 1742–1745). Parthian Books. Kindle Edition.

Roe, Lt. F. P. (1923) *A Short History of the Ulster Rifles.* Aldershot: Gale & Polden.

The National Archive, WO 95/4824, War Diary XVI Corps (Court of Enquiry papers).

Thorpe, D. R. Dr (2011) *Supermac: The Life of Harold Macmillan.* London: Pimlico.

Wakefield, A. & Moody, S. *Under the Devil's Eye: Britain's Forgotten Army at Salonika 1915–1918.* Stroud: Sutton, 2004.

Recommended Reading

Atenstaedt, R. L. Dr, *The Medical Response to the Trench Diseases in World War One.* Cambridge: Cambridge Scholars Publishing.

Foster, C. F. & Jones. E. L. (2013). *The Fabric of Society and how it creates wealth: Wealth distribution and wealth creation in Europe 1000–1800.* Northwich: Arley Hall Press.

Starling, J. & Lee, I. (2009). *No Labour, No Battle: Military Labour during the First World War: The Labour Corps in the First World War.* Stroud: The History Press.

Jones, E. & Wessely, S. (2010). *British Prisoners-of-War: From Resilience to Psychological Vulnerability: Reality or Perception.* Oxford: Oxford University Press.

Rawlinson, R. (1850). *'Preliminary Inquiry into the Sewerage, Drainage, and Supply of Water, and the Sanitary Condition of the Inhabitants of the Town of Altrincham: In the County of Chester. Report to the General Board of Health',* Public Health Act (11 & 12, Cap. 63.). London: Her Majesty's Stationery Office. Available at: https://archive.org/stream/b20423494#page/n0/mode/2up

Simkins, P. (1990) *Kitchener's Army: The Raising of the New Armies, 1914–1916.* Manchester: Manchester University Press.

Sullivan, D. (1983). *Navyman.* Clonmel: Coracle Press.

Internet Books

Buchan, J. (1917) *The Battle of the Somme.* New York: George H. Doran. https://archieve.org/details/battleofsommefir00inbuch

Hamilton, Sir Ian, G.C.B. *The Gallipoli Diary,* In two volumes l The Project Gutenberg EBook of Gallipoli Diary, Volume 1 & 2, by Ian Hamilton https://ia802705.us

Maude, Sir Frederick. (1923) *Source Records of the Great War, Vol. V,* ed. Charles F. Horne, on Operations Leading to the Fall of Baghdad, December 1916–March 1917 *National Alumni* l www.firstworldwar.com/source/baghdad_maude_htm

The 42nd (East Lancashire) Division 1914–1918 https://Lib.militaryarchive.co.uk/library/divisional-histories/library/The-42nd-East-Lancashire-Division-1914-1918/HTML/index.asp#/95/zoomed

Nicholson, G. W. L. (1962) *Canadian Expeditionary Force 1914–1919: Official History of the Canadian Army in the First World War.* Ottowa: Queen's Printer and Controller of Stationary. www.cmp-cmp.forces.gc.ca/dhh-dhp/his/docs/CEF_e.pdf

Wyrall, E. (2002) [1921] *The History of the Second Division, 1914–1918.* (Naval & Military Press ed.) London: Thomas Nelson and Sons. https://archive.org/details/historyofsecond02wyra

Field Service regulations, 1909 Reprinted with amendments by Great Britain, War Office. Published 1914 by H.M. Stationery Office, London https://www.openlibrary.org/books/OL7029903M/Field_service_regulations_..._1909

Internet References

www.williamhayes-ww1-wardiary.co.uk/index_files/Page1393.html

http://ww1.canada.com/battlefront/images-the-battle-of-vimy-ridge

www.electriccanadiaNCOm/forces/VimyWarDiaryprojectatCEFSGpdf

Researching Canadian Soldiers of the First World War l regimentalrogue.com/misc/researching-first-world-war-soldiers-part14.htm

data4.collectionscanada.ca

http://en.wikipedia.org/wiki/Second-Battle-of-Artois

https://sites.google.com/sitebowyerdicksongenealogy/memorial-day-every-day-honoring-those-who-have-sacrificed-all

www.longlongtail.co.uk

International Encyclopedia of the First World War 1914–1918 Online: Prisoners of War and Internees (South-East Europe) by Bogdan Trifunovic l www.1914-1918.invisionzone.com

www.wartimememoriesproject.com

www.acenturyback.com

www.local-local.co.uk/wwt-rememberance-stories

www.grengds.com/static.php?contentid=145

www.guardsmagazine.com/features/Autumn2015/features.autumn1505BattleOfLoos.html

www.1914-1918.net/gdiv.htm

www.firstworldwar.com/source/georgevaug1914.htm

www.cwgc.org/search/cemetery

www.ww1.cemeteries.com

www.1914-1918.net/ccs.htm

www.1914-1918.netreadcemetery.html

www.longlongtrail.co.uk/soldiers/a/-/soldiers-life-1914-1918/the-evacuation-chain-for-wounded-and-sick-soldiers/ armyunits/britishinfantry/grenadier.htm

www.wgpp.org/downloads/About-the-CWGC.pdf

britishempire.co.uk/forces/ oxforddnb.com/view/printable/40/85

gm1914.wordpress.com

https://3rdgrenadierguardsww1.wordpress.com/home/september-1916/

https://wwi.lib.byu.edu/index.php/the_Role_of_Railways_in_the_War

Repatriation of Prisoners of War.(Hansard,14november 1918) hansard.millbanksystems.com

British Prisoners of War. (Hansard, 12 October 1916) hansard.millbanksystems.com

British Prisoners of War 1914–1919 Military History Forum www.militariaNCOm

https://www.icrc.org/en/history

encyclopedia.1914-1918-online.net/article/prisoners_of_war_and_internees_south_east_europe

Prisoners of the First World War, the ICRC archives http://grandeguerre.icrc.org

ConnaughtrangersassociatioNCOm/the-great-war-1914-1918

www.iwm.org/history/podcasts/voices-of-the-first-world-war/podcast18-mesopotamia

www.1914-1918.net/mespot.htm

https://onwikipedia.org/wiki/13_(Western)_Division

www.qaranc.co/uk/mesopotamia_world_war_one_photographs.php

usacac.army.mil/CAC2/CARL/nafziger/915BXAD.pdf

The South Belfast Friends of the Somme Association www.belfastsomme.com

The Royal Irish Rifles in 1914–1918 www.1914=1918.net

Royal Irish Rifles – The Long, Long Trail www.longlongtrail.co.uk

Royal Ulster Rifles Museum www.armymuseum.org.uk

Museums l Royal Irish –Virtual Military Gallery www.royal-irish.com

www.somme-battlefields.com

Gallipolisardanelles.com/research/brigades-regiments-andbattlions-engaged-at-gallipoli/

www.gallipoli-association.org

https://en.wikipedia.org/wiki/Order_of_battle_for_the_Battle_of_the_Somme#New_Army_division

.webmatters.net/txtpat/?id=705

ia801406.us.archieve.org/1/items/medicalservicesd02macp/medicalservicesd02macp.pdf

www.eyewitnesstohistory.com/gas.htm

interactive.ancestry.co.uk

search.ancestry.co.uk

en.wikipedia.org

www.independent.ie

www.1914-1918.net

www.taoiseach.gov.ie

www.nam.ac.uk

https://en.wikipedia.org/wiki/Kitchener's_Army

Baker, Chris. 'The 31st Division in 1914–1918' The Long, Long Trail. Retrieved 11/1/17

Irish Soldiers in the First World War l l www.taoiseach.gov.ie/.../1916Commemorations-BattleOfThe Somme1.rtf

Military Service (No. 2) Bill (Hansard, 12 January 1916) hansardmillbanksystems.com

Press Censorship ('Irish Volunteer'). (Hansard, 19 Nove…) hansard.millbanksystems.com

Opinion: Did the Easter rising kill Home Rule? l The Irish Story www.theiririshstory.com

Department of Taoiseach-Irish Soldiers in the First World War web.archive.org

32nd Division – The Long, Long Trail www.longlongtrail.co.uk

Irish Free State Constitution Act 1922 Wikipedia en.wikipedia.org

John Redmond presents shamrock to American president l Century Ireland www.rte.ie

Disbandment of the Irish Regiments l Royal Irish – Virtual Military Gallery www.royal-irish.com
www.everymanremembered.org/cemeteries/cemetery/85800/page=539
www.bbc.co.uk/history/people/john_redmond
www.nam.ac.uk/soldiers-records/persons
www.historyireland.com/20th-century-contemporary-history/irish-suffragettes-at-the-time-of-the-home-rule-crisis/
Statistics of the military effort of the British Empire during the Great War, 1914–1920 l http://freepages.genealogy.rootsweb.ancest...aughr.html#bina
1914-1918invisionzone.com/forums/index.php?/topic/144904-percentage-catholics-serving-in-different-irish-regiments/
www.britishpathe.com/video/armistice-day-dublin/query/14th
https://archive.org/details/statisticsofmili00grea
Ireland's Easter Rising and how history is being twisted in celebrating the struggle for independence l www.independent.co.uk/news/politics/irelands-easter-rising-and-how-historu-is-being-twisted-in-clebrating-the-struggle-for-independence-a6820141.html
Fog of amnesia around the Great War is lifting l www.independent.ie/world-news/europe/fog-of-amnesia-around-the-great-war-is-lifting-30033956.html
Remembering the Irish who fought with Britain in 1914 l www.telegraph.co.uk/history/world-war-o/ne/11003887/Remembering-the-Irish-who-fought-with-Britain-in-1914.html
Armistice day: Remembering Ireland's sacrifice by Ronan McGreevy l www.ibtimes.co.uk/armistice-day-remembering-irelands-sacrifice-1590480
Combined Irish Regiments Association l www.ciroca.org.uk/first-world-world-war-links/infantry-regiments-1914-18
Enhanced British Parliamentary Papers on Ireland l www.dippam.ac.uk
Museum Glasnevin Cemetery and Museum l www.glasnevinmuseum.ie
Joe-duffys-list-of-children-killed-in-1916-rising.pdf
Proclamation of the Irish Republic – Wikipedia l en.wikipedia.org
Report of the Royal Commission on the Rebellion in Ireland l archive.org
Irish servicemen's attitudes to the 1916 Rising l 1914-1918.invisioNCOm
Royal Dublin Fusiliers during Easter Rising l www.dublin-fusiliers.com
Irish Battalions l Royal Dublin Fusiliers Association l http://www.greatwar.ie/ire_batmb.html
Easter 1916 l The Rising www.easter1916.ie
Easter 1916 l Rising overview www.easter1916.ie
New research suggests 485 people were killed in the Easter Rising www.irishtimes.com/news/ireland/irish-news/new-research-suggests-485-people-were-killed-in-the-easter-rising-1.2135511
An Irish soldier in the British Army l www.westernfrontassociatioNCOm/the-great-war/great-war-on-land/battles-of-the-month/5501-16th-irish-division-and-the-gas-attacks-at-hulluch-loos-april-1916.html#stha
The History Press: The secret court martial records of the Easter Rising www.thehistorypress.co.uk
John Maxwell (British Army officer) – Wikipedia en.wikipedia.org
John French, 1st Earl of Ypres – Wikipedia en.wikipedia.org
Lord Lieutenant of Ireland – Wikipedia en.wikipedia.org
UK, WWI War Diaries (France, Belgium and Germany), 1914–1920 search.ancestry.co.uk
Hulluch – UK, WWI War Diaries (France, Belgium and Germany), 1914–1918 search.ancestry.co.uk
Easter Rising 1916: Six days of armed struggle that changed Irish and British history l www.bbc.co.uk/news/uk-northern-ireland-35873316
German Plot (Ireland) – Wikipedia en.wikipedia.org
Why did Sinn Fein win the 1918 election? – Historica l republican.ie/forum/index.php?/topic/20369-why-did-sinn-fein-win-the-1918-election/
The Irish General Election of 1918 www.ark.ac.uk
BMH.WS1678.pdf www.bureauofmilitaryhistory.ie
The Connaught Rangers in 1914–1918 www.1914-1918.net
Our family at war: Letter sent from the front line l www.independent.ie/life/world-war-1/our-family-at-war-letters-sent-from-the-front line-30149160.html
Introduction to Irish Regiments l www.irishgreatwarsociety.com/introduction.htm

5th Battalion RDF during the Easter Rising l www.dublin-fusiliers.com/battalions/5-batt/5th=easter-rising.html

10th Battalion RDF during the Easter Rising l www.dublin-fusiliers.com/battalions/10-batt/campaigns/1916=10th-easter.html

The Rabble and the Republic: The Irish Story l www.theirishhistory.com

The 1918 Election – an ignored Centenary? Millstreet.ie www.millstreet.ie

Three people shot dead by British soldiers on Bachelors Walk l Century IRELAND l www.rte.ie/centuryireland/index.php/articles/three-people-shot-dead-by-british-soldiers-on-bachelors-walk

Enhanced British Parliamentary Papers on Ireland l www.dippam.ac.uk

Bill intituled an Act to amend the Government of Ireland Act, 1914 l archive.org

Model of V Beach Landings, Gallipoli – Connaught Rangers l connaughtrangersassoc.com

The Battle to Free Guillemont Village in Miniature – Connaught Rangers l connaughtrangersassoc.com

Syndicalism – Wikipedia en Wikipedia.org

http://www.theirishstory.com/2013/06/06/the-general-strike-a.. www.theirishstory.com

Limerick Soviet-Wikipedia en.wikipedia.org

The General Strike and Irish Independence l The Irish Story www.theirishstory.com

RDF A selection of photographs of the regiment l www.royaldublinfusiliers.com/online-museum/photographs/

Battle Honour St Quentin – German Spring Offensive 1918 l https://www.royal-irish.com/events/battle-honour-st-quentin-german-spring-offensive-1918

Kaiserschlacht: The German Spring Offensive www.remembrancetrails-northernfrance.com

The Battles of the Somme: https://archive.org/stream/battlesofsomme00gibbuoft#page/250/mode/... Archive.org

The Cheshire regiment and their key role in Battle of the Somme l www,chesterchronicle.co.uk/news/history/Cheshire-regiment-key-role-battle-11546389

Encyclopaedia – Trench Foot l www.firstworldwar.com.atoz/trenchfoot.htm

Trench foot l https://en.wikipedia.org/wiki/Trench_foot

War Dead of Trafford, Greater Manchester l www.traffordwardead.co.uk

The Battles of the Somme, 1916 l www.longlongtail.co.uk/battles/battles-of-the-western-front-in-france-and-flanders/the-battles-of-the-somme-1916/

Report of the Battle Nomenclature l discovery.nationalarchives.gov.uk

WWI Battles of the Somme 1916 & 1918, France l www.greatwar.co.uk

Battles of the Western Front 1914–1918 l www.greatwar.co.uk

The Chapel Street Memorial – GM 1914 l gm1914.wordpress.com

Copy-of-the-chapel-street-memorial.jpg. l gm1914.files.wordpress.com

World War One Wounded Collection: Harold Macmillan l https://www.the genealogist.co.uk/ww1-wounded/

Harold Macmillan l sparticus-educational.com

A Prime Minister's War records: From Lieutenant Macmillan to 'Supermac' – a Prime Minister's war l www.telegraph.co.uk/history/world-war-one/inside-first-world-war/part-one/10277160/harold-macmillan-war-record.html

Ask the Expert – mystery medal l Blog.main.findmypast.co.uk/2011/01/28/ask-the-expert-mystery-medal/

Distinguished Conduct Medal (DCM) The Gazette www.the gazette.co.uk

Carl's camera Altrincham www.carlscam.com

17th (Northern) Division – The Long, Long Trail www.longlongtrail.co.uk

17th (Northern) Division – Wikipedia en.wikipedia.org

Batteries and Brigades of the Royal Field Artillery – www.longlongtrail.co.uk

LXXVI11, LXXXIX, LXXX and LXXXIII (Howitzer) Brigades (17th D.. www.longlongtrail.co.uk

The Royal Field Artillery units of 1914–1918 www.1914-1918.net

Royal Garrison Artillery in the Great War- The Wa... www.wartimememoriesproject.com

The Siege Batteries of the Royal Garrison Artillery-The Long... www.longlongtrail.co.uk

Chapel-street-1934-tl3687.jpg (1550XI200) gm1914.fileswordpress.com

The Chapel Street Memorial – GM 1914 gm1914.wordpress.com

The British Campaign in North Russia 1918–1920 www.1914-1918.net

British Forces in Russia 1918–1920 – The Eastern Front-… 1914-1918.invisionzone.com

Churchill's Private War: British intervention in South Russia, 1919 hubpages.com

British Army involvement in Russian civil war 1919 l www.rootschat.com/forum/index.php?topic=544136.0

British Army in Russia 1918–1919 l Military History Forum www.militariaNCOm

The Gettysburg Address by Abraham Lincoln www.abrahamlincolnonline.org

Paragraph 392, King's Regulations l fami… myancestors.wordpress.com

South Wales Borderers – Regimental History www.forces-war-records.co.uk

Casualty details www.cwgc.org

Find War Dead www.cwgc.org

UK, Soldiers Died in the Great War, 1914–1919 – Ancestry search.ancestry.co.uk

Cheshire Regiment – Chesterwiki chester.shoutwiki.com

Measuring Worth www.measuringworth.com

SS *Kingstonian* [+ 1918] www.wrecksite.eu/wreck.aspx?96561

List of shipwrecks in April 1918 https://en.wikipedia.org/wiki/List_of_shipwrecks_in_April_1918

Great War Forum l 1914-1918.invisionzone.com/forums/index.php?/94203-ht-kingstonian/

1x Brigade l www.1914-1918.net/rfa_units_9.html

3rd (Reserve) Battalion, The Royal Welsh Fusiliers www.facebook.com

Royal Welsh Fusiliers Museum www.rwfmuseum.org.ukBBC Blogs-Wales- The Royal Welsh Fusiliers: A literary regiment: Phil Carradice l www.bbc.co.uk/blogs/wales/entries/3d274d6c-ddc8-3c3c-a70-273879f69180

'Home from Germany. 320 arrivals at Boston Yesterday'. *Nottingham Evening Post*, 21 January 1918. Image: http://www.militaryfactory.com/ships/imgs/sms-mowe.jpg

Repatriation of Prisoners of War. HLDeb 14 November 1918 vol 32 cc90-3 l hansardmillbanksystems.com/lords/1918nov/14/repatriation-of-prisoners-of-war

Repatriated prisoner – British Pathe l www.britishpathe.com

Full text of 'Prisoners of the great war. Authoritative statement of conditions in the prison camps of Germany' Carl P. Dennett l archive.org/stream/prisonersofgreat00denn/prisonersofgreat00denn_djvu.txt

Library of Congress Professional Research Service Prisoners of War: Repatriation or Internment in Wartime American and Allied Experience, 1775 to Present l https://www.loc.gov/rr/frd/rr/frd/Military_Law/pdf/CRS_Prisoners-of-War_report.pdf

Germany's Treatment of Prisoners. HL Deb 16 October 1918 vol 31 cc709-32 l hansard.millbanksystems.com/lords/1918/oct/16/Germanys-treatment-of-prisoners

The Wounded and Prisoners of War l www.roydenhistory.co.uk/eportwarmemorial/pows.pdf

Pursuit of an 'Unparalleled opportunity' Chapter 10 Successful World's Alliance POW Diplomacy: Phildius and WPA Relief Work in Bulgaria. Kenneth Steuer. www.gutenberg-e.org/steur/pdf/steur.ch10.pdf

Pursuit of an 'Unparalleled Opportunity' The American YMCA and Prisoner of War Diplomacy among the Central Power Nations during World War One, 1914–1923. By Kenneth Steuer www.gutenberg-3.org/steur/archive/AppendixA/bulgarian per cent20Prison per cent20Camps/prison_shell.html?Philippopolis

Prisoners of War. HC Deb 19 October 1916 vol 86 cc741-2W hansard.millbanksystems.com/written_answers/1916/oct/19prisoners-of-war

Philippopolis Camp. HC Deb 05 November 1918 vol 110-c1914 hansard.millbanksystems.com/commons/1918/nov/od/philippopolis-camp

Map of the Main Prison Camps in Germany and Austria, By Mrs Pope-Hennessy l digital.slv.vic.gov.au

Boston port's key role in the First World War – Boston Standard Caroline Walls www.bostonstandard.co.uk/news/business/boston-port-s-key-role-in-the-first-world-1-6223014

Three cheers for Switzerland! – the prisoners of war interned in Switzerland in 1916 by Philip Judd l lenews.ch/2016/04/06/3-cheers-for-switzerland-the-prisoners-of-war-interred-in-switzerland-in-1916/

Battle of Doiran (1917) l https://en.wikipedia.org/wiki/Battle_of_Doiran_(1917)

The Salonika Front: A. J. Mann. l https://archieve.org/details/salonikafront00mannuoft

The Times History of the War l https://archieve.org/stream/timeshistoryofwa201londoft#page/3/mode/1up

The Border Regiment in Macedonia. Compiled by Harry Fecitt MBE l www.kaisercross. com/304501/541201.html

Memorial Plaque (medallion) l https://en.wikipedia.org/wiki/Memorial_Plaque_(medallion)

James Ford 6523 R Lancs Regt-Soldiers-Great War Forum 19141918.invisionzone.com

Ourheroesinmemoriam.co.uk WW1 Soldiers Database l https://sites.google.com/site/ourheroesin-memorium/ww1-irish-soldiers-database

Population by country, 1911 and 2011 l www.cso.ie./en/releaseandpublications/ep/p-1916/1919irl/people/population

World War One: The Battle of Mons l www.the gazette.co.uk/all-notices/content/218

Convention (1V) respecting the Laws and Customs of War on Land and its annex: regulations concerning the Laws and Customs of War on Land. The Hague, 18 October 1907. www.opbw.org/int_inst/sec_doc/1907HC-TEXT.pdf

Treaties, States Parties and Commentaries: Convention for the Amelioration of the Condition of the Wounded in Armies in the Field. Geneva, 6 July 1906: International Committee of the Red Cross [CH]l https://ihl-databases.icrc.org/ihl/INTRO/180?OpenDocument

1st Battalion, Cheshire Regiment, Killed in Action www.grandadswar.co.uk

History of the Great War – Principle Events Timeline www.greatwar.co.uk

Prisoners of War – The British Library www.bl.uk

Legacy of the 1914–18 war 2: Battle for the mind: World War One and the birth of military psychiatry. Edgar Jones &, Simon Wessley l www.kcl.ac.uk/kcmhr/publivations/assefiles/2014/Jones2014e.pdf

Article by Andrew Hough 20 May, 2012: www.telegraph.co.uk/news/therooyalfamily/9148002/Personal-King-George-V-POW-letter-found-inattac-nearly-100-years.html

Surname Database: www.surnamedb.com

Navy Records Society www.navyrecords.org.uk

Naval-History.Net : World War One 1914–1918 www.naval-history.net/(Index)-1914.htm

The project Gutenberg EBook of a History of Aeronautics, by E. Charles Vivian https:www.gutenberg.org/files/874/874-h/874.h.htm

Royal Flying Corps https://en.wikipedia.org/wiki/Royal_Flying_Corps

Statistics of the military effort of the British Empire during the Great War, 1914–1918 https://archive.org/stream/statisiticsofmili00great#page/500/mode/2up

The Liverpool Shipwreck & Humane Society www.liverpoolshipwreckandhumanesoc.org/Home.html

Unit War Diary Norfolk Regiment https://www.norfolkinworldwar.1files.wordpress.com/2014/09/9-sept1914.jpg

British order of Battle Hill 60 and the Battles of Ypres 1915 l www.314th.org/Nafziger-Collection-of-Orders-of-Battle/915BXAB.pdf

'Altrincham & Bowdon: with historical reminiscences of Ashton-on Mersey, Sale, and surrounding townships' www.archive.org/stream/altrinchambowden00ingh/altrinchambowdon00ingh_djvu.txt

British Army Museums and Record at Army Museums Ogilby Trust www.armymuseums.org

How deadly was the poison gas of WWI? www.bbc.co.uk

Newspapers

Broadheath Tragedy: *Altrincham, Hale and Bowden Guardian* report, 11 March 1921.

Chapel Street Roll of Honour: *The Guardian*, Tuesday, 8 April 1919.

Chapel Street Roll of Honour: *The Guardian*, Friday, 11 April 1919.

Lodging Houses for Sale: *Nantwich Guardian*, Tuesday, 9 May 1916.

Lodging Houses for Sale: *Manchester Courier* and *Lancashire Advertiser*, 6 October 1894 (The British Newspaper Archive. www.findmypast.co.uk).

Lodging Houses for Sale and Public House: *Manchester Courier* and *Lancashire General Advertiser*, 6 July 1907 (The British Newspaper Archive. www.findmypast.co.uk).

Lodging Houses for Sale: *Manchester Courier* and *Lancashire General Advertiser*. 13 February 1858 (The British Newspaper Archive. www.findmypast.co.uk).

Soldier's Heroic Rescue: *Nantwich Guardian*, 21 November 1916 (The British Newspaper Archive. www.findmypast.co.uk).

Railway Cut. Chapel Street sent 81 men the colours out of 61 houses: *Evening Despatch-Birmingham*, 2 October 1914 (The British Newspaper Archive. www.findmypast.co.uk).

(The British Newspaper Archive. www.findmypast.co.uk).

Out of sixty houses in Chapel Street ... *Manchester Evening News*, 26 June 1915. (The British Newspaper Archive. www.findmypast.co.uk).

The Altrincham Election-Manifesto for Irish Voters: *The Times*, p.12, 9 May 1913.

Altrincham Result, Great Rise in Unionist Majority: *The Times*, p.8, 30 May 1913.

Lloyd George, Liberalism and the land by Ian Packer.

Organisations

Commonwealth Graves Commission (CWGC)
2 Marlow Road, Maidenhead
Berkshire
SL6 7DX
T: 01628634221
E: enquiries@cwgc.ord

The CWGC has many online interactive applications with simple apps to use, for example: Virtual Cemetery and the War Grave App, allowing searches of war graves at more than 23,000 locations. There is also information on video news and up-coming events. Regular themed projects that communities, groups and individuals can participate in are offered and resource material includes ideas for activities and participation, as well as raising awareness, conservation work and remembrance.

The Army
W: www.army.mod.uk/training_education/25813.aspx

As part of the Army's commemorations of the centenary of the First World War, a programme of support to schools has been developed for use by secondary schools.

The Soldiers to Schools is an initiative whereby secondary schools can request a soldier to support teaching activities in the classroom. A request form in PDF format is available on the above website address. The session has the option of being based around a theme/themes discussed between the teacher and soldier. A list of suggestions is available on the website. It is requested that consideration is given regarding booking the resource is given at least six weeks before the required date. The relevant regional Brigade will be notified, which will identify a trained soldier to make contact with you within two weeks of the request.

Sessions include: *Citizen's Workshops – KS3:* These are three different workshops, which focus on the work the Army is called on to do in times of national emergency situations, such as flooding. These have been specifically designed in conjunction with the Association for Citizenship Teaching.

Each workshop has a lesson plan with the second delivered by an Army representative, there is a Powerpoint presentation available and sessions are designed to last between 45–60 minutes. Topics covered are based on the questions: How does the local council ask the Army for help? How can people (students) help when their community is in need? Materials can be downloaded from the download materials section on the website.

Science Workshops: These are three science based challenges (biology, chemistry and physics) focusing on a humanitarian scenario. These show the real outcomes of practical science as part of the Army. The activities have been designed and developed in conjunction with the Defence Science and Technology Laboratory and the Institute of Naval Medicine. The challenges consist of questions such as: design a healthy, high energy snack with the topic link to human diet and nutrition and bacteria; design a cooling suit/vest that will remove heat with the topic link to heat energy and energy changes and transfers; design a helmet made from a composite material with the topic link to properties of polymers and composite materials.

The Army have also developed a range of resources and materials that can be used to assist teachers and careers advisors in schools and colleges. Arrangement is made via the local Army Careers Centre. Further information is available from the Outreach Team:

E: ARTD-RG-Outreachadmin@mod.uk

T: 03456008080

PDA (Formally known as Personal Development Activity): These activities involve students completing a variety of mentally and physically challenging activities (team tasks and physical fitness). The aim is to develop resilience, leadership, teamwork, confidence and communication skills.

Employability Skills: An employability skills package that includes: what an employer is seeking from a potential employee, practice interviews and communication skills.

Work Experience: These are residential courses which involve students experiencing a taste of Army life. These are five-day courses and are designed to demonstrate the training and education opportunities available in a career in the Army.

The Imperial War Museum

IWM London

Lambeth Road

London SE1 6HZ

T: 02074165000

W: www.iwm.org.uk

Free admission with twenty-minute gallery talks on key objects and stories from the collections, details from the information desk on the day. Private fee-paying tours are also available.

The National Army Museum

Royal Hospital Road

Chelsea

London SW3 4HT

T: 02077300717

E: info@nam.ac.uk

W: www.nam.ac.uk

New museum opening 2017, free admission.

The museum seeks to explore thoughts and ideas and the real stories of people, and from this to challenge the way people think about the British Army and their relationship with it. It offers: Tours, Workshops, Exhibitions, Book Club, Collections, Galleries, Online collection.

The National Archives

Kew

Richmond

Surrey TW9 9DU

T: 02088766 34444

W: www.nationalarchives.gov.uk

Free admission without booking is available to see original documents and records. Online digitised collections are available, including iconic advertising and ancient maps, podcasts and videos. There is also a live chat phone service offered Tuesday to Saturday. Free talks by experts are offered which require prior booking. They are accompanied by a document display of relevant original material held by the National Archives.

Award-winning educational resource material is available for students and teachers covering many subjects, for example: war, inter-war and post-war time periods.

Short courses are available for adults on file preparation, e-learning, cyber security, information management.

The Royal British Legion

199 Borough High Street

London

Se1 1AA

T: 02032072100

This is a registered charity which helps members of the Royal Navy, British Army, Royal Air Force, veterans and their families all year round. It campaigns to improve lives, remembers the fallen and organises the Poppy Appeal. The Legion is helping young people understand the issues of Remembrance, conflicts and the importance of peace.

Free learning pack downloads are available in PDF format along with other resources for schools, designed to assist teachers and educators working with young people to increase knowledge of Remembrance, History, English and Citizenship activities. There are also posters, videos, activity sheets, lesson plans, and Key Stage 1, 2, 3, and 4 Assembly (full set of six assemblies) information on set themes.

Societies and Associations

The Gallipoli Association

Wey House
15 Church Street
Weybridge
Surrey KT13 8NA
W: www.gallipoli-association.org
The website lists some forty-plus free online Gallipoli books, information on British school projects, international projects and a twelve-minute film of the Gallipoli Centenary Project. There is an 'On this day' feature useful for teachers looking for ideas for lessons and assemblies. There is a special membership rate for schools which enables members to join a forum, receive a journal and attend a conference.

The Salonika Campaign Society

W: salonikacampaignsociety.org.uk
The Society is marking the centenary of the Salonika Campaign (1915–1918), in a number of ways, including helping to preserve key locations of former battlefields associated with the British Salonika Force. Specific to this is an effort to preserve 'HQ House' in recognition of the part played by 10th (Irish) Division in the initial advance into, and withdrawal from, Serbia in 1915.

Details can be found on the Salonika Campaign Society website along with battlefield tour information, initiatives marking the centenary, and research and education information.

The Somme Association

The Director
233 Bangor Road
Newtownards
County Down
Northern Ireland BT23 7PH
T: (0044) 0289182 3202
E: sommeassociation@btconnect.com
W: www.sommeassociatioNCOm
The association offers a guided tour of the World War One interactive exhibition for primary school visits and a talk. Also, twice a year the museum offers A Level history conferences which are designed for AS and A2 students. The conference is hosted by academic lecturers and covers the details relevant to the school curriculum. There is a Key Stage Three tour for 10-year-old students, which covers the causes of the First World War, enlistment and recruitment, medicine and a walk through the Museum's trench experience. There is also a Community Outreach Programme where the staff of the museum offer lectures, presentations and exhibitions and a variety of events which includes visits to schools, clubs and community groups. The aim is to increase awareness and improve mutual understanding as well as supporting a more cohesive community, exploring identity and shared remembering. Some of the presentations include: The formation of the Ulster Volunteer Force and the 36 (Ulster) Division; the 10th (Irish) Division at Gallipoli; the Thiepval Wood Project; Women in the First World War.

Royal Naval Association
RNA HQ
Room 209
Semaphore Tower
PP70
HM Naval Base
Portsmouth
PO1 3LT
T: 023 9272 3747
E: admin@royalnavalassoc.com
W: www.royal-naval-associatioNCO.uk

The Not Forgotten Association, London
4th Floor,
2 Grosvenor Gardens
London
SW1W 0DH
T: 020 7730 2400
E: info@nfassociation.org
W: www.nfassociation.org
The association was founded two years after the war had ended. Its founder, Marta Cunningham, made a visit to a hospital in 1919, and was very surprised to find several hundred veterans of the war at the hospital. At that time, there were many thousands of former servicemen confined to hospital. It was her intention to ensure that men living out of the public view in hospital would know that indeed they indeed, were 'Not Forgotten'.

Today, the charity is a tri-service charity providing entertainment and leisure facilities for Service and ex-Service men and women and raises money for the provision of television sets, concert programmes, day trips, short breaks, an annual summer Garden Party and a Christmas Party through activities such as sponsored marathon races, abseiling, swimming, et cetera. They work with other charities such as BLESMA and Stoll who nominate injured veterans such as amputees, for skiing trips, for example. These types of holiday extend an opportunity for veterans of different backgrounds with a variety of injuries to come together where they can enjoy camaraderie and challenge and return home with renewed enthusiasm and determination to deal with the challenges they face.

This is a very worthwhile organisation to be involved with either individually or as classroom participation, it gives the opportunity to participate in fundraising initiatives.

The Royal Aeronautical Society
No. 4 Hamilton Place
London
W1J 7BQ
T: 020 7670 4300
E: raes@aerosociety.com
W: https://www.aerosociety.com
The National Aerospace Library is one of the world's most extensive libraries devoted to the development of aeronautics, aviation and aerospace technology. It houses journals, rare books, a repository of aviation images and photographs, artefacts, historic papers and publications.
E: the davidjonessociety@gmail.com

The War Poets Association
Anne Price-Owen (Director, UK)
c/o The David Jones Society
22 Gower Road

Sketty

Swansea SA2 9BY

T: 04179 2206144

W: www.warpoets.org

The War Poets Association promotes interest in the work, life and historical context of poets whose subject is the experience of war. In 1914, hundreds of young men in uniform took to poetry as a way to express extreme emotion at the very edge of experience. And so, war poetry became established as a literary genre. Themes explored include: identity, innocence, guilt, loyalty, courage, compassion, humanity, duty, desire, death and it asks questions about life. It explores the relationship of personal experience. The association offers poetry tours to battle sites, performances and exhibitions, conferences and symposia. It also offers good online resources including: film clips, interviews, digitised images, articles and commentaries, and important primary sources.

The Wilfred Owen Association

W: www.wilfredowen.org.uk

This is an extremely comprehensive site, well documented and thoroughly researched. All of Owen's poems are critiqued; the site features a Virtual Tour which is highly recommended. The teaching resources are second to none.

The association offers a First World War Poetry Digital Archive which is an online repository of over 7,000 items of text, images, audio and video for teaching, learning and research. It contains collections from all the major poets of the period. It offers a free teaching pack which has been created using material from the world's largest private archive of British newspapers. It is available to schools, universities, accredited institutions and libraries only at this present time. An iPad app is available at a small cost which explores the works of Wilfred Owen and forty-five of the poet's works are featured and read by women; it has been designed by Ian Bennett, a lecturer in film and media at Anglia Ruskin University (Cambridge).

Siegfried Sassoon Fellowship

W: www.sassoonfellowship.org

The fellowship offers battle tours where Siegfried Sassoon fought in Flanders and the Somme, and explores the poet's attitude to war and approach to poetry; it also specialises in literary tours and themed events. A joint membership with the Wilfred Owen Association is available.

War Memorials Trust

T: 020 7834 0200 (Learning Officer)

E: learning@warmemorials.org

W: www.warmemorials.org

The trust works for the protection and conservation of war memorials in the UK. It promotes advice and information and runs grant schemes for the repair and conservation of war memorials. The website provides a large range of resources to help discover more about war memorials and their preservation. The trust is developing a youth focused Learning Programme to educate young people in schools and youth groups about their memorial heritage.

The Wenches in Trenches Association

W: www.wenchesintrenches.co.uk

Wenches in trenches are a group of like-minded women who raise awareness and promote the memory of women in war, support members of the British Armed Forces and their families, support those with life-changing injury and illness and other worthwhile causes. Recently they funded the first memorial bench to the nurses and VADs at Lochnagar Crater on The Somme and a granite memorial. Their mission is to include the names of any women who were omitted from the war memorials after WWI in their hometowns in the UK. Many of the team's members are working in the nursing profession.

The Western Front Association

W: www.westernfrontassociatioNCOm

The Western Front Association was formed in 1980 to maintain interest in the First World War. It is a non-political association and does not seek to glorify war. It works to perpetuate the memory, courage and comradeship of all, from all sides, on all fronts.

The association has a fantastic website which offers information on learning events. Resources are available for AQA, Edexcel, OCR examination boards along with Key Stages 1, 2, 3, 4, 5. There are also post-graduate dissertations available to peruse.

List of Museums

Cheshire Regiment
Cheshire Military Museum,
The Castle,
Chester CH1 2DN
T: 01244327617
E: cheshiremilitarymuseum@live.co.uk
W: www.cheshiremilitarymuseum.co.uk

South Wales Borderers/Welsh Regiment
The Regimental Museum of The Royal Welsh
    (Brecon),
The Barracks,
Brecon,
Powys
LD3 7EB
T: 01874613310
E: info@royalwelsh.org.uk
W: www.royalwelsh.org.uk

Royal Welch Fusiliers
Royal Welch Fusiliers Regimental Museum,
The Castle,
Caernarfon,
Gwynedd,
North Wales
LL55 2AY
T: 01286 673362
E: wwwcontact@rwfmuseum.wales
W: www.rwfmuseum.org.uk

King's Own Scottish Borderers
King's Own Scottish Borderers Regimental
    Museum,
The Barracks Parade,
Berwick-upon-Tweed,
TD15 1DG
T: 01289 307426
E: museum@kosb.co.uk
W: www.kosb.co.uk/museum.htm

Gordon Highlanders
The Gordon Highlanders Museum,
St Luke's,
Viewfield Road,
Aberdeen,
AB15 7XH
T: 01224 311200
W: www.gordonhighlanders.com

Grenadier Guards
The Guards Museum,
Wellington Barracks,
Birdcage Walk,
London SW1E 6HQ
T: 0207414 3428
E: guardsmuseum@aol.com
W. www.theguardsmuseum.com

(Queen's Own) Household Cavalry & Cavalry of
    The Line
The Household Cavalry Museum,
Horse Guards,
Whitehall,
London SW1A 2AX
T: 020 7930 3070
E: museum@householdcavalry.co.uk
W: www.householdcavalrymuseum.co.uk

King's Own Royal (Lancaster) Regiment
King's Own Royal Regiment Museum,
City Museum,
Market Square,
Lancaster LA1 1HT
T: 01524 64637
E: kingsownmuseum@iname.com
W: www.king'sownmuseum.com

Prince of Wales's (South Lancashire) Regiment
Lancashire Infantry Museum,
Fulwood Barracks,
Preston PR2 8AA
T: 01772 260584
E: enquiries@lancashireinfantrymuseum.org.uk
W: www.lancashireinfantrymuseum.org.uk

Lancashire Fusiliers
Fusilier Museum,
Moss Street,
Bury BL9 0DF
T: 0161 7638950
E: enquiries@fusiliersmuseum.com
W: www.fusiliermuseum.com

Manchester Regiment
Museum of the Manchester Regiment,
Ashton Town Hall Market Place,
Ashton-under-Lyne,
OL6 6DL
T: 0161 342 2254
W: www.tameside.gov.uk

The King's (Liverpool) Regiment
Museum of Liverpool,
Liverpool Waterfront,
Liverpool L3 1DG
T: 0151 478 4545
W: www.liverpoolmuseums.org.uk

The Royal Engineers
Royal Engineer's Museum,
Prince Arthur Road,
Gillingham ME4 4UG
T: 01634 822839

Royal Flying Corps
Royal Air Force Museum London,
Grahame Park Way,
London NW9 5LL
T: 020 8205 2266
W: www.rafmuseum.org.uk

Royal Marine Light Infantry
Royal Marines Museum,
Eastney Esplanade,
Southsea,
Portsmouth
Hampshire PO4 9PX
T: 023 9281 9385
E: marines.info@nmrn.org.uk

Royal Shropshire Light Infantry
Shropshire Regimental Museum,
The Castle,
Castle Street,
Shrewsbury,
SY1 2AT
T: 01743 358516
E: curator@shropshireregimentalmuseum.co.uk
W: www.shropshireregimentalmuseum.co.uk

Somerset Light Infantry
The Museum of Somerset,
Taunton Castle,
Castle Green,
Taunton,
Somerset TA1 4AA
T: 01823 255088
E: museumofsomerset@swheritage.org.uk
W: www.museumofsomerset.org.uk

Devonshire Regiment
The Keep Military Museum,
Barrack Road,
Dorchester,
Dorset DT1 1RN
T: 01305 264066
W: www.keepmilitarymuseum.org

Recommended Images of Chapel Street

To access, type the following url: https://apps.trafford.gov.uk/TraffordLifetimes/ to the site and then type in Chapel Street (omitting Altrincham), in the dialog box along with the reference number in corresponding box.

1. Chapel Street 1919 Inhabitants. Reference Number TL0100.
2. View of Chapel Street from the top of the street. The narrowness of cobbled road and interesting steps into some houses. Rose and Shamrock signage can be seen. Reference Number TL1274.
3. View of entrance to Chapel Street and Grapes public house, off Regent Road. On right side of photograph is a view of Roll of Honour on kerbside attached to Chapel wall. The street sign can also be seen on this wall. Reference Number TL3687.
4. Chapel Street view. Unusual later photograph, well-lit and in great architectural detail. Shows terraced three-storey lodging houses (No. 7) with wooden framed windows and shutters at ground level. Of interesting note are the Board of Health recommendations: the well-appointed setts on the road, level paving, drain piping and gas lighting. Reference Number TL3688.
5. Back street view of Chapel Street showing privies, dustbins, water pails, water butts, mangles and washing lines. TL3689.
6. Later Chapel Street view, with Mrs De Courcey (mother of Patrick and Martin), and a resident of sixty years in the foreground. Reference Number TP10882.

7. Chapel Street Roll of Honour. Photograph of soldiers and dignitaries alongside the Memorial. TL2099.
8. Vivid street scene showing Chapel Street on the day of its celebration with street bunting and flags, featuring approximately fifty residents, mostly women and children. TL2973a.
9. The original telegram from King George V recognising the sacrifice of the residents of Chapel Street, Altrincham in the First World War. It is housed in a wooden frame with a photo and plaque. TL9588.
10. Rose and Shamrock public house. TL0040.

Appendix List

Appendix 1

<u>16th CORPS OPERATION ORDER No. 32</u> <u>11th April, 1918</u>

Reference Map 1/50,000

The Corps Commander notified that instructions had been received from the Commander-in-Chief of the Allied Armies that a series of active local operations is to be maintained along the whole of the Allied front in order to harass the enemy and obtain information regarding his intentions.

1. To give effect to these instructions, the Corps Commander decided as follows:-
    The 16th Corps will carry out the operations mentioned in para3 commencing after dark on the night of the 14/15 instant.
    The object of those operations is:-
    • To capture prisoners, both during the advance to and occupation of the villages named, and afterwards by means of ambush and patrol activity further forward.
    • To make the enemy think that the appearance of guns on the left bank of the STRUMA indicates preparations for a move forward, and so to induce him to send forward reconnaissance patrols.
    • To show activity on the front of the 1st Greek Division to induce the enemy to expect an attack in that direction, and so to cause him to man his forward trenches, etc., and to present targets for our artillery and aeroplanes.

2. The operations to be carried out as follows:-

<u>1st Greek Division</u>
To occupy with strong detachments BEGLIK MAHALE – KAKAKASKA – SALMHALE – KISPEKI –ADA and OSMAN KAMILA.

<u>27th Division</u>
To link up with the left of the 1st Division and occupy HOMONDOS – KALENDRA SOUTH AND NORTH WOODS _ TOPALOVA and possibly PROSENIK.

<u>28th Division</u>
To link up with the left of the 27th Division and occupy KUMLI and ORMANLI with the possibility of an extension further forward afterwards.

3. To assist in those operations Divisional Artillery to the extent of one half, and Machine Guns at the discretion of Divisional Commanders may be taken to the left bank of the STRUMA. The Corps Artillery will be disposed on the left bank of the STRUMA as attached in the table.

4. The 1st Greek Division will be responsible for the local protection of the section 153rd Heavy Battery on arrival in neighbourhood of SAJRAKTAR MAHALE.

The Corps Cyclist Battalion will provide an escort for the section of 4.5" Howitzers (D/31) on moving forward from MARIAN to the neighbourhood of KAKARASKA and until the conclusion of operations.

5. The Corps Mounted Troops will discontinue regular patrolling during the operations and will remain in Corps Reserve available to act as may be required.

6. Special instructions for the co-operation of No. 17 Squadron R.A.F. will be issued as the situation demands.

7. The order to conclude the operations and to resume normal dispositions will be issued by the Corps Commander.

H.L. Knight
Brig-General,
General Staff, 16th Corps.

Issued at 19.00

1. Copy no 1 27th Division
2. 28th Division
3. 1st Greek Division
4. Corps Mounted Troops
5. No 17 Squadron R.A.F.
6. 6 D.G. G.S.
7. D.A. & Q.M.G.
8. G.O.C. R.A.
9. D.A. & Q.M.G.
10. G.O.C. R.A.
11. C.E.
12. D.D.M.S.
13. A.D.A.S.
14. C.L.G.O.
15. A.P.M.
16. General Quarters
17.   "   "
18. War Diary
19. Office
20. Spare

Appendix 2

16th CORPS OPERATION ORDER NO 33

Reference Map 1/50, 000   18th April, 1918

1. (a) The 1st Greek Division will remain in occupation of the line of villages BEGLIK-
       KAKARASKA-SALMAHALE-KISPEKI-ADA-OSMANKA until the night 20th/21st instant
       when they will withdraw and resume dispositions.
   (b) The 27th Division will withdraw from their forward line and resume normal dispositions
       tonight but will be responsible for the protection of the left of the forward troops of the 1st
       Greek Division referred to in (a) until withdrawal takes place on the night 20th/21st instant.
   (c) The 28th Division will withdraw from their forward line and resume normal dispositions
       tonight. KUMLI will however continue to be held until the night 20th/21st instant.
2. The Corps Artillery on the left bank of the STRUMA will withdraw tonight to the right bank,
   except that in the area of the 1st Greek Division which will remain until the night 20th/21st.
3. The Corps Mounted Troops will resume their normal duties of patrolling on the morning of the
   21st instant.
4. The Argyll Mountain Battery will rejoin the 4th Highland Mountain Brigade under arrangements
   to be made by the 28th Division.

              H.L. Knight
                Brig-General
            General Staff, 16th Corps.

Issued at 1300
1. Copy no 1 27th Division
2. 28th Division
3. 1st Greek Division
4. Corps Mounted Troops
5. No 17 Squadron R.A.F.
6. 6 D.G. G.S.
7. D.A. & Q.M.G.
8. G.O.C. R.A.
9. C.E.
10. D.D.M.S.
11. A.D.A.S.
12. C.L.G.O.
13. A.P.M.
14. General Quarters
15.   "   "
16. War Diary
17. Office
18. Spare

Appendix 3
Prisoner of War List: Salonika

REGT NO.	RANK NAME	NATURE OF CASUALTY	MISSING
28442	L/C	RADFORD S.	
58352	L/C	BRACE E.	
18281	L/C	HUGHES R.	
9323	L/C	DOUGHTY C.	
315031	Pte	HEBBLETHWAITE F.	
7657	Sgt	WOODFORD F. H.	
9141	Sgt	PEARSON A.	
9930	L/Sergt	BOOTH W. E.	
15776	"	CLARKE J.	
27135	Pte. A/L/C	ALLMAN T.W.	
58696	Pte	CURTIS E.	
18549	L/C	DUNBEBBIN G.	
24872	Pte	GOULBOURNE W.	
58735	Pte	BECKLEY E. R	
18698	Pte	HOLLINGSWORTH W.	
66248	Pte	McALLISTER W. H.	
243181	Pte	ROBERTS J.	
32982	Pte	PERKS R.	
267855	Pte	WILD A.	
26642	Pte	MASSEY H.	
241204	Pte	SPROSTON N.	
315439	Pte	SWINDON J. S.	
58108	Pte	WOOD W. E.	
66424	Pte	STEWART A.	
66262	Pte	WOOTON U. L.	
58539	Pte	FURSE F. A.	
66245	Pte	BROWN E.	
315266	Pte	O'NEILL.	
54534	Pte	WEAVER T. H.	
58643	Pte	DELDERFIELD	
62808	Pte	BASON H.	
9035	Pte	HUGHES G.W.	
58722	Pte	HICKFORD C.	
27365	Pte	SIDDALL B.	
64684	Pte	MORRISON D.	
27362	Pte	NIELD S. L.	
25349	Pte	QUINN W. H. J.	

11222	Pte	RILEY J.*
36719	Pte	STAITE J. E.
58615	Pte	SPRATT J. R.
58675	Pte	TURNER H.
58368	Pte	JORDON W.
58396	Pte	WALTON E. G.
9177	Pte	PARLE S.
34982	Pte	HOLMES E.
25567	Pte	ALLEN D.
14919	Pte	ALLEN F.
26489	Pte	ASTILL J. N
26726	Pte	CLAY J.
315426	Pte	PENLINGTON W. H.
58382	Pte	SAVILLE E. J.
12516	Pte	STRETCH A.
10306	Pte	WOOLLEY A.
10409	Pte	TURNER J. T.
28133	Pte	LORD E.
8885	Cpl	JONES B.
16896	Cpl	WILDE T.
316084	Pte	TIPPER C.
25492	L/C	HALL H.

Appendix 4
Field Service Regulations
(1914)

Starting Point.

1. A point, termed the starting point, which the head of the main body is to pass at a certain time, is fixed in operation orders. If troops are not all quartered together, it may be necessary for the commander to fix more than one starting point, so as to enable subordinate commands to take their places in the column of march punctually without unnecessary fatigue to the troops, and without crossing the line of other commands. In the absence of such orders subordinate commands must arrange their own movements to the starting point. When commands are broken up for administration and discipline in quarters, the responsibility for the arrangements for the resumption of a march by the troops quartered in an area must be defined.

2. In fixing the starting point, care must be taken that each unit reaches it by moving forward in the direction of the march.

Should the march begin in the dark, the starting point will usually be marked by signalling lamps, or by fires, the method of marking it being mentioned in the operation orders. If a force, which is scattered in quarters, is required to pass a common starting point in the dark, it will often be advisable to post a chain of men, at distances of about 20 yards, between the assembly grounds of brigades, &c., and the starting point arrangements being made for collecting these men when they are no longer required.

Reconnaissance is the service of obtaining information with regard to:-

i. The topographical features and resources of a country.

ii. The movements and dispositions of an enemy.

In the latter case it may be strategical, tactical, or protective.

93. Personal reconnaissance by a commander

1. The extent of ground occupied by a large force will often prevent its commander from personally reconnoitring the whole of the ground on which his troops may be engaged. When this is the case it may often be advisable that the personal reconnaissance by commanders should be limited by commanders of divisions and smaller units, and that the commander of the force should rely upon the reports which have been rapidly transmitted from the front and prepared for him by his general staff. A personal reconnaissance which can only be partial may result in too much importance being attached to what has been seen at the expense of what has not been seen. A motor car will often enable a commander to reconnoitre rapidly an extended front, and a commander even of a large army would rarely omit to reconnoitre personally if it is possible for him to obtain thereby data for a comprehensive review of the situation.

2. Time spent in reconnaissance is seldom wasted: and unless the situation demands instant action, a commander of a division or of a smaller unit should never commit his troops to an engagement until he has made a personal survey of the ground before him.

Reconnaissance of a position:

When it is intended to occupy a defensive position, the chief points to be noted are:-

3. The best distribution of the infantry, and the means of protecting the flanks.

4. The positions for the artillery.

5. The positions which the enemy may endeavour to seize in order to develop an effective fire against the position.
6. The probable positions of the enemy's artillery.
7. Any points the possession of which may exert a decisive influence on the issue of the fight.
8. The most favourable lines of attack.
9. The most favourable ground for the counter-attack.
10. Ground to be occupied by the general reserve, by the cavalry, and by the other mounted troops.
11. Positions to be occupied in case of retreat.

Protection:
Action of a rear guard to a retreating force.

The first requirement of a defeated force is to be relieved from the pressure of pursuit. This is affected by detaching a portion of the force, the strength of which will depend on the situation, as a rear guard to impede the enemy's advance. The remainder of the force is thus enabled to move in comparative safety, and to recover order and moral.

2. A rear guard carries out its mission best by compelling the enemy's troops to halt and deploy for attack as frequently, and at as great a distance, as possible. It can usually effect this by taking up a succession of defensive positions which the enemy must attack or turn. When the enemy's dispositions are nearly complete, the rear guard moves off by successive retirements, each party as it falls back covering the retirement of the next by its fire. This action is repeated on the next favourable ground. All this consumes time, and time is what is most needed by a retreating force. A rear guard may also effectively check an enemy by attacking his advanced troops as they emerge from a defile or from difficult country.

3. In occupying rear guard positions it is important: (i.) to show as strong a front as possible to the enemy; (ii.) to make sure of good lines of retreat.

7. A point of great importance to the commander of a rear guard is to judge accurately the proper time to retire. He must constantly bear in mind the difficulty of withdrawing infantry that has once become engaged. If he retires too soon he is only partly carrying out the work required from the rear guard; on the other hand if he falls into error of trying to dispute every inch of ground he may become seriously involved and run the risk of being cut off from the main body, or oblige the latter to halt and reinforce him.

8. When a rear guard halts to fight, every moment separates it from the main body, whereas with a pursuing force every moment brings its reinforcements closer; in regulating the distance of the main guard from the main body the chance of the enemy interposing between the two must be considered. The distance, however, must be sufficient to prevent the main body being shelled by the enemy. This is especially important during the passage of a defile. The commander of the main body should periodically keep the commander of the rear guard informed of his progress, and *vice versa*.

9. It is always advisable to send an officer to the rear to note the next favourable position for defence on the line of retreat. The lines of retirement from position to position should not converge.

The positions should be sufficiently far apart to induce the enemy, after seizing one, to re-form column or route before advancing against the next.

10. Before withdrawing from a position, arrangements should be made to cover the retirement of the portion of the rear guard which is still engaged, by the disposition of the troops that have already retired.

94. Tactical reconnaissance by patrols.
As the commander of a force will form his plan of action on the result of the tactical reconnaissance, officers and scouts employed on it must be highly trained, have considerable technical knowledge, be quick and intelligent observers, be possessed of judgment and determination, and, if belonging to a mounted arms be well mounted.

Inter-Communication and Orders
10. The subordinate commanders will, in turn, frame their own orders on receipt of the superior's order, of which only so much will be embodied as is necessary. Their orders should however, be sufficiently full to enable those under them to appreciate the situation properly and to understand how they may co-operate with others.

138. The advance.
1. Before the troops move off from the position of assembly it is essential that the orders should be clearly explained to all ranks, so that everyone may know:-

   i.   The object in view and the direction of that objective.

   ii. The formation to be adopted at the disposition of deployment.

   iii. The part he has to play.

   iv. His action in case the enemy is not surprised.

Night Operations

130. The reconnaissance.

1. A thorough reconnaissance is an essential prelude to a night advance or to a night assault, and should rarely be dispensed with in the case of a night march. Under exceptionally favourable conditions, e.g., when good roads, reliable guides, and good amps are available, a night march may be successfully carried out without this preliminary, but every commander who orders a night operation which is not preceded by a complete reconnaissance increases the risk of failure and incurs a heavy responsibility.

2. In a reconnaissance for a night march the route should be examined both by day and by night. The best method of protecting the march and the column should be ascertained (Sec.132,3). All points where checks are likely to occur, the position of the branch roads or of places where the column might go astray and the best method of marking them should be noted. (Sec.132, 10). The general compass direction of the march should be taken and should be mentioned in the operation orders. It is often difficult for a column to know when it has reached its destination in the dark; this should be some easily recognizable landmark or should be marked in some prearranged manner; its appearance by night should be noted, and a description of it should be inserted in the operation orders, or, if it is desired to keep it secret, communicated confidentially to the commanders concerned.

3. In the case of a night advance or of a night assault, reconnaissance from a distance is insufficient. Information should be obtained as to:-

   i.   The distribution of the enemy's forces as far as possible and the positions of his outposts.

   ii. The nature and position of his entrenchments.

   iii. Whether there are any obstacles either natural or artificial which might hinder his advance.

   iv. The position of any landmarks which might assist the advance. (Sec 136).

It will rarely be possible to obtain this information without fighting, which will usually fall to the advanced troops and take place in daylight (Sec 92).

Subordinate commanders and regimental officers who are immediately responsible for the leading of the troops should carefully study the ground over which they will have to move, subject to such limitations as the commander of the force may impose. When in proximity to the enemy, advantage should be taken by all officers of pauses in the operations, to gain knowledge of ground over which they may at any time be required to lead their men by night.

Selected scouts from the units to take part in the operation should usually be sent out in the direction of the proposed advance, to study the ground and to note the position of the enemy's outposts and any of the defences or obstacles he may have erected. These scouts should assist in guiding their units in the subsequent advance.

Appendix 5
Divisional Structure
1915

- Divisional HQ
- Infantry: 3 brigades
- 4 battalions (with 4 machine guns each)

Mounted troops:
- 1 cavalry squadron
- 1 cyclist company

Artillery:
- HQ Divisional Artillery
- 3 field artillery brigades (each of 4 batteries of four 18 pounders and one ammunition column)
- 1 heavy battery (four 60 pounders with an ammunition column)
- 1 divisional ammunition column

Engineers:
- HQ Divisional Engineers
- 3 field companies

Signals Service:
- 1 signal company

Pioneers:
- 1 pioneer battalion (with 4 machine guns)
- 3 field ambulances
- 1 sanitary section
- 1 mobile veterinary section
- 1 motor ambulance workshop
- 1 divisional train

Number of troops and equipment:
- All ranks: 19,614
- Horses and mules 5,818

Guns:
- 48 x 18 pounders
- 16 x 4.5" howitzers
- 4 x 60 pounders
- Vickers machine guns: 52
- Assorted cart & vehicles: 958
- Cycles: 19
- Cars: 11
- Lorries: 4
- Ambulances: 21

Appendix 6
The British Expeditionary Force by 1918

Army Structure	Formation	Number of Men
ARMY		
CORPS	2 or more Divisions	25,000 to 50,000
DIVISIONS	3 or more Brigades or Regiments	10,000 to 15,000
BRIGADE	3 or more Battalions	1,500 to 3,500
BATTALIONS	4 or more Companies	400 to 1,000
COMPANIES	2 or more Platoons	100 to 250
PLATOONS	2 or more Squads	16 to 50

Regiments had expanded from pre–1914 composition of two Regular Battalions and one Reserve Battalion, to numerous battalions by 1918.

Appendix 7
Medals and Emblems

Gallantry Medals and Emblems

The recommendation for a Gallantry Medal was usually given by the Commanding Officer using Army form W3121. When the award was granted, the details were used in the citation. Almost all the recommendation forms were destroyed by enemy bombing in World War Two.

The Victoria Cross, the Military Cross, the Distinguished Service Order and the Distinguished Conduct Medal generally received a full citation in the *London Gazette* newspaper. To be published in this way, was to be referenced as 'Gazetted'.

Distinguished Service Order (DSO)

The Distinguished Service Order is an operational gallantry award given for highly successful command and leadership during active operations.

Military Cross (MC)

The Military Cross is an operational gallantry award given to all ranks of the services in recognition of exemplary gallantry during active operations against the enemy on land.

Distinguished Conduct Medal (DCM)

This medal was awarded to warrant officers, non-commissioned officers and men for 'Distinguished, gallant and good conduct in the field'. For all ranks below commissioned officers, it was the second highest award for gallantry in action after the Victoria Cross (VC). The DCM came with a stipend of £20, and an extra sixpence per day if the man was entitled to a pension.

The Military Medal (MM)

The Military Medal was established on 25 March 1916. It was the other ranks' equivalent to the Military Cross. Recipients of the medal are entitled to use the post-nominal letters 'MM' after their name. Over 115,000 awards were made for actions during the First World War.

Spray of Oak Leaves

This bronze emblem was awarded for a Mention in Dispatches in place of a medal, for notable acts of gallantry, and was usually worn on the ribbon of the Victory Medal.

Campaign Service Medals

1914 Star – Known as the 'Mons' Star

This bronze medal was authorised by King George V for those who served in France or Belgium between the periods 5 August 1914 to midnight on 22 November 1914. There were approximately 378,000 1914 Stars issued. Recipients of this medal will have seen service in the Battle of Mons, the retreat to the Seine, the Battles of Le Cateau, the Marne, the Aisne and the First Battle of Ypres. A clasp sewn on to the ribbon and bearing the dates '5th August – 22nd November 1914', shows that the recipient had served under fire from the enemy, during that period. Those who received the medal with the clasp were also entitled to attach a small silver heraldic rose to the ribbon when the ribbon was being worn.

1914–1915 Star
The medal was awarded to all who served in any theatre of war against Germany between 5 August 1914 and 31 December 1915, exemption was for those eligible for the 1914 Star.

The Allied Service Medal
The front of this medal depicts a winged classical figure representing victory. Eligibility for this medal was more restrictive and was not awarded singly, but was awarded to those who received the 1914 Star or 1914–1915 Star.

The British War Medal 1914–1918
This silver medal was awarded to those who saw service at home or entered service overseas between 5 August 1914 and 11 November 1918.

Appendix 8
Chapel Street Residency

South-East Side

3 & 5 Burns Martin, lodging house keeper; Clarke family.

7, 9, & 11 Decourcey Mrs Bridget, lodging house keeper: Frank Collins; Morley; James Murray; Michael Groark, Samuel Wood, William Hulme.

13 Hennerley Dennis, general dealer.

15 Hughes William, labourer; James Bell Houlden.

17 Norton.

19 Ratchford.

21 Naughton William.

23 Mongon Patrick, bricklayer.

25 Madden Patrick, labourer.

27 Naughton, Mrs Charlotte.

29 O' Connor Thomas, labourer.

31 Groark Patrick.

33 Lace George, Musician.

35 Brennan John.

37 Starrs Harry.

39 Haughton William.

41 Morley Peter.

43 Peers Tom, labourer.

45 Corfield Thomas.

47, 49, & 53 Collins Mrs Margaret, lodging house keeper: William Ratchford.

51 Green John.

55 Scanlon John.

57 Kirkham John, hawker.

59 Drinkwater James.

61 Walker Harry, labourer.

63 Tyrell.

North-West Side

2 Tracey William.

4 DeCourcy Patrick.

6 Hollingsworth; Albert Oxley.

8 Hennerley.

10 Hanley James, labourer.

12 Griffin Michael, labourer.

14 Ratchford Michael, lodging house keeper; Thomas Ratchford.

16 Tayfe James, labourer.
18 Rowan John, beer retailer.
20, 22 & 24 Oxley Alfred, lodging house keeper; Charles Croft.
26 Burns Martin, lodging house keeper.
28 Bagnall William, labourer.
30 Burns Martin, lodging house keeper: Joseph Arnold.
32 Gilligan Peter, lodging house keeper.
34 Egan Thomas, labourer.
36 Haughton Mrs Mary, lodging house keeper: Edward Caine.
38 McCarty James, farm labourer.
40 Booth.
42 Burns.
44 Andrews John, labourer.
46 Wyatt Frank, labourer.
48 Ralph Ryan.
50 Booth John, labourer; Taylor Family.
52 Reeves Mrs Mary; Wyatt family, Thomas Tyrell.
54 Hindley Mrs Mary.
56 Ratchford James, labourer.
58 Leonard John.

The
History
Press

The destination for history
www.thehistorypress.co.uk